THE
TOMORROW
TRAP

*Unlocking the Secrets of
the Procrastination-Protection
Syndrome*

KAREN E. PETERSON, Ph.D.

Health Communications, Inc.
Deerfield Beach, Florida

This book is intended to provide accurate and authoritative information about the subject of procrastination. It is sold with the understanding that the publisher and the author are not engaged in rendering psychotherapy or other professional services. If psychotherapeutic services are needed, the services of a competent mental health professional should be sought.

Library of Congress Cataloging-in-Publication Data

Peterson, Karen E.
    The tomorrow trap: unlocking the secrets of the procrastination-protection syndrome/Karen E. Peterson.
    p.   cm.
    Includes bibliographical references.
    ISBN 1-55874-417-7 (pbk.)
    1. Procrastination.   I. Title.
BF637.P76.P48   1996   96-34323
155.2'32—dc20   CIP

Publisher: Health Communications, Inc.
                3201 S.W. 15th Street
                Deerfield Beach, FL 33442-8190

Author photo by Scherley Busch
Cover illustration ©1996 Master Series
Cover design by Lawna Patterson Oldfield

For Steven,
my favorite attachment

The fundamental joke with
Laurel and Hardy, it seems to me,
was that they did their best with every test.
They never failed to bargain in good
faith with their destinies.

—Kurt Vonnegut, *Slapstick*

Contents

The Two Types of Procrastination
• The Procrastination-Protection Syndrome
• The Human Condition As a Template for
Procrastination • Procrastination As Protection:
Pendulum, Prison or Prophet?

Gaining Access to the Winner Within
• Autonomy • Creativity • Confidence • Effort
• Spontaneity • Solitude

Figures

Acknowledgments

I would like to take this opportunity to thank so many people who were helpful in the preparation of this manuscript, including Elisa Albo, Audrey Bahrick, Norma Carreras, Dwayne, Iris Elliott-Mosconi, Mac Fancher, Estella Fransbergen, Leahanne, Bob Lunior, Maureen Malone, Abby Nelson and Beau Wilder.

I would also like to thank authors Gerald Costanzo, Paul Levine, Bernie Siegel and Les Standiford for granting me their time for interviews, which they have graciously allowed me to reproduce in this book.

I thank Denise Levertov and Kurt Vonnegut for their words of inspiration so many years ago, when they had no idea who I was or how much I needed it.

Special thanks go to Betty Yuen-Torres, for her perceptive insight in reading the right side of my brain so as to produce just exactly what I wanted in terms of illustrations for this book, and to Ron Wilder, for his perceptive ability to tell the right side of my brain to settle down long enough to allow the left side of my brain to get this book published once and for all.

A special breed of thanks goes also to Stasia Peterson and Cosmo Carreras, for their unswerving canine and aviary companionship during the many hours it took to create and type this manuscript.

I would also like to extend my feelings of appreciation in particular to Marlene Colangelo, Maryann Dolson, Dottie Gifford, Cora Llera, Steven Warner and Vitor Weinman, for their special assistance in the preparation of the right side of my brain in order to publish this book.

I would also like to thank my editor, Christine Belleris, as well as Randee Goldsmith, Peter Vegso, Kim Weiss, and the staff at Health Communications for their patience, professionalism and unswerving belief in the power of my words.

My deep gratitude goes out to Gail Lois Jaffe, friend and faithful writing companion, for her long hours of editorial and spiritual support as well as her offers to share an occasional heated brownie, even at 10 o'clock in the morning.

My eternal gratitude goes out to Tom Woolison, friend and effervescent spiritual inspirateur, whom I can still see in the outer purple ring of every rainbow.

My spontaneous gratitude I offer to Nicolas Andrew Carreras, who knows more about bargaining in good faith with destiny at the ripe old age of two months than I do at the age of 42.

And to Steven Andrew Carreras—for your excellent research skills, countless trips to Kinko's, sublime sense of irreverence rivaled only by the likes of the Marx Brothers, and most of all your ongoing support and honesty—I say, quite simply, "Thank you."

PART I

Exploring the
Tomorrow Trap

Introduction

"I have all the books and tapes on time management and motivation, and I know what they say is true. But when I try to make the behavioral changes they suggest, there's always this *thing* in the back of my mind."

Although these are the words of a client suffering from procrastination, they could just as easily have been my own. This is the book I needed to read 20 years ago—while fighting a never-ending battle with procrastination, stuck in the clutches of the perennial "tomorrow trap."

Unlike other books that focus on mere behavioral change, this book offers right-brain, emotional techniques—such as nondominant handwriting, indirect interviews, photohistory and the unique five-stage psychoautobiographical writing— for discovering and eradicating that "thing" in the back of our minds. This "thing" is a universal, unconscious sense of shame that is a normal part of the human condition.

This underlying shame, which can trigger procrastination, is usually rooted in the first few years of life—regardless of one's upbringing. Because our memories of these pre-verbal years are stored primarily in the right brain, we must utilize right-brain techniques to eliminate problems with procrastination.

In response to each of these normal, everyday childhood experiences, a droplet of unconscious shame is added to a gradually expanding pool that may resemble an irritating, muddy puddle; a deep, dark lake; or a raging sea. This pool corresponds to our level of procrastination, which can be of low, mid- or high intensity. Regardless of our level of procrastination, it's much easier to be ashamed about being late than it is to feel ashamed about finishing the task or making the decision, only to be told we've performed poorly. In this way, procrastination actually protects us from tapping into this pool of deeper feelings we'd just as soon avoid. For procrastinators of all levels, this book will offer a program for living more than just "half a life," as a colleague once said to me.

Procrastination, which starts at birth in terms of what we were born into (family and environment) and what we were born with (genetic templates for physical flaws and problems), is actually a gift that can provide us with clues about our spiritual destiny. Whether we call our life situations our "cross to bear" or "karma," the fact is that many people procrastinate on tasks and decisions that are of great importance to them. However, by allowing procrastination to serve as a guide to our inner shame, we can take charge of our lives and learn how to embrace our essential destinies.

Each chapter contains composite case examples (to preserve confidentiality, all identifying data have been changed or omitted) from my clinical practice, along with my own history of procrastination, to illustrate the self-help techniques of recovery that I have discovered over the years. These techniques are geared toward allowing individuals to break free from the procrastination patterns of the past and embrace a new way of living, working and believing. If I can do it—while simultaneously conquering premenstrual syndrome, depression and seasonal affective disorder (I'm bracing myself for menopause)—you can, too.

Care to come along for the ride?

1

Earth or Bust: Understanding the Procrastination-Protection Syndrome

*Beyond talent lie all the
usual words: discipline, love, luck,
but, most of all, endurance.*

—James Baldwin

Ever watch *Star Trek?* Well, even if you're not a science fiction fan, you'll probably see yourself aboard the Starship Enterprise by the end of this story. During one recent episode, I was instantly reminded of the vicious cycle of what I call the "psycho-evolutionary" patterns of humanity.

As I watched Captain Picard and his fearless crew trapped in a space/time distortion, unwittingly repeating the same events for 17 days in a row, I felt increasingly upset each time their "day" ended in the complete destruction of the ship and its crew. I wanted to reach through the TV screen and say, "But wait, you don't have to keep repeating the same events that will result in your total destruction!"

As Captain Picard and his crew became increasingly alert for signs of *déjà vu* moments, trusting that their instincts were correct, they were finally able to give themselves a clue to avoid the inevitable collision in this repeated "day," and out of the loop they went—free at last from "the tomorrow trap." However, after the ship had broken out of the space/time distortion, Captain Picard hailed the captain of the other ship and quickly realized that the other ship's crew was as yet completely unaware that they, too, had been repeating the same day—but for over 80 years.

So what's all this going around in circles have to do with procrastination? Essentially, this book is the "clue" I needed to give myself 20 years ago, when I was stuck in the repetitive, destructive cycle of procrastination. In my case it took the form of writer's block, which I now view as an unconscious form of procrastination. With an intense desire to write, I knew that something was wrong with my life, but I couldn't begin to figure out what or why. Although I saw a variety of fine therapists over the years, none was able to help with my procrastination regarding the writing process until I was ready to deal with underlying issues.

As an English composition teacher, I was also aware that some of my students had problems with writer's block and procrastination, and it seemed to have more to do with the student than with the writing project per se.

During those years, I searched for information to help sort this all out. I found some interesting books and excellent research material, but none of them started me writing again.

My earliest clues regarding what I now feel is the true source of procrastination came while researching my doctoral dissertation in psychology—a project in which I studied the relationship between "self-monitoring style" (how much of one's "true self" is shown to others) and one's level of writing anxiety, writer's block or procrastination.

This book is a composite of all that I've learned about procrastination—both as a survivor of this negative pattern and as a psychologist who has worked with procrastinators for the past 10 years. In my workshops across the country, I have seen the same patterns over and over again that have plagued me, as well as my clients. And just as Captain Picard invited the other starship's captain aboard to help him out of his 80-year entrapment, so, too, do I offer you this book to help you out of your particular prison of procrastination, a prison that does indeed protect you from facing the real issues underlying procrastination, but that also keeps you caught in the teeth of the tomorrow trap.

* * * *

The Two Types of Procrastination

Let's examine briefly the level to which you feel ensnared by the tomorrow trap. Try to respond to the items that follow with your first gut-level reaction. Once you have assessed your particular pattern of procrastination, we'll know which of the two types of procrastination is keeping you trapped in this uncomfortable pattern.

Procrastination Pattern Quiz

1. I procrastinate regarding:
   _____ making decisions.
   _____ paperwork.
   _____ creative activities.
   _____ academic activities.
   _____ my job.
   _____ household tasks.
   _____ financial matters.
   _____ my personal relationships.
   _____ self-care.
   _____ relaxation and leisure time.
   _____ my hobbies.
   _____ my hopes and dreams.
   _____ other: _____.

2. When I hear the word "procrastination," I think of:
   _____.

3. When I hear the word "procrastination," I feel:
   _____.

4. When other people procrastinate, I feel _____
   _____, and I think _____
   _____
   _____.

5. I procrastinate _____ percent of the time.

6. I procrastinate mostly when it comes to _____
   _____, and _____
   and _____.

7. I rarely procrastinate when it comes to _____
   _____, or _____
   or _____.

8. What bothers me the most about my procrastination
   is _____
   _____.

9. Procrastination has caused me trouble in terms of my:
   _____ job _____ relationships
   _____ self-esteem _____ fulfillment
   of my dreams.

10. The reasons that I think I haven't stopped procrasti-
    nating are: _____
    _____
    _____.

In looking at your answers to item #1, notice whether your procrastination relates to one area, a few or many. If your problems are just with one area, you could be dealing primarily with a simple case of what I call "task-related procrastination" (TRP). This suggests boredom and low frustration tolerance regarding an aversive task. In this case, the application of time management principles would help.

However, the more negative your responses were to items #2-10, the more likely it is that you may be experiencing what I call "person-related procrastination" (PRP). This suggests the possibility of unresolved interpersonal issues (issues between you and another person) or unresolved intrapersonal issues (issues residing within you from previous life experiences). And yes, if you're really lucky, like most of us, you can have both TRP and PRP at the same time.

A few case examples will illustrate:

Robert, a 45-year-old architect, relocated to Florida to accept a management position with a large architectural firm. He came for counseling at the suggestion of his employer, who had noticed that Robert had a difficult time completing tasks that involved minor paperwork or conducting meetings.

When I questioned Robert, it appeared that he had no other problems with procrastination outside these two areas at work. Prior to being promoted to manager, Robert had shown no evidence of postponing tasks or low morale. He enjoyed the creative aspects of being an architect.

However, when it came to writing memos to or setting up meetings with the junior members of the firm, Robert tended to put off the chore. Although he would never be so blunt with his employer, Robert stated to me that these were "boring and meaningless" tasks that "distracted" him from his real purpose: creatively designing buildings and other structures. He added that although he appreciated the substantial hike in salary, he yearned for the old days when he could focus more closely on being creative, rather than on such boring tasks that he now "had" to do.

Robert's case is a clear example of task-related procrastination. On a daily basis he faced aversive tasks that prevented him from doing what he enjoyed. When we explored the fact that he was in a management position by choice, even with all the "aversive tasks," Robert began to see his situation in a different light.

When I asked if he'd like to step down from his new, lucrative position, he exclaimed "no." He said that with two sons in college, he and his wife had never had the money to travel. With his new salary, they were already planning a trip to Europe. I pointed out that perhaps all the paperwork was worth it, given the financial results of his management position. Reluctantly, he agreed.

What Robert needed was a daily reminder of these positive consequences regarding the performance of such "meaningless" tasks. I suggested a form of time management, a behavior therapy technique called "contingency management," in which a reward for behavior depends upon performance. It calls for breaking an aversive task into manageable steps, then rewarding oneself after each step is completed. Robert needed immediate and tangible gratification after each bout of "boring" paperwork.

We decided to try breaking his tasks into half-hour blocks. He agreed that for each half-hour of time he spent writing memos, he'd deposit $25 in a new European vacation savings account. For each half-hour spent conducting staff meetings, an additional $25 would be put in an account for one getaway trip each month for Robert and his wife.

Once Robert realized he was being amply rewarded for performing these relatively unpleasant tasks, he was able to execute his job well without the need to procrastinate.

Such cases of task-related procrastination are usually fairly clear-cut and relatively easy to remedy. However, in cases of person-related procrastination, the causes and solutions are more complex. Another case example will illustrate.

Cynthia, a 27-year-old computer whiz, yearned to be a writer. Although she had a comprehensive library of motivational tapes and books on time management, Cynthia was a classic case of procrastination. Not only did she put off expressing herself via her writing, she also delayed doing her job since she saw her work as an obstacle to writing her novel. To deal with her frustration, Cynthia often ate compulsively; she had gained 75 pounds since completing graduate school. As a result of her weight gain, she put off joining clubs and professional groups where she could meet men. She feared rejection based on her appearance.

Upon closer inquiry, it became apparent that Cynthia was trying to maintain her balance on a tightrope of approval—with one parent at each end. Her father, who had insisted that Cynthia follow his career path, was always reminding her that if she did well enough, she might take over his multi-million-dollar business. He also constantly admonished her and was never forthcoming with praise or approval —a negative pattern that had started when Cynthia was a small child. Cynthia was sure he would "practically disown" her if she spent time on such a "frivolous" activity as writing a novel.

Similarly, Cynthia was unable to reap any approval from her mother—an aloof woman who spent the bulk of her time pampering herself. She constantly reminded Cynthia that it would be "impossible to get a man" because of Cynthia's weight.

Unlike Robert's task-oriented procrastination, Cynthia's problem was more complex. It required focusing on her interpersonal issues with her parents, as well as on her feelings regarding her own sense of shame, low self-esteem and lack of independence.

More often than not, procrastination is usually a mixture of task-related and person-related factors.

For example, suppose your supervisor is on vacation and you must write a report—a task you find aversive. The president of the company is expecting the report for the annual meeting in a week.

If you were in this situation, most likely every time you thought about this project, you would start to feel _____, and you'd probably be thinking thoughts such as: _____ _____, or _____ _____, or _____.

If your feeling about the report is solely related to the task itself, then you probably would experience the sensation of being overwhelmed, overworked or frustrated. You might think:

_____ I wish I didn't have to write this long report.

_____ I'm too busy to do this report.

_____ I hate to write—this is so overwhelming.

_____ I don't even know where to begin.

_____ This will take huge amounts of my time, so I'll put it off until I have a few free hours.

Compare these five statements to your responses with the fill-in-the-blank statements in the previous paragraph. The five statements above are focused on the fact that you must perform an arduous and unpleasant task. Your negative feelings and thoughts are focused upon the task itself. This would be a clear example of pure task-related procrastination. Your responses, however, may suggest a deeper form of procrastination.

This project may also produce a form of procrastination that is interpersonal or intrapersonal in nature—a case of person-related procrastination (PRP). When you start to feel extremely angry, victimized or helpless, you may be experiencing a deeper form of procrastination.

Perhaps you think your supervisor takes too many vacation days, and that this report is another example of his or her selfish expectations that you will "cover." Naturally, you would not want to jump headlong into this project, let alone complete it on time. Or perhaps you just don't want to write this report because you feel resentful toward the company's president for commanding you to write it, instead of asking politely. Why would you want to start or finish an aversive task (TRP) for two people who are treating you badly (PRP)? This would be a perfect example of procrastination due to interpersonal factors as well as task-related factors.

But suppose you feel so enraged that you cannot work on the project even if you want to. Then it's no longer just a case of "I'll do it later." This incapacitation may be because your supervisor reminds you of your mother, who has never been supportive of you, left most of the housework for you to do, and never had to answer for it. And suppose that the company's president reminds you of your father, who constantly assigned tasks without ever asking politely. In such a case, procrastination would also be classified as intrapersonal because the task of writing the report is forcing you to tap into unresolved feelings from the past that still reside within you.

As a result of these unresolved feelings about your parents' dysfunctional behaviors, you have probably internalized their voices, so that now you are your own worst enemy.

This is where a case of serious procrastination can develop, often with severe consequences. Once we understand that procrastination protects us from other issues not yet faced, then we are already on the road to recovery.

* * * *

The Procrastination-Protection Syndrome

Procrastination is a multifaceted phenomenon. When people ask me what causes it, they usually want a quick, one-word response. I could simplify the definition by saying that procrastination is used primarily for "protection." However, the reasons why we procrastinate are much more complex.

Here's another simple quiz to illustrate some of the unique components of the procrastination-protection syndrome (PPS). Check off any items that may apply to you. Answer spontaneously, without thinking too deeply.

The Procrastination-Protection Syndrome Quiz

____ 1. I know that I need to practice some of the basic principles of time management, but I just can't bring myself to do it.

____ 2. I don't like to be alone, so I often put off tasks that require solitude.

____ 3. Even if I stopped procrastinating, sometimes I'm not sure I deserve much more than I already have in life.

* * *

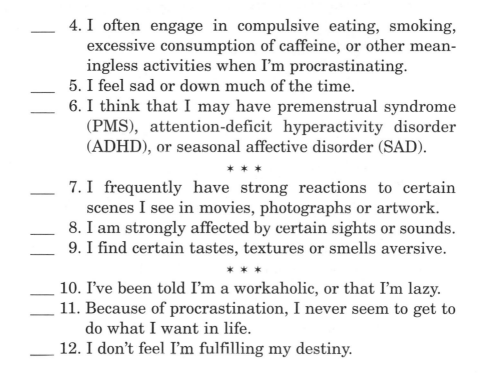

___ 4. I often engage in compulsive eating, smoking, excessive consumption of caffeine, or other meaningless activities when I'm procrastinating.

___ 5. I feel sad or down much of the time.

___ 6. I think that I may have premenstrual syndrome (PMS), attention-deficit hyperactivity disorder (ADHD), or seasonal affective disorder (SAD).

* * *

___ 7. I frequently have strong reactions to certain scenes I see in movies, photographs or artwork.

___ 8. I am strongly affected by certain sights or sounds.

___ 9. I find certain tastes, textures or smells aversive.

* * *

___ 10. I've been told I'm a workaholic, or that I'm lazy.

___ 11. Because of procrastination, I never seem to get to do what I want in life.

___ 12. I don't feel I'm fulfilling my destiny.

If you checked off any of items #1-3, then you are probably allowing procrastination to protect you from underlying issues that you will learn more about as you read this book.

If you checked off any of items #4-6, then you may have some physiological issues that are either triggering or aggravating your problems with procrastination.

If you checked off any of items #7-9, then it's possible you have already tapped into some of the underlying clues to your procrastination problems that are hidden in the right side of your brain.

Finally, if you checked off any of items #10-12, you are allowing procrastination to limit your ultimate destiny.

Most of us would check off at least one item in each of the four categories listed above. However, all four of these categories are bound together by the notion of shame—that universal, unconscious part of normal childhood development that we are now beginning to understand as simply part of the human condition.

* * * *

The Human Condition As a Template for Procrastination

Like Cynthia in the case example earlier, you've probably purchased at least one or more books on time management. You may also have listened to a variety of motivational tapes or attended seminars on the subject. The behavioral changes suggested are usually valid, but chances are you haven't put them into action.

What was missing for me in all those books was the information I needed to create the cognitive and emotional change in order for me to stop procrastinating. I remained trapped in a prison of my own making, a prison surrounded by a deep moat of shame.

This shame is a universal, often unconscious feeling that arises as a normal part of the human condition, particularly during the first three years of life, regardless of our upbringing. Even if we feel as though we grew up on the set of *The Brady Bunch* or *The Donna Reed Show,* we still have a residual pool of unconscious shame—however deep or shallow—that can subtly contaminate our perceptions and behaviors.

This shame arises from the simple fact that as infants we are extremely egocentric. As babies, we respond to many temporary separations as if we have done something wrong to make our caregivers "abandon" us so. Recent research indicates that even babies with healthy attachments to a guardian still respond with a small amount of shame once they are reunited—even if the caregiver just stepped out to buy a lottery ticket! This shame can lead to problems with procrastination later in life if it is combined with shame from other sources. The more intense our shame, the more intense our procrastination can be.

No matter how loving our caretakers were, they could not have been there for us perfectly at all times. Our childhood caretakers—parents, babysitters, grandparents, aunts, uncles, siblings, neighbors, teachers, clergy or anyone else with whom we came into contact—were mere human beings trying to raise us in the middle of their complicated lives, perhaps along with several other children, temporary unemployment, or broken hearts. As hard as they may have tried to be perfect, they were flawed, just as we are. And because they were flawed, they may have been unable to love us the way we needed to be loved. This loss of love—however temporary—is experienced as shame. In her excellent book entitled *The Role of Shame in Symptom Formation* (pp. 30, 32), Helen Block Lewis states: "Shame is an inevitable human response to the loss of love. . . . Shame is the empathetic experience of the other's rejection of the self."

Now, you may be thinking: "But I wasn't affected by my childhood." Well, if that's the case, consider this: Imagine a child with healthy parents (there's got to be one out there somewhere). The child grows up appreciated and respected, with healthy rules and appropriate limits, and plenty of love and guidance. Would you expect this child to become a serial killer? Or would you expect that this child's self-esteem level would be healthy because of his or her positive family experiences? If that's the case, then how can we say we're "not affected" by childhood? The reality is that unless we are automatons, we are all affected by our experiences, particularly when we are so impressionable as children. And even if you did have relatively healthy parents or primary caretakers, does that exclude you from the possibility of colliding with any unhealthy people for the rest of your early childhood and later life? Children are exposed to so many people at school, clubs, church, or on the street—many of whom are never even introduced to the children's parents.

In the psychoevolutionary scheme of things, our caretakers have usually maintained the flaws they were born with or born into, and for the most part, passed them on to us. This is because we are only just now, as a race, beginning to understand what it takes to raise a child with healthy self-esteem. Our parents and grandparents couldn't flip on *Oprah* and find out how to make up for the fact that they grew up during the Great Depression and passed their financial fears onto us. They didn't mean to make us so insecure about money—and life. It was simply part of the times in which they grew up. That doesn't make them "bad" people, but the effects are still here in us today.

So unless we were literally "born yesterday" into the current *zeitgeist* of self-help and delicate self-esteem surgery we're all encouraged to get nowadays, we have all had some sort of psychological "injuries," however unintentional or meaningless they may seem now.

Now, as an adult, it's certainly easy to say, "Well, of course I understand why I never felt loved enough by my mother—when I was born, my brother had just started into the Terrible Twos, my father had just lost his job, and we had just moved to a new city where my mother had no friends, so I can understand why she wasn't perhaps as loving to me as I would have liked." This all sounds well and good, but try to explain this to a nine-month-old child.

But even if you had a relatively healthy childhood, unfortunately the potential for shame is still there. In *The Role of Shame in Symptom Formation* (p. 33), Helen Block Lewis points out that shame—exemplified by the universal "gaze aversion" of downcast eyes—is an inevitable part of life even for the healthy child with secure attachment bonds:

> *Videotapes of "secure" infants responding to their mothers' return after separation show that even while they are seeking and accepting reunion, there is at least brief gaze aversion or a blank expression on their faces. Even with secure attachment, reunion after separation is apparently experienced with a mixture of pleasure and some hint of shame.*

We all have some residual pool of shame, however shallow, as a result of these minute but often chronic and cumulative moments of perceived loss of love, simply because our guardians were human. The capacity for an infant to understand any absence is limited because the child is egocentric. Any temporary loss of love is perceived as rejection, which in turn engenders tiny droplets of shame. Does this mean that every waking moment must be spent with a child until he or she is old enough to understand? Of course not.

You might be thinking, "Life's tough—I can't sit around and weep and wail and gnash my teeth about every little thing. Life's not a bowl of cherries." You're right. There are lots of pits in that bowl, and most of us get by all right in spite of that. As children, we are amazingly resilient.

However, it's when you find more pits than cherries that the real problems set in. If the negative outweighs the positive, the psychological ramifications can last a lifetime.

On the other hand, even the smallest positive influence can help a child who is otherwise bereft of support. Therapists' files abound with stories of people who have suffered severe deprivation or neglect as children, but who remained surprisingly positive because of a kindly neighbor, an attentive teacher or a peer who gave support. In other cases, some individuals who have been raised in a fairly nurturing home grow up desolate and self-destructive.

How do we account for these discrepancies?

Research suggests that some individuals are born feistier than others, but there are many factors that must be accounted for. Simply put, people react differently to the amount of shame that they carry around from childhood and/or adult experiences.

The cumulative effect of each droplet of shame can lead to a rather large pool of unconscious shame, which in turn leads to procrastination. In the next two chapters (through a careful analysis of psychological research and composite clinical case examples), I will explain how procrastination protects us from dipping into this universal pool of unconscious shame. After all, it's much easier to feel ashamed of your procrastination than it is to complete the job or make the decision, only to find that your work or your decision was somehow inadequate—meaning that somehow *you* are inadequate. And if you start to feel ashamed and inadequate, you just might dip into that residual pool of unconscious shame.

For some people, those I call low-intensity procrastinators, this pool of shame is relatively shallow. But the waters are too cold for comfort, and murky. Who knows what kind of dangerous snakes or Loch Ness monster eggs might be lurking at the bottom of this pool? These people, who often experience mild relationship difficulties and loss of sleep accompanied by late-night caffeine binges, will put off projects and important decisions in spite of the fact that they feel anxious. They most likely have endured nontraumatic but chronic shame-based events.

For those who function in the mid-intensity range of procrastination, this pool of unconscious shame probably looks more like the famous "Blue Hole," a clear blue pond, maybe 10 feet in diameter, known to be immeasurably deep—or so the tourist attraction pamphlet said as I gazed upon this mini-abyss when I was a small child. People with this type of shame pool are chronic procrastinators who live under the constant threat of losing jobs and relationships. Just like the Blue Hole, it is quite "clear" that the problem is indeed one of procrastination, but you can't see to the "bottom line" in order to find out why you are procrastinating so much. These individuals most likely have endured numerous types of chronic shame-based events, or a few very intense, traumatic events.

Then there are the high-intensity procrastinators, whose pools of shame are like raging dark seas on a wind-whipped night. The icy black waters are dotted with large sharp-edged floes of ice that could sink a Titanic of self-confidence in a millisecond. It's certainly not safe to sail—unless you want to meet up with the *Doppelgängers* of your own drowned self-confidence from Titanic days past. Such is the nature of the shame pools within procrastinators who have lost jobs, marriages and sometimes even their own lives due to procrastination. These are people who have experienced chronic and traumatic shame-based events such as childhood neglect or childhood abuse.

Most of the composite case examples discussed in this book are mid- to high-level procrastinators, since those individuals are most likely to seek therapy. If you are a high-level procrastinator, it may be helpful to review the exercises in this book with a licensed psychotherapist who can help you interpret some of the insights you will discover about yourself.

Even if you consider yourself to be a low-intensity procrastinator, the suggestions I offer can help you to break free from the cycle of procrastination once and for all.

You will be offered various techniques to discover and "drain" your pool of residual unconscious shame that has been triggering your procrastination for so many years. And by trusting your instincts, you will be empowered to release yourself from the tomorrow trap—and well before the 80-year mark!

* * * *

Procrastination As Protection: Pendulum, Prison or Prophet?

Procrastination protects us from dipping into our pools of unconscious, cumulative shame. But what is perhaps most insidious about procrastination is that it changes its appearance—acting sometimes like a pendulum, other times like a prison, and yet at still other times as a prophet offering clues to our spiritual destinies.

The Pendulum of Protective Procrastination

How many times have you said to yourself, "It's the middle of January and I haven't even started putting into practice any of my New Year's resolutions yet"?

At that point an overwhelming wave of shame rolls over you, and then you go back to doing whatever you feel like doing—anything *but* doing exercise, making plans to go back to school, calling that singles club, finally contacting a divorce attorney, starting that book project, or actually implementing that plan you enjoyed creating at the office. You would rather be doing something else—something more gratifying. You want instant gratification, not boredom. As you sit at your desk doodling on scratch paper, or in front of the television numbing out over sitcoms, you have swung the pendulum of destiny away from the "work" zone and locked it back into place at the "play" zone.

The momentum that swings your pendulum is called procrastination, and the velocity of the pendulum's movement is determined by your level of unconscious shame.

Ideally, most of us would like to spend a healthy amount of time in the "work" zone, meeting our goals as we fulfill our destinies, then balancing out our lives by spending a healthy amount of time in the "play" zone, where we take time out for relaxation and leisure activities. However, most of us tend to spend a great deal of time in the "play" zone in order to avoid work (or other tasks or difficult decisions), and then, at the last minute, we swing over and lock ourselves into an all-nighter in the "work" zone. Work then becomes associated with anxiety, frustration and helplessness, and so we spend even more time in the "play" zone with each swing of the pendulum.

Or, conversely, we may spend so much time in the "work" zone that we never take time out for the "play" zone, allowing cherished magazines to pile up for years without ever taking the time to allow ourselves the luxury of sitting down to read them.

Obviously, we all know on some level that the answer to procrastination is time management or some form of contingency management in order to make an unwieldy task more manageable and worth doing, by offering ourselves a reward after each step of the task is completed. Why is it that such a gold-star system works for our children, but not for us? If we all know what works, then why don't we do it? What keeps us from having the ability to delay gratification long enough to finish our work, and what keeps us from feeling that we deserve to take time out for relaxation, leisure time and fun?

* * * *

Protective Procrastination As Prison

Twenty years ago, in my quest to find an answer to such questions regarding my own problems with writer's block, I ran into this same dilemma. I knew what to do, but I couldn't do it. What I didn't know at the time was that procrastination not only causes shame, it comes from shame. It feels more like a prison than a pendulum. The layers of imprisonment that procrastination forms to protect us can be overwhelming and all-encompassing.

Figure 1 illustrates the ways in which shame, like a pebble in a pond, can produce outer waves of pain that in time prevent us from following our dreams, attaining our goals, or reaching a higher level of spirituality. The life cycle of procrastination may be summarized as follows:

1. The original source of procrastination is unconscious shame emanating from common, "normal" issues that originate at birth or during childhood. They include perceived or real physical imperfections, flawed or disrupted parenting, neglect, or even abuse (zones 3-4). Whether one refers to these unresolved issues as destiny, "a cross to bear" or "karma," the fact remains that these issues must be worked through in order to lead a productive, meaningful life.
2. Research shows that this childhood shame surfaces under the various guises of such clinical symptoms as perfectionism, fear of solitude, fear of rejection, fear of failure or success, anxiety, depression, co-dependence, powerlessness and anger against authority figures—in other words, the underlying dynamics of procrastination (zone 5).
3. Later in life, genetic physiological sources of shame may aggravate procrastination patterns. These include

Figure 1. The Life Cycle of Procrastination

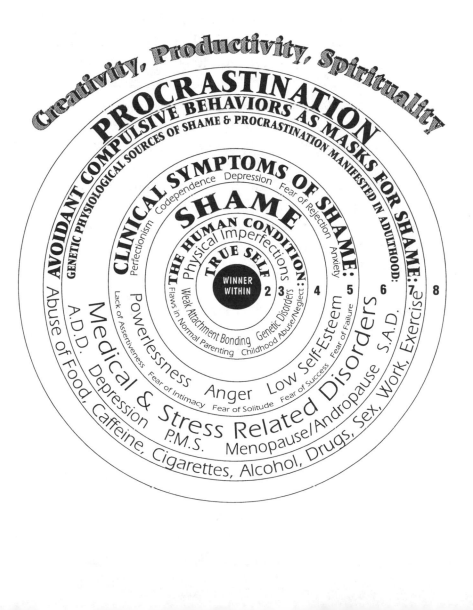

the genetic blueprints for such problems as attention-deficit/hyperactivity disorder, seasonal affective disorder, depression, premenstrual syndrome and even menopause (zone 6).

4. Behavioral sources of procrastination—compulsive behaviors—are used to mask childhood shame as well: overindulgence in sugar/white flour products, coffee, alcohol, cigarettes, drugs, sex and even workaholism (zone 7). Because these compulsive behaviors create an altered state of consciousness by restoring mood-altering brain chemicals (such as endorphins, serotonin, dopamine and norepinephrine) that are depleted by shame and depression, these compulsive behaviors can become addictive as ends in themselves, thereby leading to further procrastination.

5. The final result of a lifetime of procrastination (zone 8) is a deficit of spirituality, since one's lifelessons are never learned—one's "karma" is never worked through—and no legacy of human improvement is passed to the next generation.

Looks like an airtight system, doesn't it? But it's not. Although figure 1 is an accurate representation of how we usually feel about procrastination, figure 2 offers a more accurate portrayal of the way we need to think about the life cycle of procrastination: as a fortress of the mind. Although the various barriers to productivity may appear to be a mile high and 100 miles long, there are many gaps in these walls. The way out is simpler than you think.

Thus, you may start at the outside barrier (zone 8) by admitting to yourself that you have a problem with putting off tasks, decisions, or activities. However, you may run into difficulty at the next wall of resistance—compulsive behaviors such as

Figure 2.

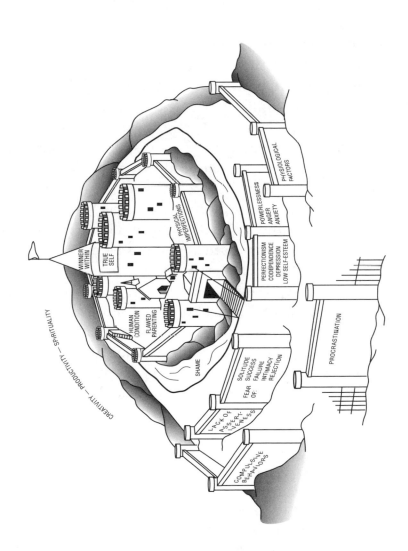

overeating, alcohol abuse, or workaholism that help us delay important decisions or tasks even more (zone 7).

Perhaps upon tackling this wall of addictive behaviors, you soon begin to realize that you have relied on them not only to assist you in procrastinating, but also in order to cope with certain physiological factors that may aggravate problems with creativity or productivity—problems such as attention-deficit/hyperactivity disorder (ADHD), premenstrual syndrome (PMS) or seasonal affective disorder (SAD; zone 6). These problems not only contribute to procrastination by increasing shame and by decreasing concentration and motivation; they also reduce our levels of mood-enhancing brain chemicals, thereby leading us to replenish these chemicals via overindulgence in food, cigarettes, alcohol and caffeine and through other addictive behaviors.

Even if you are fortunate enough to be exempt from such problems as ADHD, PMS or SAD, you must still attempt to scale the next wall—or walk around it. This wall is composed of the clinical manifestations of shame, issues such as perfectionism, co-dependency, anger against authority figures, depression, anxiety, fear of solitude and powerlessness (zone 5). As you approach zone 5, perhaps you will focus on only one issue, or perhaps you will address several at a time—for example:

> **Perfectionism**—*you can't create anything because it won't be perfect the first time.*
>
> **Co-dependency**—*you don't work on your project or attempt to follow your dreams because you spend so much time performing tasks for others.*
>
> **Depression**—*you can't make any decisions or produce anything because you are so unmotivated and unable to concentrate.*

These issues are all a direct outgrowth of shame (zone 4). Once you see that shame is the true source of your "impostor syndrome"—the feeling that you don't have the right to make healthy decisions, to express yourself creatively, or to fulfill your dreams—then you are ready to cross the drawbridge and enter the arena of childhood (zone 3). This arena is brimming with your feelings about real or perceived physical imperfections, as well as disruptions in parenting patterns.

However, once you have used the techniques offered in this book as a drawbridge over the moat of shame and found the way to your inner self (zone 2), your winner within is not far behind (zone 1).

In studying this system of defense, it is important to avoid becoming overwhelmed. Instead, focus upon how often you have been able to spontaneously bypass the barriers inherent in this imposter syndrome by just jumping past ALL the barriers when no one is looking—you'll say you had a burst of creative energy or decisiveness as if it came from outside of you, when in reality such bursts of productive energy indicate that, for whatever reason, the winner in you felt safe enough to circumvent this system of defense and just plain and simple come out to play. The trick, of course, is to gradually penetrate this system of defense while simultaneously creating a level of safety in your own world so that you can be decisive, creative and productive in all aspects of your life.

So you're thinking: *All right, just what am I supposed to do about all of this—blame my procrastination on my parents, like so many self-help experts and television talk-show hosts suggest that I should do?*

Well, not exactly. It's more like blaming "the human condition." Yes, your parents are a part of the human condition—as were their parents before them and their parents before them, etc., all the way back to the amoebas—but then, so are you. There's really no one to "blame." Rather, it's more like you deciding to take responsibility for filling in those holes that have been blasted in the foundation of your self-esteem by any one of a number of random events.

Let me offer a hypothetical example. Suppose your great-grandmother died while giving birth to her fourth child. Her husband, overwhelmed by the responsibility, decides to keep the two boys on the farm and places the two girls in a nearby orphanage. Thus, your grandmother spends an isolated childhood in an orphanage, growing up without much affection or bonding, and is hardly equipped to enter the world of healthy, reciprocal relationships.

Your grandmother enters college in 1920 but is quickly dissuaded by her first beau to drop out and marry him. He has only a ninth-grade education, and it just won't do to have a woman outshine her husband, a notion that your grandmother readily accepts. After all, she's never had anyone say "I love you" before. Later, she gives birth to several children, one of whom is destined to be your mother. As a result of your grandmother's emotionally deprived childhood, she is unable to offer her daughter the kind of love and nurturing that is necessary for healthy self-esteem.

And there you have it: Due to an earlier tragedy in your great-grandmother's shortened life, you end up being born into a household that cannot sustain you emotionally. Your mother, suffering from the lasting effects of maternal deprivation, unwittingly marries a man who is equally as insecure as your grandfather.

You try to survive with an emotionally vacant mother and self-centered father, but the foundation of your self-esteem looks like Swiss cheese.

If you're wondering how I know so much about this family, the woman who died while giving birth was my great-grandmother. You'll hear more about the ramifications of her misfortune by and by. But first, one by one, let's attack those barriers between zones 1-8. Obviously, I got past all of this in the fortress of my own mind—all the way into zone 1—or you wouldn't be reading this book!

* * * *

Protective Procrastination As Prophet

In *Zen in the Art of Writing,* Ray Bradbury says: "I finally figured out that if you are going to step on a live mine, make it your own. Be blown up, as it were, by your own delights and despairs" (p. 15).

If you feel that your own "delights and despairs" are inaccessible, or unspeakable, keep in mind that noted psychologist Dr. Albert Ellis estimates that 95 percent of college students suffer from procrastination—in other words, from the effects of the human condition.

So is it any wonder that far too many of us live lives of quiet desperation without fulfilling our dreams, without any sense of purpose in our lives?

We must learn how to conquer this lack of motivation in order to avoid a diminished sense of spirituality in our lives, regardless of our religious orientations. As you begin to investigate the source of your procrastination, you will chance upon various clues that will help you to understand some of the driving forces in your life. In other words, if you're willing to listen to your procrastination as prophet, you just may find your way clear to the path you'd rather be on. By putting an end to procrastination and taking charge of your life, you are literally choosing to fulfill your own destiny.

It is the central tenet of this book that once the underlying issue of shame has been discovered and systematically released, procrastination can be reduced or stopped completely. Until this is done, one cannot fully enjoy a successful life either materially or spiritually. We must learn to overcome the obstacles that we are handed at birth, both major and minor. And no matter whether you are an agnostic or a member of a specific religious group, it is clear that overcoming such obstacles is a necessity for healthier, enlightened living, whether now or in some sort of afterlife.

For example, in some Eastern philosophies, it would be said that by overcoming these obstacles—which can produce shame and subsequently procrastination—we are working through our "karma," barnacles of old issues that need to be resolved in order to achieve perfection and oneness with God and the universe, a state of being known as *moksha* in Hindu philosophy or as *nirvana* in Buddhist terms. Similarly, Christians might call this "karma" their "cross to bear," a remnant of "original sin" that must be absolved by God before one can enter heaven.

No matter what your spiritual orientation may be, the humanistic element of psychological balance between work and play—the antithesis of procrastination—is often not far behind. For example, according to Hindu philosophy, we must work through such life obstacles or karma in order to achieve the four goals of humankind: *dharma, artha, kama* and *moksha*. To work through such "karma," which is often exemplified by one's childhood and family-of-origin issues, individuals must ascertain and perform their *dharma,* or life duties, such as performing adequately at work, creating works of art, or even doing household chores. If one procrastinates in performing such *dharma* (in other words, if one does not work through one's "karma"), then one is never freed up to achieve the subsequent goals of humankind: *artha*—material success; *kama*—enjoyment of life, the arts and sensuality; and *moksha*—emancipation of the spirit.

This is analogous to Freud's definition of the healthy individual: the person who can manage the pleasure principle by balancing work and play. In essence, procrastination prevents individuals from living their lives to the fullest—or with a sense of purpose. Instead, we must, as Kurt Vonnegut says regarding the effervescent optimism and fortitude displayed by Stan Laurel and Oliver Hardy, learn how to "bargain in good faith with destiny."

So you see, procrastination isn't so bad after all. It's actually there to provide us with clues about our life lessons, since it leads us back to shame—the emotion we most like to avoid—and the issues underlying the shame that keep us locked in the tomorrow trap. We can learn to see procrastination as a signal in the vast chasm of destiny, a voice in the darkness saying, "Get thee to nirvana!"

Ready to take a step or two in the right-brain direction?

2

Who Are You?
Essential Traits of the
Productive Person

Courage is not the absence of despair;
it is, rather, the capacity to move
ahead in spite of despair.

—Rollo May

Procrastination: even the word sounds overwhelming. But it doesn't have to be. All it takes is commitment—yes, the C-word. Right now, by reading this chapter, you are making a commitment to understand something more about the process of putting off until tomorrow what we all know we *could* do today. This is the first step in changing your life.

To start, notice the way you feel when you read the following sentences. Which ones feel "right" to you?

_____ I should stop procrastinating.
_____ I have to stop procrastinating.
_____ I need to stop procrastinating.
_____ I want to stop procrastinating.
_____ I choose to stop procrastinating.

Most people feel that they "should" or "have to" stop, but it usually takes a while before they can progress into the area of "choosing" to stop.

41

If it were that easy, you wouldn't be reading this book, and I certainly wouldn't have written it!

Most people don't know what causes procrastination. But they know enough to feel badly about postponing important tasks or decisions. By "important," I mean important to you, even if it is just tackling a good book you've been wanting to read. Remember, procrastination involves only the "unnecessary delay of tasks," according to expert researchers such as Laura Solomon and Esther Rothblum. Sometimes when we think we are procrastinating, we're really prioritizing. However, I have a feeling that in at least one area of your life, you're not just struggling with a skewed sense of priorities, but rather with a stronger sense of helplessness when it comes to leading the life you'd really like.

Awareness about the roots of procrastination is crucial in stopping this cycle of leading an unfulfilled life. Of course, you already know a good number of things about procrastination. For example:

1. **It keeps you riddled with anxiety:** *What's going to happen to me if I don't finish* _____ _____?

2. **It makes other people angry with you:** *How will I be able to face* _____ *when he / she finds out that I'm not going to finish this on time?*

3. **It keeps you from enjoying life:** *I wish I could go to this social event, but I can't because I have to finish* _____.

4. **It keeps you from getting the love you need:** *I'd really like to start dating again now that the divorce is final, but I won't have time to until I finish* _____.

5. **It keeps you from living your dreams:** *I've always wanted to* _____,

but I can't do that until I finish _____

_____.

It keeps you from being happy.

It never seems to go away.

It interferes with your life.

But although procrastination sounds like a very powerful force in your life, there is a way out. By making a commitment to understanding *why* you procrastinate, you can begin to eliminate this controlling factor in your life.

But how do I do this, you're asking. *You make it sound so easy.* Well, it is. Let's take a simple test to see if you are ready to bail out of procrastination prison. It goes like this:

Q: How many psychotherapists does it take to change a light bulb?

A: Only one, but it has to *want* to change.

And that's a fact. After years of research on what makes psychotherapy clients change for the better, psychologists have consistently found that one of the most potent predictors of change is whether or not the client WANTS to change.

Well, guess what? You've just passed the test by showing that you do want to change. By filling in the blanks on questions 1-5 earlier—mentally or with a pencil—you've already noticed a thing or two about procrastination that you didn't already know. You've already taken step one of the process: awareness. And you have achieved this new awareness by keeping the commitment you made—to yourself—in the first paragraph of this chapter.

And try to remember that you are not alone as you take these steps in the confusing process of procrastination recovery. There—listen, can you hear it? The sound of thousands of pencils scratching their way across the pages of this book—in bus stops, offices, studios, kitchens, bedrooms, banks and diners all over the world. Remember, we're all in this together. Procrastination is simply part of the human condition—part of our evolution as a species that we're just now beginning to understand.

✶ ✶ ✶ ✶

But I'm getting ahead of myself. Allow me to explain how I came to understand that procrastination is an inherent part of the life cycle that must be overcome in order to reach a higher level of spirituality.

And allow me to acknowledge that you'll find here and there an asterisk-break like the one above, a stopping-off place, if you will. Sometimes we forget to stop and rest on our journeys, to savor what we've just seen around the last bend. For example, right now you could say that already, you now realize something new about the issue of procrastination, namely that it can affect your life by _____ _____, and that really makes you feel

_____.

Surprise, surprise. You're taking control of procrastination already. Remember, you have to understand how it works before you can tame it.

Before I understood how it works—or why it works—I first had to understand that procrastination played a major role in my life. Although I was always able to achieve academically, it was often under the repressive dictatorship of procrastination fueled by all-night caffeine binges that I became so successful, and it was this same repressive dictatorship that kept me from fulfilling my dream of writing novels. But now that I've learned how to practice what I preach in this book, I am enjoying the process of writing not just one novel, but several.

Yet 20 years ago, although I was successful academically, inside I was deeply pained. And what about on the job? As an

English teacher, I took pride in my role as a writing mentor to my students, spending a great deal of time in personal meetings with each student—but torturing myself with late-night binges of paper-grading induced by procrastination. Similarly, in my role years later as a psychology intern, I spent inordinate amounts of time seeing clients in therapy, but procrastinated when it came to the paperwork. What could have caused this? Was I more comfortable being with people than being with papers? In other words, was I uncomfortable with the solitude necessary for doing paperwork? Or was I just being passive-aggressive, defying authority by resisting the university's rule of grade assignment and the university counseling center's rule of accountability?

* * * *

The answer is both—and a lot more. Let's take a look at how you're feeling about my story of recovery right now—and how it may be similar or dissimilar to yours. Try to answer the following questions:

1. When I think of my own problems with procrastination, I feel _____
   _____.

2. When I think of my own problems with procrastination, I think _____
   _____.

There is probably a slight difference in the way that you feel as opposed to the way that you think about procrastination. Now, answer these two questions, but this time switch hands and write or print with your nondominant hand.

1. When I think of my own problems with procrastination, I feel _____
   _____.

2. When I think of my own problems with procrastination,
   I think _____
   _____.

Again, there may be a difference in the way you feel and
the way you think about your problem. There might even be
different answers when you switched hands. By using your
nondominant hand you may have accessed other parts of
your brain that are less likely to contain your conscious
thoughts. (If you've read John Bradshaw's excellent book on
childhood, *Homecoming,* you may remember this technique
as a powerful one.)

This is due to the phenomena of "hemispheric lateraliza-
tion and specialization" as well as "hemispheric dominance"
in the brain. In other words, the two sides of the brain spe-
cialize in different areas, almost as if we had two separate
brains. However, keep in mind that although the left hemisphere of the brain controls the right hand, and the right
hemisphere controls the left hand, the left brain is dominant
in nearly everyone, regardless of whether you are right- or
left-handed. The left brain is the hemisphere specializing in
such areas as language, logic and conscious thought.

The right brain—which is nondominant in most individuals, whether you are right-handed or left-handed—is the
brain hemisphere specializing in creativity, spatial skills,
sensory memory (sight, sound, smell, taste and physical
touch), diffuse emotional states and unconscious thought.
By using your nondominant hand, you have accessed the
less dominant portion of your brain and perhaps some
deeper emotional material that is normally less available to
your conscious mind.

Using your nondominant hand throughout this book
might offer you a deeper level of insight into issues that you
feel you've already been over and over—but not deeply

enough. If you're not sure about all of this, try answering each question in this book twice, once with your dominant hand and again with your nondominant hand. Quite often, you'll get divergent answers that may lead you closer to the source of your procrastination.

Regardless of the types of answers your right and left hands have provided you in response to the questions just asked, do you notice that procrastination for you results in feelings of shame or guilt? Does it make you think less of yourself, or worry that others will somehow judge you harshly?

Ask yourself which of the following statements you'd prefer.

"I could have done better if only I'd had more time or started a little earlier."

OR

"I started the project early, worked diligently on it to the best of my ability and finished it well before the deadline, but I still didn't meet the standards of success, so that must mean I'm inadequate."

The first choice allows us to save face, while the second one leads directly to our nemesis: shame.

Most of us prefer the first sentence. Why? To find the answer, let's take a closer look at what personal qualities we need to release our unconscious shame and access the winner within.

Gaining Access to the Winner Within

To the untrained eye, the world of procrastination may appear confusing and intimidating. After all, most of us like to think that if we want to do something, then we can, or should, just do it. Why, then, don't we jump into action?

What's stopping us from accomplishing even the simplest task?

We all know that we're supposed to break up the project into smaller tasks so that it's more manageable and less overwhelming. According to researchers in the area of contingency management, such as psychologist Robert Boice, if we add in a reward after each smaller task is completed, then we are more likely to be successful in completing our task.

In one of Boice's studies, he even found that writers who used such contingency management strategies not only produced more work than writers who did not use contingency management, but the writers who used contingency management also produced work that was rated by independent judges as being more creative. So much for our claims that we have to wait until the muse or mood strikes us before we can work on a given project!

So, if all this contingency management works so well, why don't we do it? If we can fill out little charts for our children to clean their rooms and earn their gold stars toward an allowance or a trip to the movies at the end of the week, why can't we seem to fool ourselves into such a scheme for task completion?

There are several reasons. As you might guess, at least part of the problem is rooted in a deep sense of shame. First of all, contingency management involves both work (the task) and play (the reward). Aside from the fact that our society values work much more than play (how many supervisors would be thrilled to hear that you spent Monday afternoon playing golf instead of finishing the monthly report?), most of us feel that we must work in order to justify our existence. When we have a chance to relax and "play," we usually feel guilty, as though we don't deserve time to play.

Where do we get this sense of guilt, this sense that we don't deserve to play until all of the work this side of the

Mississippi is done? Why do we forget how to balance the pendulum of our lives between work and play, wedging a block beneath the pendulum once it swings over to the work zone? We'll explore the answers to these questions in the following chapters, and you'll see again and again that procrastination is nearly always rooted in a sense of unconscious shame—something we all have, but most of us don't know that it's simply part of the human condition, let alone that it's part of our life's work to discover and recover from the source of our shame.

After we have discovered and released our feelings about the sources of shame that restrain our creative, productive inner selves, we then have the option of freeing ourselves from the prison of procrastination. We can do this by using contingency management or any other time management program we've already read about that may suit our personal styles, such as David Burns' *Feeling Good* version of "The Antiprocrastination Sheet," in which we actually measure the before and after levels of the difficulty and satisfaction regarding task completion. But before we begin our journey toward freeing our inner selves, we must come to understand certain qualities about this winner within in order to gain ACCESS to him or her, as illustrated in table 1 below.

TABLE 1
Gaining ACCESS to the Winner Within

A Autonomy
C Creativity
C Confidence
E Effort
S Spontaneity
S Solitude

Autonomy

Even the sound of this word suggests a connotation of emptiness: automatic, automation—there's something inherently inhuman and negative about this word. And yet all it really signifies is the ability to function on one's own, the ability to be self-directed, unrestricted, unfettered by the demands of others.

How do you define and perceive this word? Answer each question below twice: once with your dominant hand and once with your nondominant hand.

Dominant Hand

When I think of being autonomous, I think _____
_____.

When I think of being autonomous, I feel _____
_____.

Nondominant Hand

When I think of being autonomous, I think _____
_____.

When I think of being autonomous, I feel _____
_____.

You can probably see a difference between the way you think and feel about autonomy.

In many societies, the word "autonomy" is not always perceived as positive. The notion of not needing others is considered antisocial. In his book *Solitude,* psychiatrist Anthony Storr speculates about the assumed negativity inherent in the notion of autonomy: "The majority of psychoanalysts, social workers, and other members of the so-called 'helping professions' consider that intimate personal relationships are the chief source of human happiness (p. 5)." Storr then points out that the autonomous individual who spends a great deal of time in solitude—even if he or she is a successful artist—is viewed by many people as somehow mentally imbalanced.

Thus, society values intimacy and personal relationships more than individual autonomy. The rule seems to be: You must maintain relationships with others before you can maintain your relationship with yourself. This notion affects our level of productivity, particularly those of us who have small children and/or numerous other relationships to maintain, both personal and professional. Honestly, how can one expect to take time alone for an important task when your children's laundry isn't done?

Well, would you tell your toddler that he or she cannot play with any toys whatsoever until *all* the housework is completed? (Translation: Skip the notion of having a child-hood.) Of course not. And yet that's the way most of us treat our inner child who seeks to be productive and creative.

To be a fully productive person, one must master the art of being self-directed. For example, while I was typing this sentence, no one stopped by to give me a nod of approval. As a matter of fact, anyone who knows me has been made quite aware that Tuesdays and Thursdays are off limits: I wouldn't take a conference call from the United Nations on my writing days. There was no brass band to applaud the ending of the previous paragraph. It's a beautiful day, and I can hear people splashing about in the public pool outside my window, and there are people in my life who would love to get a return phone call from me today, and yet here I sit at my computer spilling out these words in complete isolation from the rest of the world. Needless to say, you have to have a certain amount of autonomy to get away with all this—and I earned mine the hard way.

In the next few chapters, we'll explore how shame prevents the development of autonomy in one's life and look at ways to attain a higher degree of autonomy.

* * * *

Creativity

Let's take another look inside, twice, with each hand.

Dominant Hand

When I think of my creativity, I think _____
_____.

When I think of my creativity, I feel _____
_____.

Nondominant Hand

When I think of my creativity, I think _____
_____.

When I think of my creativity, I feel _____
_____.

Are your responses different or consistent? If your responses are inconsistent or negative in tone, this is probably an area of conflict for you.

If you want to be creative but are unsure if you can be, ask yourself, "Have I ever had an original thought?" or "Have I ever stated something in an original or entertaining way?"

If the answer is yes, then you've probably got what it takes. If the answer is no, then you probably still have what it takes—you just haven't let your inner self out of that blasted fortress yet. And you haven't yet built a drawbridge over that threatening moat of shame you're likely to fall into if you should dare to come out and show yourself to the world. Until your winner within has been released, you will most likely have the appearance of lacking creativity, but the reality is that we are all capable of creative behavior.

Creativity has been defined by many theorists and researchers in numerous ways. In this book, it will be defined as follows: the ability to take elements and put them together in a manner that is new, interesting and entertaining, and that evokes emotion or provokes thought. Now, with this definition in mind, why do we all have so much trouble being creative?

We may shed some light on this issue by examining another definition of creativity. In his classic work, *The Courage to Create* (p. 56), Rollo May states that "creativity is the encounter of the intensively conscious human being with his or her world." And therein lies the problem. It is often our encounters with the outside world that stifle our creativity in the first place. Over the years, other people have had the power to squelch our creativity by telling us, implicitly or explicitly, that our efforts aren't good enough or creative enough.

Consider the hypothetical case of two-year-old Sally, who, while wearing her new, lacy white dress, makes her very first mud pies 15 minutes before she is scheduled to be whisked off to Easter Sunday Mass. Do you think Sally's parents will clap their hands with joy at their daughter's first creative act, thereby encouraging her to exercise her creative spirit?

It's more likely Sally's parents will disapprove of her first attempt at sculpture. They'll probably reprimand Sally verbally or even physically, thereby teaching Sally that her creativity is not only unworthy of approval but is actually something "bad" that must be avoided, since it can bring shame and emotional pain—perhaps even physical pain. After all, she's only two years old—she can't understand that a $50 dress is supposedly worth far more than her self-esteem.

Before we jump into the judgment zone regarding Sally's parents, we must ask ourselves how many parents can afford not to teach a child that "money doesn't grow on trees." (Personally, I can honestly say that as a child I checked those spring buds on our maple trees myself several years in a row, just to be sure.) How many times have we reacted in anger, only to apologize moments later for our inappropriate outbursts? However, unless the apology is immediate and later efforts at creativity are rewarded, Sally's self-esteem is likely to suffer.

One healthy choice—but not one that most would expect to see as a knee-jerk reaction by parents on a limited budget—would be to praise the child's first creation, telling her that because her mud pies are so beautiful and important, you're going to select some special clothes for her to wear whenever she wants to create more mud pies (translation: those worn-out toddler overalls you nearly pitched last week). Then, as you clean up the child and change her into a different dress, you mentally write off the formerly lacy and now mud-laden white dress as a $50 investment in your child's self-esteem bank account (which Valerie Wells so aptly describes in *The Joy of Visualization*), remembering that you can't put a price tag on self-esteem. Fifty dollars wouldn't even cover your child's first psychotherapy session! And then you resolve to keep making these approval deposits in your child's self-esteem account, just as you might for a college fund.

Again, unless your parents came back from the future through one of those sci-fi movie portals, we have to remember that most parents and other caretakers of children are only now just beginning to understand how important their approval—or disapproval—can be to the self-esteem of a developing, impressionable child. We all no doubt have experienced numerous similar events, with or without mud pies, at home, at church, at school, in the neighborhood, at club meetings, or, in later life, in college or on the job—and this common dispensation of disapproval is only one of many factors that can inhibit the creative spirit through the mechanism of shame.

The inhibition of this creative spirit can be inherently damaging. In a recent interview with bestselling thriller writer Les Standiford, he discussed the fact that if we ignore our inner drive to express ourselves, we'll pay for the negative consequences accordingly:

> *I get depressed if I go for very long without doing writing. . . . I feel like I'm letting myself down. . . . It's a part of the self that needs to be exercised, and if it doesn't get exercised, I feel out of sorts.*

In whatever endeavors you may be delaying, such a feeling of being atrophied can cause you to feel an even deeper sense of shame, which in turn can lead you to kick yourself while you're already down—certainly not fair play when it comes to trying to help yourself out of procrastination prison.

* * * *

Confidence

Before we examine this essential ingredient for creativity and productivity, let's take another brief look inside.

Dominant Hand

When I think of my self-confidence, I think _____
_____.

When I think of my self-confidence, I feel _____
_____.

Nondominant Hand

When I think of my self-confidence, I think _____
_____.

When I think of my self-confidence, I feel _____
_____.

When I think of self-confidence, it reminds me of an experience I had several years ago when I served on a panel of speakers for the American Pen Women's Association.

In a very humble manner, considering he is a bestselling author, Dick Francis described his annual plan for writing. He usually finished a manuscript in the spring, mulled over his next book during the summer, got down to the hard work of writing in the fall and finished up again in spring: a yearly cycle of productivity. Although he joked about the expectations of his publisher, it was obvious that Francis liked his life and was confident in maintaining his work as a writer. Francis also mentioned his mother as someone who was always supportive of his endeavors.

This story of success, confidence and familial support is contrary to the stories I hear from clients suffering from procrastination and creative inhibition. Since I don't know about Dick Francis's relationship with his mother, I cannot say for certain that such positive support helped build his confidence as a productive person, but it certainly didn't hurt. Interestingly enough, in a recent interview published in *The Writer's Handbook,* Francis stated that he never experiences writer's block.

Other words of wisdom about self-confidence came during an interview with the prolific bestselling author, Bernie Siegel, M.D. When I asked him about writer's block, he said: "The worst grade I got in college was in creative writing."

Obviously, he didn't let anyone's negative evaluation of his writing demolish his self-confidence.

We all know that confidence isn't usually something that can be faked. If we try, it doesn't ring true. However, it is something we can build up gradually.

For a variety of reasons, most of us lack confidence at one time or another. Even if we are willing and able to access our creativity, that doesn't mean we'll have the faith to follow through. Suppose our efforts don't measure up to certain standards. How can we continue in the face of possible failure?

Such failure might bring about a sense of inadequacy, leading us to tap into our pools of unconscious shame. The result is that we're less likely to continue our efforts, even though we believe we have the talent and stamina to complete the project. In later chapters, we'll see just how far astray our confidence can go.

* * * *

Effort

Recently, when I interviewed bestselling thriller writer Paul Levine, he said that he doesn't have problems with writer's block. I asked him what advice he'd give to aspiring but procrastinating writers, and he said: "Six words: Stick your ass in the chair." But after offering this straightforward "solution," he agreed that completing a task such as writing a book isn't easy:

> *You are not punching a clock, you don't have a supervisor, you are not working in an office environment where there is peer pressure. . . . So you have to find it in yourself, and it is just plain old self-discipline and organization. That is what you have to do.*

Author Les Standiford agrees:

> *It has a lot to do with understanding the . . . necessity of practice and time. . . . It requires great effort and diligence and a schedule of activity. . . . Inspiration is more likely to arrive in the workroom than anywhere else.*

If what these prolific, successful authors are saying is true, why don't we do it? What's stopping us from making the effort to sit down and begin a given task or contemplate the factors involved in an important decision?

Let's take a look inside and see once again if the right hand knows what the left hand is doing.

Dominant Hand

When I think of "making an effort" at something, I usually think _____

_____.

When I think of "making an effort" at something, I usually feel _____

_____.

Nondominant Hand

When I think of "making an effort" at something, I usually think _____

_____.

When I think of "making an effort" at something, I usually feel _____

_____.

Chances are your answers are rooted in your childhood. Did your family set goals and complete them? Were you taught by your caretakers that reaching an important goal usually takes time, effort and persistence? Or did they give you the impression that they were entitled to have life handed to them on the proverbial silver platter because they'd had it rough in the past?

We must not minimize the effects of "hard times" on our caretakers—just living through the Great Depression and World War II warrants some sort of gold medal in and of itself. However, did your caretakers make an effort to change their "lot in life"? Or did they resign themselves to their situation, too exhausted, depressed or fearful to channel their efforts into a positive mode?

Many of our caretakers had a different and in some ways more difficult road to follow than we do. They did not have the luxury of psychotherapy, support groups or self-help books. Thus, for many of us, the legacy of our caretakers involves a certain amount of "learned helplessness," and even though we may know that such an attitude is painful and futile, we may hang onto it just out of habit, especially if that's the ONLY legacy we received from our caretakers.

This concept of "learned helplessness" is one psychological explanation for depression, as illustrated by Martin Seligman's research in the 1970s. The results of his work have been helpful in understanding why people don't make an effort to change their lives, even when it seems clear that they have the option to do so.

Seligman conducted a series of experiments in which two groups of matched dogs were delivered a series of very mild, but uncomfortable, electric shocks. Of course the animals initially got up and walked around, trying to avoid the discomfort of the shocks. The first group of dogs had to learn to press a panel to escape. For the second group of dogs, there was no escape, unless their matched "partner" dogs from the first group pressed the panel in their boxes.

Eventually this second set of dogs became accustomed to the discomfort of the stimulus. And since they were not in charge of their own escape, when they did get out, it appeared random.

However, what is most striking about these experiments occurred in the next stage.

Both groups of dogs were again subjected to the same mild intensity of electric shock, but with the possibility of escape for both groups by jumping a hurdle. The first group, which had had control in the previous experiment, learned to jump the hurdle to escape. However, even though they could see a clear mode of escape, the dogs in the second group, which had had no control in the previous experiment, were unable to learn to escape by jumping the hurdle.

Accepting the discomfort of what they perceived to be their only choice, these animals had developed a sense of "learned helplessness."

Similarly, individuals learn the same lesson after life's many defeats. Even though we might say,"But our caretakers could have done something about their problems—they could have improved our lives," it's important to remember that learned helplessness has a powerful effect on behavior. As such learned helplessness can become a transgenerational problem, with each generation in a family adopting such an attitude as part of the family's psychological legacy.

What if we don't want to remain helpless in reaching our goals in life? What keeps us from making the effort necessary to change our habit of procrastination when it comes to our careers and relationships?

Sometimes the payoff runs something like this: Keeping our caretakers' legacy of learned helplessness and self-neglect is like wearing a comforting old sweater woven from the DNA strands of our ancestors. Although our caretakers' learned helplessness is a very negative legacy, keeping it around is a way of keeping our caretakers with us, so that we don't really have to see ourselves as alone and solely responsible for our lives. If we have suffered neglect or abuse from our caretakers, keeping their legacy—even if it's downright destructive—is a way of fooling ourselves into thinking they DID give us *something,* some kind of love, after all. The only problem is, we don't need that kind of "love" if we want to have fulfilling lives.

Instead, we can sew a silk lining in that scratchy old wool ancestral sweater, or perhaps lengthen the sleeves a little: We can choose to change our attitudes and beliefs about setting and meeting our goals, and start accepting the fact that it's really up to us to put forth the effort to change our lives. For example, in my work, I see many aspiring writers who are so intimidated by the effort involved in the process of researching, writing, editing and publishing a book—especially with no guarantee that anyone will ever read those pages for which one expends so much blood, sweat and tears—that they never even try to start.

There are two ways to respond to this type of intimidation. The first step is to recognize that your project—whether it's writing a book, getting a divorce, starting a relationship or choosing a career—can and must be broken down into smaller tasks so it's not so overwhelming. A first effort might be reading two related articles for the writer, calling two daycare centers to assess post-divorce financial costs for the unhappily married, calling two organizations or clubs for the person seeking a relationship, or calling two universities and requesting admissions brochures for the college-bound.

The second and perhaps even more potent antidote to the poison of what I call "project intimidation" involves the following realization: If you don't finish your project, who will? You can't worry about anyone appreciating your efforts until you show the world what you can do. We will see how the feeling of shame stops us before we can even begin.

* * * *

Spontaneity

Let's see what your views are on this essential factor in the creative-productive process.

Dominant Hand

When I think of spontaneity, I think _____
_____.

When I think of spontaneity, I feel _____
_____.

Nondominant Hand

When I think of spontaneity, I think _____
_____.

When I think of spontaneity, I feel _____
_____.

You may find that your answers reflect two different points of view. First, it's not okay to be too spontaneous; it may be viewed as irresponsibility. A second view would be that spontaneity is a positive part of life, a matter of remaining childlike—rather than childish—in a world that could stand some lightening up, to say the least.

No matter what your view, it's quite obvious that in order to be a fully productive and creative person, one must have the capacity to be rational and organized and to plan if a project is ever to be undertaken, let alone completed. But what about our emotional, more spontaneous side—the inner self who must be freed up to access our creativity? The inner self is the part of us who feels, not just thinks, about creative projects and important decisions to be made. The problem is, far too many of us can't feel anything anymore. Many of us live within the boundaries of a restricted range of emotions. Since we cannot fully express ourselves, our creativity and productivity suffer.

Author Les Standiford, who also teaches creative writing to graduate students, said he sees this inability to feel a broad range of emotions, particularly unpleasant emotions, as a major block for many inexperienced writers.

> *Only trouble is interesting. You've got to identify with your character, you've just got to—but to the extent you're living that character's life when you're writing about that character, and then that character's got to have terrible trouble? Well, who wants to go through that? . . . I know there are many, many people who have great difficulty with this . . . because we don't want conflict in our lives. To write convincing fiction means living vicariously the life of this person in trouble. . . . So sometimes I think it's just plain simple old avoidance: "I don't want to do that. It's not pleasant."*

Any form of psychological discomfort that comes early enough or is painful enough can trigger a fear of strong emotion. This restriction of emotions, both pleasurable and distressing, can lead to severe problems with procrastination.

All of us have our own personal reasons for limiting our feelings. Suppose you have had some sort of heartache—perhaps a lingering sense of hurt from the effects of flawed parenting, coupled with the effects of a recent divorce and perhaps a child who has a debilitating disease. Each of these painful situations, whether alone or in combination, can bring about a restriction in your emotions.

So you can just imagine what can and often does happen to the emotional range of people who have endured childhood abuse, a traumatic first sexual experience during the teen years (nowadays we call it date rape), the death of a loved one, or a terrifying stint as a soldier at war—the list is endless. In other words, all of us living on Planet Earth have a reason or two or 10 as to why we should restrict the range of our emotions. But if we restrict them too much, then our productivity and creativity are likely to suffer.

For instance, one client had a severe case of writer's block. This 40-year-old man had horrific experiences as a soldier in Vietnam, one of which left him unable to walk without a cane. Alex's range of emotion was so constricted that you could have set off a bomb in my office and he wouldn't have blinked. He had steeled himself against emotional reactions to survive the war. Now that coping mechanism was no longer useful and, in fact, was detrimental, since Alex was unable to face his emotional side long enough to write. It seemed as though he was afraid of his own unconscious.

Sometimes imagination is just a little too close to memory—they both reside in the right side of the brain, which is much more likely to encode negative rather than positive memories—and Alex wasn't about to go traipsing around any place filled with so many potential land mines. He'd already done enough of that as a soldier.

Even if your lifelong litany of painful events doesn't rival being a witness to the horrors of war, your pain, though you've probably minimized it, could still be affecting you. You may think that others have had it much worse than you—but you've got to look both ways on the continuum of human suffering. Yes, you can always find someone worse off. But look the other way, and you'll see those who had it better than you—always a reminder that you, too, deserved being treated with more love, dignity and respect.

The reality is, it could have been better for that other person as well as for you. Other people didn't have to be raised by a single parent—they had two parents show up for Parents' Day in elementary school. Other people didn't get bullied by the neighborhood gang—they had good friends to play baseball with. In other words, your pain—though it may not emanate from domestic violence or a serious car accident—is still very real. You wouldn't say to a two-year-old with a broken arm, "Oh, just get over it—you don't need any medical attention; you could have broken your neck." So why treat your inner self that way?

Whatever your inner self has suffered, to avoid feeling pain, you may restrict your emotions and close off your imagination. Spontaneity will not be an option. For if we behave in a fashion that is not predictable, we may dip into that pool of residual emotions, with that old layer of unconscious shame at the bottom. It is as if all of our unexpressed emotions—which normally come up to the heart level—are backed up all the way to the eye level, and, like the brimming spoonful of water that awaits that one last drop to break its surface tension and cause its overflow, we, too, sense (consciously or unconsciously) that our emotions can erupt into tears of sadness or anger at any moment. So we hold back, fearful that even the slightest sensation of emotion will release an onslaught of uncontrollable tears. Thus, when we attempt to make an important decision or take on a project, we are not fully present; only half of us is there. And of course, we are much more likely to put off doing something that requires our total presence.

Although this may seem like a foolproof system for avoiding painful emotions, we must also realize that when we restrict our range of emotions, we hold back all of our feelings, even the pleasurable ones. It is as if our emotions, like the beats of our hearts, are registered in spikes and valleys on the graph produced by an EKG. But if we raise up the lower edge of the EKG apparatus so as to avoid any deep, intense negative emotions, we simultaneously pull down the upper edge of this emotional apparatus as well—the two borders comprise a connected set. They do not move independently of one another, just as our eyes cannot work independently. Thus, we feel neither pain nor joy. And once life becomes joyless, depression can set in. This not only decreases spontaneity, but also increases procrastination by lowering the motivation and concentration necessary to make a decision or complete a task.

We usually restrict our emotions because we assume that negative feelings will erupt and overwhelm us. We think that once we tap into our sadness, anger or hurt, we'll never stop crying. We imagine that negative emotions are permanent, even though we know that positive emotions are not.

Imagine that you're in front of a cozy fireplace with friends or family after a hearty meal, laughing over old times as the sun sets. You feel relaxed and satisfied. You wish that this evening would last forever, but you know such positive moments and feelings are transient.

While you are aware that such positive emotions are temporary, you may have convinced yourself that negative emotions are permanent. How can that be? Obviously, it can't. Below is a brief exercise that will help to illustrate the idea that both positive and negative emotions are transient. Just think of one or two words that can accurately describe how you felt during the specified times.

Right now _____

9:00 P.M. yesterday _____

5:00 P.M. yesterday _____

3:00 P.M. yesterday _____

12:00 P.M. yesterday _____

11:00 A.M. yesterday _____

9:00 A.M. yesterday _____

2:00 P.M. last Sunday _____
10:00 A.M. last Sunday _____
11:00 P.M. last Saturday _____
4:00 P.M. last Saturday _____
1:00 P.M. last Saturday _____
11:00 A.M. last Saturday _____

Notice how your emotions can change; they come and go, a constant ebb and flow. Children are a perfect example: a four-year-old can be playing and giggling, then fall down, skin a kneecap and start wailing. Two minutes later that same child is laughing and playing again. Children don't question the spontaneity of emotion. If we were able to access that inner child and experience the full range of human emotions, our creativity would blossom. Instead, most of us restrict our self-expression and our productivity as well.

If you are unable to feel joy or any other positive emotion, then you may be at higher risk for workaholism. As you'll see in chapter 7, workaholics often procrastinate in fulfilling their underlying dreams—they don't feel they have the right to enjoy life at all. Because they are unable to be spontaneous or playful, they often come to resent their daily work, so they begin to procrastinate on those tasks as well. Ironically, they end up procrastinating at work as well as play—hardly an enviable life.

* * * *

Solitude

The last essential element of the creative-productive process is solitude, which differs from the concept of autonomy. Autonomy is the ability to be self-directed, whereas solitude is simply spending time alone, whether you are highly autonomous or not. An autonomous person might begin writing a paper even before it is assigned, but that person could still be afraid of isolation and choose to work on the task only if others are nearby—such as in a library or restaurant.

Essentially, one must be autonomous to tolerate long periods of solitude. However, an autonomous person doesn't necessarily feel comfortable alone.

Dominant Hand

When I think of solitude, I think _____

_____.

When I think of solitude, I feel _____

_____.

Nondominant Hand

When I think of solitude, I think _____

_____.

When I think of solitude, I feel _____

_____.

Fear of solitude is perhaps one of the most common and most debilitating sources of procrastination. For many tasks, and for making important decisions regarding relationships or careers, we eventually need to spend time alone. There's just no getting around it. Yet people will resort to just about anything rather than face themselves alone. Just ask yourself, when you've tried to sit down and perform a task or make an important decision, how many times you've procrastinated with the help of the following behaviors:

_____ Doing meaningless or menial tasks
_____ Eating compulsively
_____ Getting a cup of coffee
_____ Lighting up a cigarette

_____ Having a drink
_____ Lighting up a joint
_____ Snorting cocaine
_____ Engaging in sexual activity
_____ Engaging in compulsive shopping
_____ Engaging in compulsive exercise
_____ Working compulsively on another project

Although most people instantly recognize themselves in at least one of the first four avoidant behaviors, I have also worked with clients who regularly use the last seven compulsive-avoidant behaviors as part of their delaying techniques. These actions help us avoid anxiety by triggering the release of mood-enhancing chemicals that temporarily alleviate the anxiety accompanying solitude. So while we may feel good, the task or decision at hand never gets completed or resolved.

When I am trying to clarify the exact nature of a procrastinating client's anxiety, I'll often suggest that prior to a regularly scheduled psychotherapy session, the client come and use a desensitization room that I call "The Writer's Floe"— an island of safety in an otherwise tempestuous sea of procrastination. There are no telephones, books or any other distractions in the room—just tablets of paper, pens, pencils, crayons and markers of every color and style you might imagine. The room is decorated in bright but soothing colors, with prints of Monet's water lilies and various photographs on the walls. The client is asked to use the room for 15 to 30 minutes—free of charge—and to write about his or her anxiety regarding procrastination, or to actually try to perform part of the task being procrastinated (such as studying, making an outline for an academic paper, doing a character sketch for a novel, writing a letter of good-bye to a spouse, brainstorming a list of possible new careers).

Although many clients are drawn to this colorful room when they first walk past it before they know its purpose, once they are asked to use the room—in solitude—many of them are quite resistant, even though they are aware that a therapy session will immediately follow their stint of solitude, so that whatever anxiety comes up can be dealt with immediately. The threat of solitude is just too great.

In my clinical work, I have noted that fear of solitude seems to stem from two primary sources: separation anxiety and fear of painful emotions that may surface once you're alone without distractions.

Separation anxiety comes from childhood when our primary caregivers were unreliable, neglectful or abusive. The fear of experiencing repressed feelings of hurt or rejection during solitude may relate either to these earlier years or to later shame-based experiences. Often this cycle will repeat itself. This example will illustrate just how much fear can come from the forces of solitude.

Sandy, 25, a bright college student, was so uncomfortable with the idea of studying that he would procrastinate until the last few days of the semester, then drink caffeine nonstop for days. The result was usually a set of C's when he knew he could get A's. This was not simply a case of boredom. Sandy enjoyed his courses in engineering and planned to be a successful engineer. It soon became clear that his procrastination was related to a fear of solitude emanating from separation anxiety.

During the last year of his marriage, Sandy's wife had lived in another town, 600 miles away, in order to attend the college program of her choice. During this separation, she told Sandy to study, since she was away. Instead, Sandy came to resent the time away from her. Being alone with his studies only served to highlight his loneliness.

Even long after the divorce, whenever Sandy tried to approach his studies, he would alternately feel lonely and angry. He had developed a conditioned response to studying. To cope with the anxiety that preceded his negative feelings, Sandy would eat compulsively while watching television. The resulting weight gain lowered his self-esteem even further.

To make matters worse, Sandy's residual feelings of separation anxiety regarding his parents were also triggered when he was alone. Through such techniques as photohistory and the indirect interview (discussed in chapter 6), Sandy determined that his childhood as an "Army brat" had resulted in separation anxieties many times over. His parents moved four times before he was three years old. They were often preoccupied with the pragmatics of moving and with feelings of loss relating to relatives and friends left behind. As a result, Sandy's parents were emotionally unavailable to him. Gradually, Sandy began to see the connections between his old feelings of shame, rejection and abandonment, and his current life situation.

Once he was able to work through his feelings of abandonment regarding his wife and parents, Sandy was able to start studying in restaurants where he would not compulsively overeat, then in the procrastination desensitization room at my office (where there was no food), and finally alone at home, starting with 15-minute segments of study time without compulsive eating. Once he had mastered the art of solitude—an essential ingredient in the creative, productive person—he stopped abusing himself with all-night study binges and compulsive eating.

The words of author Les Standiford may also be instructive here. He discussed the fact that although he is by nature a very social and gregarious person, he realizes that enduring long periods of solitude has been essential for his success as a writer:

> *That just goes with the territory. . . . It isn't the fun part, but I'll tell you, when I'm writing. . . it's as if I am the person I'm writing about. . . . As a result, the characters whom I'm writing about—they're out there having a social life, and so am I, too, vicariously. . . . At that point, I'm no longer alone.*

Standiford's words can certainly offer us hope that even while we may have trouble enduring solitude, the very nature of our work, if it involves creative writing, can help us to overcome such feelings of being "too alone." However, not all people can relate to this level of "vicarious living" as an antidote to the pain of solitude, and not everyone has problems with procrastination that simply relate to the area of creative writing.

Any task that requires solitude, such as making a decision, writing or expressing oneself artistically, doing paperwork or reading, may be avoided if being alone makes one uncomfortable. Such fear of solitude can mask deeper problems relating to issues of shame. In the next chapter, we'll find out why many of us are unable to develop the essential traits of the productive person—all the while keeping in mind that the only thing to fear is fear of the self, a notion we'll dispel in part two of this book.

3

You're Free to Go Now:
The Development
of Autonomy During
Childhood to Prevent
Procrastination
in Later Life

*The capacity to be alone,
first in the presence of the mother,
and then in her absence, is also related
to the individual's capacity to get in
touch with, and make manifest,
his own true inner feelings.*

—Anthony Storr

Throughout the first few chapters of this book, I have suggested that shame emanating from early childhood is the triggering factor for the development of procrastination in later life. In chapter 2, I suggested that certain qualities were essential for the development of a "productive" personality. In this chapter, we'll explore how normal child development can set us up for problems with procrastination in later life.

Autonomy vs. Shame

Autonomy versus Shame—sounds like two heavyweights vying for the World Wrestling Federation title, doesn't it?

According to noted psychologist Erik Erikson, these two concepts represent an essential conflict that must be resolved during the developmental stage we all face between the ages of two and four. Unfortunately, you can probably guess which word usually wins the match.

What happens between birth and age two, during the battle of trust versus mistrust, will also affect this battle between autonomy and shame—as well as the level to which you may procrastinate in later life. It's hard to imagine being an infant or toddler, let alone to recall how either autonomy or shame won out in the battle over your self-esteem in the first place. Most of that information is locked in the right side of the brain, since that is where our pre-verbal and more emotional memories are stored (remember: the left brain starts storing data after age two or three, since it handles language-based memories).

To take a closer look at how that battle was fought and won, let's begin with a simple self-assessment, first with your dominant hand, then with the other:

Dominant Hand

When I think of my self-esteem, I feel _____
_____.

My self-esteem is lowest when _____
_____.

On a scale of 0 (self-esteem of an amoeba) to 100 (highest self-esteem possible), I'd rate my self-esteem as usually being between _____ and _____.

Nondominant Hand

When I think of my self-esteem, I feel _____
_____.

My self-esteem is lowest when _____
_____.

On a scale of 0 (self-esteem of an amoeba) to 100 (highest self-esteem possible), I'd rate my self-esteem as usually being between _____ and _____.

I have suggested that procrastination is a direct result of unconscious shame that accumulates during our early years. In essence, unless we had an absolutely perfect childhood, a certain amount of shame will be a predictable result. In response to this idea, check off the statements below that apply to you.

_____ I have no deep sense of shame—I've never done anything that terrible.

_____ I didn't have any major childhood traumas.

_____ I had a happy childhood.

_____ I had some rough times growing up, but I've put them all behind me.

_____ I wasn't affected by my childhood.

If the answers to the first three statements are true for you, you are likely to be envied by the rest of us. However, even if you had truly loving parents who had no residual problems from their own childhoods—no illness, no financial pressures, no divorce —you are not exempt from life's troubles. As a matter of fact, I actually worked with a client who, because he'd had such a loving childhood, came in for psychotherapy to help him adjust to the pressures of living in Miami, the capital of capital offenses!

Even though your parents may have provided you with a relatively healthy environment, what about grandparents, aunts and uncles, neighbors, baby-sitters and other potentially toxic people outside of the family? Shame also can develop from events in later life, like mistreatment at the hands of an alcoholic stepparent or enduring an emotionally abusive marriage.

But let's go back to where it all began.

* * * *

The World According to Baby

Imagine that you are a newborn—a fresh, new spirit in a tiny, fragile body. You have brought with you the innocence and purity of the universe in its clearest form. Your only goal is survival.

Until your birth, your sensory input was limited to the comforting warmth and sounds from or near your mother's body. Suddenly you are in the world, bombarded by a host of confusing and intense stimuli.

You begin to adjust to these sights, sounds, textures, smells and tastes, communicating through your five senses. Curled up in your crib or in anyone's arms, you are one tiny ball of sensation and emotion.

You have no sense of self yet—no sense that you are separate from all of these sights and sounds and stimuli. You don't know yet that you are what we call an individual—a unique, living entity who is separated from all other entities by the boundary of skin. From an Eastern philosophical perspective, perhaps it can be said that you are still perceiving yourself as part of the One or God from whence you came, and thus you expect that love will be mirrored right back to you wherever you may look.

But from a sensory level, as far as you are concerned, you are literally part and parcel of everything around you. Those flowered curtains are not seen as separate from you. That chair your Aunt Esmerelda is sitting on is part of you, and so is she, for that matter. She might be more interesting to you because she moves (let's hope in later life you'll find a few other good qualities about her), but she ranks right up there with the chair and flowered curtains for now.

Within two weeks after birth, you begin to prefer the human voice over other sounds. Soon you realize that human beings are interesting, and they feed you. Food is most important, whether you are bottle- or breast-fed. By four weeks of age, you prefer the voice of your mother, or primary caretaker, over all others.

You also discover something wonderful when you look into the faces of your primary caregivers—or at least you're supposed to see something wonderful there. What you are supposed to see, given a fairly loving caretaker, is an expression of kindness, love and approval—a mirror image of the One of which you may still feel a part. Because you have no idea yet that these caretakers are separate from you, it's like looking in the mirror when you look into the faces of your caregivers because they are, as far as you know, part of you.

You must depend on the mirroring of your "self" in the eyes of your caretakers in order to begin developing a sense of "self." If what you sense in the eyes of those around you is love, then you feel that you are "love-able,"or worthy of love. If, however, what you see in this emotional mirror is distress, aggravation, anger or shame, then you feel that you are distressing, aggravating, anger-provoking and shameful. Whatever is reflected back to you in the faces of your caregivers is what you experience as your "self."

Of course it is impossible for any caregivers to be so perfectly attuned at all times to a child's needs.

Our parents or caretakers had problems: trying to raise three children under the age of five, coping with a dying grandparent living in the home, struggling for food during the Great Depression, grieving over a lost loved one in a war, living with infidelity or violence. And of course our caretakers couldn't be expected to mask all of their feelings in response to such problems. Instead, it's more likely that these emotions of fear, grief and anger were prominently displayed in the expressions of our caretakers, and unbeknownst to them, unconsciously transmitted to us.

A child can sense when a guardian is displacing aggression or withholding love. I once saw a toddler whose mother, grieving over the death of her husband, had teased the child in a subtly frightening way, whereupon the child immediately turned to a complete stranger, called her "mommy," and jumped into the person's lap. Of course, the child immediately returned to the mother, her primary source of attachment. But the bond had been ever so subtly contaminated with the mother's frustrated reaction to her husband's death, displaced as anger onto her child.

Recent research by Mary Ainsworth and Carolyn Eichberg indicates that such a loss in the caretaker's life can have a profound negative effect on the caretaker's attachment bond with his or her infant, unless the caretaker has worked through and resolved the emotional pain of such a deep loss—an unlikely prospect if our parents were raising us before the era of self-help. Regardless of the child's behavioral response to disrupted or flawed parenting, the result is shame when such loss of love is experienced.

What happens if this "loss of love" is long-lasting? Children must have a mechanism to avoid absorbing the toxic emotions of unhealthy caregivers. Infants break this emotional mirror through the inborn mechanism of shame. Yes, I did say "inborn." Researchers around the world have consistently found that the universal sign of shame, gaze aversion, is present even in infants. Gaze aversion, or downcast eyes, is what we usually do when we feel ashamed. Even animals do this—Fido's telltale "gaze aversion" often gives you fair warning as you approach the new carpeting that he's just christened.

So how does this work with babies? Infants will usually return your gaze by instinct, since they need to bond with caregivers in order to guarantee the caregivers' continued presence for the baby's survival. Within the first few months, the human face will bring delight to an infant: hence, the appearance of the "social smile." However, if the caretaker's gaze is toxic—and we're talking about not just parents, but also siblings, relatives, neighbors, baby-sitters and the like—then the infant will break eye contact: the universal sign of shame. It's as though the baby knows that it is unsafe to bond with an unhealthy person.

I came across a clear example of such gaze aversion one day while waiting in a hair salon. I saw a photo in a magazine of a high-fashion model and her four-month-old baby. Aside from the model's comment that it would have been "easier" if they had "rented a baby for this shoot," I was struck by the vacuous look in her eyes and the look of apathy mirrored in the baby's face.

Perhaps it was only for the sake of the photo shoot, but I couldn't help noticing that the model's eyes were devoid of love, carrying the cold expression of a mannequin that no doubt she'd been trained to exhibit. In every photo, this mother's eyes were met by the baby's complete gaze aversion, even when the mother's face was only inches from the baby's eyes. Again, perhaps this was the intended effect of the photo shoot—to show that high-fashion models can have babies and still be working models with trim figures— but what struck me was that nowhere in the article did anyone mention the baby's gaze aversion. The focus simply was not on the baby. For the sake of this baby not being exposed to this toxic display of apathy, I wish they *had* "rented" a baby—a mannequin. Again, in all fairness to this particular high-fashion model, she may very well be a loving and attentive mother in other situations. But what is significant to me is the fact that the pictures were taken in this toxic manner at all in the first place. As a society, we often just don't get it.

In general, by "toxic," I mean a person who consistently displays apathy or negative emotions. Toxicity comes in varying degrees. Even caregivers who are non-toxic can become so during a postpartum depression, recurring pre-menstrual syndrome (which can become worse after each pregnancy), a painful divorce or the death of a loved one.

All of these, plus the caretaker's unresolved childhood pain, can severely impair his or her capacity to mirror love and give a healthy sense of self-esteem to a child. Instead, the infant sees anger, hurt, disapproval and pain, all of which not only diminish the infant's capacity for feeling good but also deepen the pool of shame that is just begin-ning to develop. Although this shame is initially helpful and essential to the baby's avoidance of a toxic bond, the shame itself becomes toxic if the child is not exposed to healthier caretakers, such as relatives or perhaps a dedi-cated day-care worker, because the child then comes to believe that he or she is not worthy of love. And in rolls the next cloud of shame.

Now, there are many people who might say that such notions are ridiculous: The baby isn't engaging in "gaze aversion," she's just "looking around." However, if we exam-ine some of the classic research on attachment bonding and shame, we'll see that such notions are indeed ones that we'd better take more seriously if we ever, as a race, want to raise enough healthy children to finally hit any sem-blance of "nirvana."

* * * *

Attachment and Bonding

The classic research of the '40s, '50s and '60s by John Bowlby, Harry Harlow and Mary Ainsworth offers impressive evidence of the need for infant attachment bonding. Later research supports their theories.

Perhaps the best known of Harlow's experiments involved a group of infant monkeys who were separated at birth from their mothers. Harlow offered the newborn monkeys two options. Side by side were two surrogate mother wire-mesh monkeys with buttons for eyes. Attached to one cold, wiry surrogate "mother" was a baby bottle full of milk. The other surrogate mother monkey had no food to offer, but its wire-mesh body was covered in a soft terry cloth material. Surprisingly, Harlow found that the infant monkeys were willing to forego food for a chance to cling to the soft warmth of the cloth monkey. Harlow concluded that the need for the comfort of physical contact and attachment bonding is a primary element of survival.

Bowlby's research, commissioned by the World Health Organization in the 1940s, provided even more direct evidence that attachment bonding is crucial to a child's growth. Normally, between the ages of six and 12 months, infants develop a strong preference for their mothers and other primary caretakers. This is exemplified by the normal development of "stranger anxiety." The infant at this age often expresses alarm when exposed to strangers.

Bowlby studied infants and toddlers whose attachment bond had been broken by a long separation, such as hospitalization of the child or the mother. Once away from their mothers, the children would protest loudly for prolonged periods of time. Then came despair and finally detachment. When children believe the mother will not return, they become depressed. If they are abandoned by a primary guardian, children believe that they are the cause. They feel that they must be "bad" because if they had been "good," the caretaker would not have left.

In Bowlby's research, the children who were reunited with their mothers often reacted with detachment and apathy. It was as if, in an attempt to avoid the shame of being unwanted and unworthy of love, the child was saying, "I didn't need your love anyway."

Since "abandonment depressions" are so emotionally painful, the child must detach in order to avoid such pain. These abandonment depressions, whether due to physical or emotional abandonment, are often relived in adulthood, and here is where procrastination comes in. If as a child you suddenly lost or were separated long-term from your primary guardian, then an abandonment depression most likely occurred. For example, situations such as divorce and/or remarriage often involve suddenly removing the child from the primary care of a parent or grandparent, and if a strong attachment bond has formed, the child senses this loss. If those feelings of sadness are unexplored and unresolved, they don't simply go away but remain in the form of fear of intimacy and procrastination.

Here's how it works. If you are a consistent procrastinator, then you're probably always turning down social engagements because you "don't have time" since you "have to work on _____." In other words, procrastination protects you from developing deeper, more intimate relationships, which always carry the threat of rejection and abandonment. And because you have rarely tried to develop deep, intimate relationships, you have probably had negative experiences with being hurt. You don't know how to peel back the layers of trust like an onion, one layer at a time. Instead, someone cuts right into the middle of that onion, with too many tears as a result. And intimacy is once again thwarted.

Procrastination can also protect you from feeling lonely or alone if you always have that project to come home to. For a young couple who came for counseling, this was a serious problem.

Essentially, Ben took second place to Sara's house, which she was always working on in one form or another—a convenient way to avoid intimacy for a woman who had been deeply hurt as a child by her mother's alcoholism. Sara was never really "alone," since she always had projects in the works. At the same time, she avoided true intimacy with Ben, and kept him orbiting at a safe distance by keeping herself busy all the time. In a sense, she was doing to Ben what her mother had done to her, keeping Ben bonded to her but without any true depth of communication or vulnerability on her part.

In a similar case, I worked with a client who had been "ABD," all-but-dissertation, for 25 years.

While trying to finish her Ph.D., Rose had deprived herself of most human contact, interacting only on a superficial basis at work. Upon closer scrutiny, it became clear that the pain of early maternal rejection had led Rose into stage three of Bowlby's model: detachment. She didn't believe that she needed other people, let alone intimacy. Her job and her dissertation research were enough.

Rose gradually began using alcohol to dull her anxiety about the dissertation. In reality, this alcohol abuse masked a deeper, painful sense of shame brought on when she was a child. Through the process of photohistory, Rose became aware of the depth of her feelings of rejection. When her mother was pregnant with Rose, she was forced to give up her career as a dancer and marry a man she didn't love. In nearly every picture that Rose retrieved from the family albums, her mother was scowling at her. There was always a desk or a chair or just plain empty space between mother and daughter—no touching allowed.

With the help of this and other techniques, Rose was able to release her hurt and anger, stop her compulsive use of alcohol and join a support group in order to develop the social skills necessary for the human relationships she had always craved.

As her social life developed, Rose relied less and less on her dissertation project as her "friend." Once she saw it as an albatross blocking her career path, she was finally able to begin using contingency management (completing small goals, followed by rewards) to work on the project.

So what does all this have to do with you and your procrastination? Perhaps more than you think. As we progress further you may find that your habit of putting things off has its roots in your childhood, when you had little or no control over your life.

Remember, no matter what you find on this journey within, it is yours, and it is up to you to learn from it and move on. And there's no shame in that.

* * * *

Healthy Attachment As a Basis for Safe Exploration of the Environment

As you can see, the need for a healthy attachment is directly linked to survival. Infants instinctively bond with adults in order to assure a permanent caretaker who will fulfill their basic needs.

But what happens when the child no longer needs the caretaker's constant attention? How does he or she achieve a separation while still maintaining an attachment?

Jean Piaget, who scientifically studied his own children, found that this phase of separation/individuation occurs gradually between the ages of 24 to 36 months. By that time the child has developed a sense of object permanence, which means that an object continues to exist even when it can't be seen. Notice how an infant won't go looking for a particularly loud, obnoxious toy once you put it out of the baby's view behind the couch. The infant simply assumes the object no longer exists. But a toddler will go right behind the couch and retrieve that obnoxious toy—and of course as a perfect, loving and highly enlightened parent, you rejoice in your child's development of object permanence in spite of your toy-induced migraine, right? (More than likely, you scheme as to how the toy might break or become "lost" by the end of the day and hope that your child will take a renewed interest in Mister Rogers.)

Needless to say, this concept applies also to people in the child's life. Even though you can hand a newborn or a four-month-old over to just about anyone, between six and 12 months, when the child knows who the primary caretakers are, quite a fuss will be made when the child is held by any-one else. Such "stranger anxiety" has caused many an uninformed or frustrated child care worker or baby-sitter to berate or even slap a child—something the parents (out at last, to the movies, alone!) will probably never even know.

By 24 months, the child frequently explores the world, returning to touch or gaze at the primary caregiver every few minutes for reassurance. Thus, the child is safe in the knowledge that a loving, reliable caretaker is waiting in the background. That fact established, the child will begin to explore the environment even more, thereby developing a sense of autonomy, a.k.a. "the Terrible Two's." Because many adults do not understand how important it is for a child to develop this sense of independence, the Terrible Twos—the "just say no" phase of toddlerhood—are often a time when children are at greater risk for child abuse, and thus the development of shame rather than autonomy.

Even though I've yet to hear any parent or caretaker say, "Thank God for the Terrible Twos," it's extremely important to recognize that this sense of independence is essential to the child's ability to tolerate the solitude necessary for task completion in later life. A child who does not feel securely attached to a healthy adult will not be comfortable exploring the environment alone. Rather, the child will be afraid to let the guardian out of sight, fearing he or she will disappear. (Children who have actually lost primary caretakers will often go to the place where they last saw the deceased persons, hoping to find them there still.)

Mary Ainsworth's studies of Ugandan and American infants in the 1960s demonstrated just how universal this phenomenon is across cultures. She found that toddlers with a secure attachment bond had mothers who were sensitive to their children's needs, had very few competing interests or problems outside of rearing the child, interacted enthusiastically with the child and adapted their behavior to the child's rhythms rather than superimposing their own style or pace upon the child. This description stands in great contrast to the typical hectic modern family life, where parents often unwittingly impose their frenetic pace onto a child who cannot keep up.

In contrast to the mothers of securely attached infants, Ainsworth found that mothers who disregarded their infants' signals or responded to them inappropriately produced two other types of attachment patterns in children: those with insecure-resistant attachment (also called insecure-ambivalent attachment) and those with insecure-avoidant attachment.

Children who had developed an insecure-resistant attachment pattern displayed symptoms of discomfort even during normal play, were excessively distressed by separations and appeared confused when reunited with the inconsistent caretaker. These children would act as if they wanted close physical contact, and at the same time they would resist it.

On the other hand, babies who had developed an insecure-avoidant attachment pattern rarely cried during periods of separation from their mothers and tried to avoid their mothers once reunited with them. (In her later work, Ainsworth states that more recent research has confirmed the existence of a third type of insecure attachment pattern: insecure-disorganized or insecure-disoriented, a pattern in which the infant appears immobilized to either seek the mother's nonexistent comfort or to avoid the mother's rejection.)

Thus, since abandonment is forever a possibility with an unreliable, inconsistent or apathetic caregiver, exploring one's environment is not an option, and the seeds of procrastination due to fear of solitude are sown once again. Indeed, recent research by Gordon Flett and his associates has indicated a higher rate of procrastination behaviors among college students who had insecure attachments to their primary caregivers—regardless of the type of insecure attachment pattern.

The importance of a responsive, reliable primary caregiver in early life cannot be underestimated. This fact may cause some alarm for working parents who leave their children with relatives or place them in private or public daycare centers. However, parents who cannot be with their children during the day can maintain a healthy attachment bond as long as they are consistently responsive and sensitive to their children's needs when they are together.

This was clearly demonstrated in a recent study sponsored by the National Institute of Child Health and Human Development (a division of the National Institutes of Health). After following 1,300 families in the U.S. between 1991 and 1996, researchers demonstrated that the sense of trust felt by 15-month-old children toward their mothers was not affected by the fact that a child was put into day care, by how many hours a child spent in day care, by the quality or type of day care, by the age they entered day care, or by how many times day care arrangements were changed. On the other hand, what affected this bond of trust between mother and child was the mother's level of responsiveness and sensitivity to her child's needs.

However, when the mother was not responsive to her child's needs, problems with attachment bonding were shown to be increased by child care that was of poor quality, involved more than 10 hours per week, or was changed several times. The researchers did suggest that higher quality of day care should always be sought, as indicated by more adults per child, smaller groups of children and more sensitive caregivers (see Ellen Tauscher's *The Child Care Sourcebook* for help in selecting good child care).

What makes a caretaker unreliable or apathetic? The results of research published in 1991 by Ainsworth and her associates found that many women who had lost an attachment figure during their own formative years had not fully faced their grief. Of the mothers who had never resolved their sorrow, 100 percent had children who were not securely attached.

Instead, these mothers, who were laden with residual childhood sadness, had offspring who were disorganized and anxious and who behaved as if their mothers were sources of stress rather than pillars of support and sources of love. The mothers who were struggling with their unresolved feelings of loss were unable to become appropriate attachment figures to their own children.

Similarly researcher Marian Radke-Yarrow has found that children of depressed mothers are more likely to develop an insecure attachment, while Juliet Hopkins has found that a primary caretaker who rejects a child by withholding physical affection usually produces an insecure attachment pattern as well.

And researchers such as Ainsworth and Eichberg have discussed the work of Mary Main and her associates, who studied the childhood attachment history of new parents and then compared these attachment patterns with the way these new parents related to their own infants and toddlers. In a startling demonstration of the transgenerational nature of attachment patterns—both healthy and unhealthy—these researchers found a 75 percent match between the mother's childhood attachment pattern (with her own mother) and her infant's attachment style, and a 69 percent match between the father's childhood attachment pattern (with his own mother) and his infant's attachment style. In other words, consciously or unconsciously, we tend to treat our babies the same way we were treated.

Furthermore, these same researchers also found that infants with "insecure-disorganized" attachment behavior—that is, when under stress, they avoid environmental exploration as well as the attachment figure, leaving these infants in a frozen zone that sounds a lot like the experience of procrastination—tend to come from homes where the mothers, prior to reaching adulthood, have lost a parent through death.

However, do not despair in the case of your own children if you have suffered a deep loss, particularly during your child's toddler years. Main and her associates have demonstrated that it is not the loss per se that leads to insecure attachment styles in children, but rather whether or not the loss has been resolved. So if you haven't already started working on your unresolved loss, now is as good a time as any.

On the other hand, considering the fact that most of our parents and grandparents probably did not have a complete library of self-help books stacked up next to that Donna Reed dinette set, it's likely that many of our caretakers' losses remained unresolved, at least during our toddler years, and most likely influenced our attachment patterns and subsequent ability to explore the environment with confidence. And bear in mind that what might have helped our caretakers to cope with any such early loss—according to researchers such as Main, family support and psychotherapy as well as a secure, autonomous attachment style to begin with—quite possibly wasn't available at that time, either.

If you're not sure whether or not your attachment years were healthy, try reading such classic books on healthy parenting as T. Berry Brazelton's *Touchpoints: Your Child's Emotional and Behavioral Development,* Penelope Leach's *Your Baby and Child: From Birth to Age Five,* or *Bonding: Building the Foundations of Secure Attachment and Independence* by Marshall Klaus and his associates (a book with very helpful suggestions on how to include fathers in the initial bonding process during those first few hours after a baby's birth). Then ask yourself just how much of this information your caretakers had access to during your toddler years—information that may even affect our ability to choose and maintain a successful career in later life, according to researcher Nancy Ryan and her associates.

Some people, because of their reluctance to be alone as a result of poor bonding, will procrastinate for years, even on tasks that are highly important to them.

Consider the case of Joyce, a writer who had suffered emotional neglect during childhood, when she had been banished to her room so as not to be "such a pest" to her parents, both of whom had been neglected themselves as children. Because of her reluctance to be alone, Joyce had delayed writing. The idea of spending so much time alone, as writers must do, was too unsettling for her.

Whenever Joyce would try to write, she would find herself beating a well-worn and embarrassing path to the kitchen. Her compulsive eating would ease her anxiety, and the task of writing was then successfully avoided as she found herself once again preoccupied with cleaning the kitchen or attacking the piles of paperwork on her dining room table—mindness activities that served to numb her, a sort of "activity addiction."

After exploring her childhood via photohistory, art therapy and self-hypnosis, Joyce began writing a few minutes at a time. Knowing that I was close by, and that her session with me was just a few minutes away, she was able to tolerate a small amount of solitude.

Gradually, she was able to tolerate longer periods of isolation. She began to focus her efforts on one book in particular, sometimes outlining and sometimes just freewriting a rough draft of a section or two. At times she became frustrated with the process of writing a book (it isn't easy, even if you like living alone on the rock of Gibraltar for years at a time). But the important thing was that Joyce had begun to overcome her fear of solitude, to feel more secure in her ability to explore the world of creativity and writing on her own.

Joyce's story is representative of many procrastinators with whom I have worked over the years. But suppose you really did have healthy parents who had absolutely no

major losses during their own childhood, no major issues
that might engender shame in a growing child. Until you've
conducted an indirect interview as described in chapter 6, I
wouldn't be too sure about that. Suppose your mother's closest friend had just moved away a week before your birth, or
your mother was anemic and therefore exhausted during
your first year of life, or your mother was a chronic dieter
before you were born and projected all of her body shame
onto you as an infant. Any of these scenarios could create a
deficit in the amount of genuine love, affection and tender-
ness you would have perceived at the time, and shame
would have been the result.

Even if there were no problems such as this during your
first few years of life, does that necessarily exclude you from
the possibility of colliding with any unhealthy people for the
rest of your life?

Below is a partial list of those who may have been harm-
ful to your self-esteem via emotional neglect and/or verbal,
physical or sexual abuse. Place a check mark next to anyone
on this list around whom you have felt uncomfortable in the
past or the present.

_____ Parents
_____ Siblings
_____ Grandparents
_____ Uncles
_____ Aunts
_____ Cousins
_____ Step-parents
_____ Step-siblings
_____ Step-grandparents
_____ Baby-sitters
_____ Baby-sitters' friends
_____ Adult neighbors

_____ Older neighborhood children
_____ Parents of your childhood friends
_____ School bullies
_____ Teachers
_____ Coaches
_____ Cub Scout/Boy or Girl Scout troop leaders
_____ Cub Scout/Boy or Girl Scout members
_____ Summer camp counselors
_____ Summer camp members
_____ Clergy
_____ Day-care center personnel
_____ Janitors
_____ Friends or relatives of any of the above-listed persons

If you have a long standing problem with procrastination, the chances that any of these individuals were in any way hurtful to you and caused you shame, via disrupted or unintentionally flawed caretaking, neglect or abuse, is quite high.

I have worked with numerous clients whose procrastination stemmed from shame related to events that happened without the knowledge of their loving, healthy parents. Until the recent acknowledgment by society that child abuse does indeed exist—and in large percentages—most children suffered the inappropriate actions of others silently. And it's still happening now. If you have a severe, protracted case of procrastination, to deny that you may have had any shame-inducing experiences that could be triggering your problems probably means either one of two things. Either you don't recall the shame-inducing events, or perhaps you have minimized them, thinking that "it wasn't that bad" or "it didn't really affect me—I had good parents." This is like saying, "When I get a promotion or a new house, I am happy, but when I get fired or become homeless, then I'm not affected at all." Hardly a logical statement—it's called denial.

If your problem is one of repression—in other words, the feelings associated with shame are still trapped in the right side of your brain—you may find that the self-help techniques in part 2 of this book will assist you in recalling and identifying any sources of shame. But if your problem is one of denial—"I've put it all behind me"—let's take a quick test to see if this is true. Chances are, if you haven't been in therapy, you probably have not released the emotional residue from past hurts or losses. You may be still holding onto it, replicating it in current relationships or burying it so deep that you can only feel the tip of the iceberg in the form of anxiety.

Imagine a situation, recently or in the past, in which someone hurt, disappointed, humiliated or angered you. Picture the person standing right in front of you. Your persecutor is in shackles, having been arrested for the crime of neglecting or abusing you, with armed guards on either side to insure that the persecutor cannot hurt or attack you in any way. As you look into your persecutor's face, think of exactly what he or she said or did to you—picture the setting, too. As you begin to feel the emotions of hurt, anger or shame welling up, allow these words to continue to build up all the negative energy accompanying them. In a moment, you will release these emotions by simply shouting one word—"NO!"—that will encapsulate the following ideas:

NO—you didn't get away with it!
NO—I didn't deserve to be treated that way!
NO—you cannot hurt me anymore!

Feel the emotions welling up. They're somewhere in your chest right about now. And as you take a deep breath, on the count of three—ONE, TWO, THREE—shout "NO!" as loudly as you can.

Notice that although you feel some relief, there's still some emotion trying to make its way out of your throat. So, once again, on the count of three—ONE, TWO, THREE— shout "NO!"

Notice how you feel even more relieved, but perhaps you still have some residual hurt, anger or shame to release. Again: ONE, TWO, THREE—"NO!"

Notice how your throat is less constricted. But your heart is still pounding, and you still feel the shakiness of adrenaline—anxiety's messenger—throughout your body. Let's release any of this tension by simply breathing it out of our bodies through the top-to-bottom method:

1. Inhale deeply through the nose while counting from one to three. Imagine that you are inhaling molecules of strength and tranquility from your environment.
2. Hold the breath while counting from one to three. Imagine your lungs distributing this strength and tranquility throughout your body.
3. Exhale through the mouth while counting from one to three. Imagine that you are exhaling tension and residual negative emotions, envisioning these discarded molecules of negativity dispersing into thin air.

Last but not least, if you still feel any residual anger, hurt or shame, imagine exhaling these feelings into a balloon. Once you have released all of these emotions into the balloon, let it rise up into the sky and watch it drift upward until you can no longer see it.

So what's the point of this exercise? It's to let you feel the fact that old painful emotions—all of which are fostered by underlying shame—don't just go away if you don't express them. They're still inside of you, putting you on overflow like a spoonful of water so that any present-day threat that might cause you to feel further shame is avoided in order to maintain the surface tension atop the spoon, thereby preventing these emotions from spilling over. Just one more drop and then you'd start to feel how painful they are.

Most people are afraid to face distressing feelings. That's where procrastination sets in. I have worked with numerous clients who had put off business reports or academic papers to avoid facing their hypercritical supervisors or professors. Remember, it's a lot easier to accept criticism for procrastinating than for not doing a good job. Instead of finishing their tasks and facing whatever criticism they might have to endure, these clients simply avoided the task completely. Through the course of therapy, the clients were able to see from whence sprang the original pool of shame they were so terrified of tapping into. Most of them had been handed over by the universe to flawed caretakers, and the cycle of transgenerational shame had begun.

Regardless of the way you perceive the impact of your childhood issues on your adult life, it's important to remember that no matter what the universe may have handed you, it is going to affect you, whether it is positive or negative. As a matter of fact, a basic tenet of Eastern philosophies is that it's all *supposed* to affect us, so we can learn. Similarly, many Western religions focus on having "a cross to bear," while at the same time implying our spiritual duty to come to terms with such burdens.

No matter how you look at it, we are living in a world of colliding egos and shame-inducing events. However, it's up to each of us individually to take responsibility and learn from these collisions. Onward, procrastinating soldiers!

* * * *

Healthy Self-Esteem:
The Antidote to Procrastination Poison

Self-esteem can be viewed as a bank account. Just as mud-pie Sally's parents could either make a withdrawal (spanking) or a deposit (praise), so can other significant persons in your life. Sadly, some of these people keep withdrawing all your funds, so that you end up bouncing checks all over the place. Then it's time to make a serious deposit in your self-esteem account.

But what if you can't? Suppose that when others seem to take away your self-esteem, you haven't the wherewithal to build yourself back up again, let alone to take their names off your self-esteem account or challenge how they got them on there in the first place. If this is the case, you are likely to avoid situations that may threaten your self-esteem, particularly situations in which you are being judged or evaluated.

These situations that threaten to close your self-esteem account via evaluation can be personal (procrastinating regarding your divorce because of the shame of "failure") or work-related (procrastinating regarding paperwork to be scrutinized by a dreaded supervisor). And, since any threat to self-esteem will usually produce anxiety, your productivity is likely to be further inhibited, since anxiety tends to reduce cognitive processing capacity and the ability to concentrate.

So why would we feel threatened in the first place? Why isn't it okay to just perform the task and chalk it up to experience if we are relatively unsuccessful in this task? Does a toddler, after one or even many attempts at walking, fall down, stay down and simply say, "Okay, forget it— that's it, you're going to have to carry me around for the rest of my life"? Of course not—the child laughs or cries, releases the emotion and then moves on. There is usually no shame at that point in the old "try, try again" syndrome.

Somehow by the time we reach adulthood, or perhaps even during late childhood or the teen years, this willingness to "try, try again" starts to fade. We become reluctant to face any threat to our self-esteem that may tap into our residual pools of shame. The degree to which we procrastinate depends on the amount of shame we carry, which in turn depends on the amount of approval and love versus disapproval and abuse we've encountered.

Notice how situations on the job, in academia, or in relationships tend to mirror these childhood dynamics. Will we get:

_____ Approval? (Probably occasionally)
_____ Disapproval? (Probably frequently)
_____ Abuse? (Possibly occasionally)

Notice how most of us still get—on the job, at school and in relationships—what we got as children: some approval, the possibility of occasional abuse and frequent disapproval.

Keep in mind that approval, which builds a sense of self and self-esteem in the developing child, also can build a sense of encouragement in adulthood. However, constant inappropriate disapproval will diminish the sense of self and self-esteem, and can inhibit attempts at productivity or creativity in adulthood. And abuse, which damages the self and self-esteem, can severely restrict one's capacity for productive or creative behavior in childhood or in adulthood, since it would no longer be safe for that inner self to "come out and play." Instead, your motto becomes: "Better not to try."

Thus, your level of procrastination depends on the type and amount of dysfunction you were exposed to as a child.

However, as you proceed through the next few chapters, searching for the headwaters of the rivulets—or rivers—of shame that have at times put you on overflow, keep in mind that the sole purpose of this journey within is for you to heal. You picked up this book because you are tired of living only half a life. You are tired of living in a constant state of anxiety. And most of all, as far as procrastination goes, you are especially tired of _____

_____

_____.

Regardless of what just popped into your mind in answer to the above item, I'll bet it's related to some sort of self-neglect or self-abuse patterns. In the next few chapters, we'll see who taught us to continue their pattern of neglect or abuse of that innocent, deserving infant we once were—and still are.

Think about it: If you see a baby on an elevator, everyone smiles, and perhaps some people will dote on the child in those few moments. But before showing affection—verbal or physical—to the baby, no one asks the baby, "Did you get an A on your math test?" or "Haven't you got a job yet?" The infant doesn't have to do anything to get that love and approval—he or she gets that just for being alive. And that's what we all deserve. But since our caretakers weren't perfect, and, like us, needed to learn some life lessons, we didn't get what we deserved. Part 2 of this book will help you to see just which building blocks are missing in the foundation of your self-esteem, as well as offering you the new bricks and mortar with which to rebuild that foundation—a foundation that will no longer support the habit of procrastination.

* * * *

Now Is the Time

Now that we have explored the parameters of the tomorrow trap, let's take a moment to reflect on what we have learned before we make our moves to escape from this uncomfortable pattern.

As illustrated by figures 1 and 2 in chapter 1, the relationship between shame and the ability to be decisive, creative or productive (between our fears and the ability to gain ACCESS to the winner within) appears quite complex, but it isn't. In considering the fact that both shame and creativity/productivity as well as decision-making involve discomfort with being "exposed," the situation becomes a bit more clear. Simply put:

1. To make effective decisions or to be creative and productive, one must develop certain qualities (autonomy, creativity, confidence, the ability to make an earnest effort, spontaneity, capacity for solitude) that are the direct result of a healthy childhood.

2. If one does not have a healthy childhood (due to disruptions in parenting from accidents, illness, unintentional flaws in "normal" parenting, or intentional neglect and abuse), then one cannot adequately develop these qualities that are necessary for being decisive, creative or productive. Instead, one develops qualities that prevent a healthy pattern of decision-making, creativity and accomplishment.

3. Therefore, childhood issues may result in difficulties with such abilities if these issues remain unresolved. They may lead to compulsive avoidant behaviors that may interfere with the decisive/creative/productive process (see chapter 7). This, in turn, may aggravate other physiological factors in adulthood (see chapter 8)

and lead to a sense of meaninglessness in one's life (chapter 9).

So there you have it: In order to develop a sense of meaning and purpose in life, we must overcome procrastination. Once we can effectively utilize the various techniques outlined in part 2 in order to conquer these problems, we can release that winner within from its prison in the right side of the brain.

In the words of a highly successful writer, the most important ally on this journey within is you. In *Zen in the Art of Writing* (pp. 65-66), Ray Bradbury has said of the younger self within:

> *He has written my stories and books for me. . . . He is the skin through which, by osmosis, all the stuffs pass and put themselves on paper. I have trusted his passions, his fears, and his joys. He has, as a result, rarely failed me.*

Once trusted, your inner self won't fail you, either. So start typing: "Now is the time for all good people to release the winner within . . ."

PART II

Escaping the
Tomorrow Trap

4

Did I Ask for Any of This? Tracing Your Experience of the Human Condition

*Shame is initiated
by the exposure of the self
before another.*

—Helen Block Lewis

A variety of factors and events stemming from childhood can trigger shame, which can later manifest itself as procrastination. These factors include real or perceived physical imperfections, disruptions or flaws in normal parenting, neglect and abuse. While most people are exposed to disruptions or flaws in normal parenting, others are subjected to more severe problems such as abuse. Keep in mind that although you may be thinking that "other people had it worse," even the less traumatic events listed in this chapter can trigger shame and subsequent problems with procrastination, especially if there is an accumulation of such events, as the case examples in this chapter will illustrate.

Perceived or Real Physical Imperfections

Let's explore some of these childhood factors by first checking off any of the following items that may have triggered shame at some point in our lives.

_____ I am not happy with my body.

_____ I dislike certain parts of my body, such as my
_____, _____, _____ and
_____.

_____ In grade school, I felt ashamed and/or was teased
because:

    _____ I wore glasses.

    _____ I was overweight.

    _____ I was considered unattractive by others.

    _____ I had poor hygiene.

    _____ other reasons: _____.

_____ I do not measure up to society's standards of beauty.

_____ I was born with physical problems, such as: _____
_____
_____.

_____ I feel inadequate sexually because I have.

    _____ small or deformed breasts.

    _____ a small or deformed penis.

    _____ other reasons: _____.

_____ Other physical problems: _____
_____
_____.

Although some of these problems may seem petty, it is the reaction of others or our perception regarding our physical flaws that can cause shame. This is more likely if there is little or no parental support regarding the physical problem, or if there are other problems in the child's life, such as inappropriate parenting patterns, which may intensify this sense of shame. At times, individuals will create an illusion of a bodily flaw in order to have something to blame their shame on. After all, it's much easier to be angry with your body, even though it may be relatively normal, than it is to be angry with an apathetic or overcritical parent, or with a feared perpetrator of abuse.

One of the more common results of shame due to perceived or real physical "imperfections" is weight gain. Since many procrastinators use food to quell their anxiety, obesity can become a problem. Children who were neglected or abused often become compulsive overeaters; the cycle of shame seems never-ending. Residual shame from childhood neglect or abuse can trigger the overeating, which in turn engenders more shame.

While the extra weight serves as a bandage to cover old emotional wounds, shame is the inflammation that won't let these injuries heal. How many times have you avoided being in the spotlight in order to avoid the shame of public exposure regarding your weight or your appearance? Often, it's just easier not to win the award in the first place, and let procrastination protect you from winning the right to such public "exposure." How often do you procrastinate regarding exercise, even though you know it will help with your weight and will make you feel better from stress relief via the release of mood-enhancing endorphins? On some level, because you have not made yourself a priority, you don't feel that you deserve to feel good in your body. Such feelings emanate from shame.

This was the case of a 23-year-old college student who came to me for help, ostensibly for his compulsive eating. Sam had always been overweight, even as a child, and was often the butt of cruel jokes by his schoolmates. As an adult, he was 150 pounds overweight. He had tried every diet but could not maintain a weight loss. He was aware that his procrastination regarding exercise was a primary factor in his inability to raise his metabolism enough to lose the extra weight, but he still could not bring himself even to go for a 10-minute walk.

Sam was so ashamed of his body that he would avoid taking required courses in college that involved public exposure (such as public speaking) or physical contact (such as a course on CPR in which students must practice on one another). He had also delayed his dream of becoming a writer. Although he was talented, he was terrified of being singled out in his writing classes and feared drawing attention to himself.

However, once Sam uncovered the emotional deprivation he'd suffered as a child after the sudden death of his mother, he could see the link with his problems of body shame, procrastination and compulsive eating. His overweight body gave him something other than maternal abandonment to feel ashamed about. It also gave him an excuse to procrastinate in order to avoid public attention and the threat of exposure. Once Sam decided to take charge of his life and stop neglecting his body the way his father had unintentionally neglected him (while raising three rambunctious older siblings), Sam began to change his life.

Other physical problems can also trigger shame and procrastination as another case example will illustrate.

One young man was so ashamed of his congenital deformities in one hand that he avoided almost all social contact outside of his job, though he longed for friends. Along with suspending his social life, Mark had also delayed making a change in his career, even though he was terribly bored with his job. Now, why would this man allow himself to be so beleaguered by shame and procrastination when there are people who have no hands at all, yet who have high self-esteem, full social lives and rewarding careers?

It was only after Mark acknowledged and released his shame regarding his mother's verbal abuse that he was able to let go of his physical deformity as a protection against these residual feelings of humiliation as well as his shame about being "different." Once Mark realized that his misshapen hand had "taken the rap" all those years for the shame he felt as a result of his raging, alcoholic mother, Mark was actually able to joke about his hand during group therapy. The group became a healthy forum in which he could practice his social skills and publicly acknowledge his shame, thereby releasing it.

There are numerous other cases of procrastination that *appear* to be triggered by shame regarding a physical problem. But this physical problem is usually not activated as a source of shame unless there are other shame-inducing problems in one's early life.

For example, I have worked with a number of men whose self-imposed shame about penis size was a central element in their procrastination. In a few cases, with the clients' permission, I conferred with their urologists, who did not think the clients' genitals were abnormally small. Thus, it was the clients' perception that had triggered the shame. The greatest fear with these men seemed to arise from "the imposter syndrome." This would entail thoughts such as, "If I stop procrastinating and become successful, then I'll be noticed. And if I'm noticed, then I may be scrutinized. And if I'm scrutinized, they'll see how inadequate I am."

However, in every case, the shame about having an allegedly undersized penis was a mask for the residual shame these men carried as a result of neglect by a mother or father who was depressive, alcoholic, or otherwise emotionally absent during the client's childhood.

In these and other cases where people have procrastinated due to physical imperfections, real or imagined, it is
important to remember that even if a person is physically
attractive to others, he or she may feel "ugly" inside as a
reflection of inner residual shame.

> *For example, I once worked with a beautiful young
> woman who would never wear anything but long-sleeved
> blouses because of the "horrible scars" on her arms. Gloria,
> who lived in sunny South Florida, had limited her social
> life considerably, fearful that she'd be questioned about
> wearing long sleeves, even in 90-degree weather.*
>
> *As part of her treatment for depression, I referred Gloria
> to a dermatologist, who, with Gloria's permission,
> reported back to me that the scars were nothing out of the
> ordinary, just the usual remnants of faint scar tissue from
> childhood scrapes and scratches. Because Gloria had such
> low self-esteem as a result of flawed parenting, she had
> transferred her feelings of shame to her arms. After all, it's
> much easier to hate your arms than to hate your parents.*

When a physical flaw appears to be at the root of an individual's procrastination, it is important to recognize that
such flaws, real or imagined, are usually tethered to other
shame-based issues that must be explored as well.

* * * *

Disruptions in Normal Parenting

As you check off any applicable items that follow, you will
notice that many of them are normal, everyday experiences.
However, they can create feelings of abandonment, rejection

and shame in children. Again, this is because children are so egocentric and impressionable—they cannot possibly understand that Mother having another baby at the same time that Grandmother is dying obviously limits the amount and quality of caregiving Mother can offer.

_____ During the first three years of my life, my mother gave birth to another baby.

_____ During the first three years of my life, my mother or primary caretaker (father, nanny, other family member, older sibling) was also caring for other children who were under the age of five.

_____ During the first three years of my life, my mother or primary caretaker was caring for more than two children (of any age).

_____ My primary caretaker(s) was/were preoccupied with a sick grandparent/relative who came to live with us.

_____ One or more of my primary caretakers or siblings had a serious health problem when I was a child.

_____ One or more of my primary caretakers suffered from bouts of mental illness (bipolar disorder or manic-depression, schizophrenia, etc.) when I was a child.

_____ During my early childhood, one of my siblings died.

_____ During my early childhood, one of my primary caretakers suddenly left.

_____ During my early childhood, one of my primary caretakers did not live with me because he or she took a job for a long time elsewhere.

_____ During my early childhood, my parents were separated or divorced.

_____ During my early childhood, one of my primary caretakers died.

_____ During my early childhood, someone very close to one of my primary caretakers died.

_____ Just before I was born, or just after I was born, my mother or father lost a dear friend or very close family member because the person moved away or died.

_____ As a child, I was left with a baby-sitter or slightly older siblings most of the time.

_____ Both of my parents worked.

_____ My single parent worked full-time, and it seemed as though we had a different baby-sitter every week.

_____ I was sent to boarding school from first grade on.

_____ I was raised:

  _____ in foster care.

  _____ in an orphanage.

  _____ by numerous caretakers at different times.

_____ During my early years, my family endured a serious accident or natural catastrophe.

_____ Just before I was born, or just after I was born, my father or mother lost his or her job.

_____ Just before I was born, or just after I was born, my family moved to another home or city.

_____ Other: _____

_____

_____.

These are some of the potential events that can disrupt healthy parenting patterns and lead to the development of shame in children. Youngsters are egocentric and do not understand why parents are sometimes emotionally unavailable.

Some of these situations are very common, such as being "dethroned" by a new sibling. Other situations, such as having a parent with mental illness, are relatively uncommon, but they do happen.

I once worked with a very talented photographer who was terrified of pursuing his talents after spending his childhood with a schizophrenic father, who alternated between being lucid and loving, and at other times being completely bizarre, apathetic and/or cruel toward Jack. Of course Jack had no idea why his father's parenting pattern would suddenly change, and as a result, Jack had become very restricted in his emotional reactions in order to survive his father's irrational wrath. Jack's inner child, his creative side, did not feel it was safe to come out and "play." Instead, Jack established a pattern of procrastination.

* * *

Another client, whose mother was bipolar (manic-depressive), was never able to understand why his mother was sometimes gentle and at other times full of rage. It was only in adulthood that Bob was finally told "what was wrong with Mommy"—after the damage was long since done. But once Bob released his childhood shame and confusion about his mother, he was able to see that his procrastination regarding the need to divorce his emotionally abusive wife was a clear recapitulation of his desire to remain with his mother even though she had been filled with rage. The feeling of loss associated with the pain of separation was too great to bear.

Like other psychotherapists, I have worked with numerous clients who had unresolved feelings of loss and shame regarding their parents' divorce, the sudden loss of a grandparent, or the death of a primary caregiver.

A graduate student with a rocky marriage who had delayed his schoolwork so long that he was in danger of failing two courses came to me for counseling. It soon became apparent that his procrastination was clearly related to separation anxiety. As a child, George's parents had divorced, and he was sent to live with his mother. The pangs of grief that George felt regarding the loss of his father went unexpressed and unnoticed. Years later, when George's wife said she would divorce him upon his receiving a degree, George put off his schoolwork to guarantee not passing. Thus, he could avoid another very painful separation—this time, from his wife.

* * *

Another client, a highly successful businesswoman, was both a workaholic and a procrastinator. Sara worked feverishly for years, yet she always put off taking time for herself. This caused conflict with her spouse, who wanted Sara to take time off to relax and enjoy life. Sara would even put off buying small items that would please her, even though she could well afford to buy thousands of hammocks or big-screen televisions. Her attitude about enjoying even the simple things in life was summed up in her words: "What's the point?"

The roots of this woman's apathy became apparent as we explored her early history. For the first year of her life Sara had enjoyed the loving approval of her parents. However, Sara became aware that her father's death, when she was a toddler, had affected her deeply. Whenever she had gazed into her mother's eyes, she saw only grief and hopelessness. The birth of a sibling two months after the father's death ("dethroning" Sara as the center of attention) only served to heighten Sara's loss of love and the resulting shame.

Thus, Sara learned to adopt a pessimistic attitude, and she restricted her range of emotions so she wouldn't feel the pain of loss—or the joy of life's simple pleasures.

There are numerous other events that could cause a disruption in healthy parenting and the resulting sense of loss internalized as shame. The death of one's sibling can cause a parent to retreat into grief and depression. Without intending any harm, the parent thereby triggers an abandonment depression and a sense of shame in the surviving sibling. The death of other loved ones, the birth of a seriously ill sibling, the loss of a job, or even a natural disaster can also cause a major disruption in the quality of a child's care. Again, because children are inherently egocentric, unless their fears are addressed and resolved, they will automatically assume that this withdrawal of parental love is their fault, thereby triggering the domino effect of shame and subsequent procrastination in later life.

* * * *

Flaws in Normal Parenting

Imperfect parenting is perhaps the most common cause of shame-based procrastination. Our parents, grandparents and great-grandparents had no role models for healthy parenting. Instead, they were prey to the transgenerational ignorance regarding childrearing that continues to plague us today. This is not to say that you have no right to be angry with your caretakers for putting you down or restricting the expression of your emotions. You have the right to be angry and the right to release that anger and its accompanying shame (emotions that don't necessarily have to be expressed in front of your caretakers). But first, let's take a look at which type of parenting flaws were prevalent in your family.

_____ One or more of my parents/primary caregivers was often critical of me regarding my physical, mental or emotional attributes (this includes long-term baby-sitters, child-care workers, or nannies).

_____ As a child, I was told that children should be seen and not heard.

_____ As a child, I was told that if I had nothing good to say, I shouldn't say anything at all.

_____ Showing anger was not allowed in my family.

_____ Crying was not allowed in my family.

_____ Talking about feelings was not allowed in my family.

_____ Success was not allowed in my family.

_____ Failure was not allowed in my family.

_____ Showing affection was not permitted in my family.

_____ We did not discuss problems openly in my family.

_____ I was not permitted to disagree with my parents.

_____ I was given "the silent treatment" if I misbehaved.

_____ I was afraid of my primary caregivers.

_____ I was often compared with my more successful sibling(s).

_____ I was often compared to "the black sheep" of the family.

_____ I was shunned or ostracized by my parents/family because I am not a heterosexual, a fact of which I was dimly aware even at a very young age.

_____ Other: _____

_____.

In *Homecoming,* his popular book on childhood issues, John Bradshaw asserts that much of what passes for "normal parenting" can actually be seen as "abuse," since we are just beginning to understand what it takes to raise a healthy child. Our parents and grandparents used the popular child-rearing styles of their day—techniques that we now know can create great waves of shame in an impressionable child. All we have to do is peruse the pages of such books as *Playful Parenting* by Denise and Mark Weston or *Positive Parenting from A to Z* by Karen Joslin, and we can see that our parents probably didn't know half of what they needed to know in order to raise us with healthy self-esteem.

Throughout her many books on childhood, such as *Thou Shalt Not Be Aware* and *Breaking Down the Wall of Silence,* Alice Miller has been a leader in scrutinizing how the parenting styles of yesteryear—all the way back to biblical times—have damaged whole generations of children, who then of course grow up and repeat the same flawed parenting styles with their children. Such flawed parenting that diminishes rather than heightens the child's self-esteem is implied in the following statements. Check off any that apply to your childhood experiences, either at home or elsewhere.

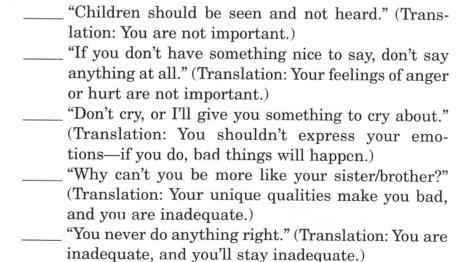

_____ "Children should be seen and not heard." (Translation: You are not important.)

_____ "If you don't have something nice to say, don't say anything at all." (Translation: Your feelings of anger or hurt are not important.)

_____ "Don't cry, or I'll give you something to cry about." (Translation: You shouldn't express your emotions—if you do, bad things will happen.)

_____ "Why can't you be more like your sister/brother?" (Translation: Your unique qualities make you bad, and you are inadequate.)

_____ "You never do anything right." (Translation: You are inadequate, and you'll stay inadequate.)

_____ "How can you be so stupid?" (Translation: If you make a mistake, you are inferior.)

_____ "You'll never amount to anything if you don't stop thinking like that." (Translation: You are not able to survive or be successful without your parents—it's not okay to have your own ideas.)

Like other therapists, my files abound with such cases of flawed parenting styles—all of which tend to generate huge waves of shame in impressionable children.

> *One client, a talented painter, was particularly affected by such statements. Joan, one of four children, was the only one with artistic leanings in a family that valued hard work on the farm. Joan grew up feeling the pain of an absent father who worked from dawn to dusk, then collapsed into bed each night. Her overwhelmed mother was verbally explosive. Her reaction to Joan's artistic attempts was usually, "Why can't you be more like your brothers and sisters? What's wrong with you?"*
>
> *In contrast, Joan's teachers encouraged her artistic efforts, and she won a scholarship to a prestigious university. But her procrastination in finishing assigned projects put her in danger of being asked to leave the program. Joan had learned early on that to express her creative spirit meant that she was "bad."*

Other cases have involved:
- a student with writer's block whose teacher reminded him of an overly critical parent;
- a man trying to pass the bar exam, which had come to represent the intimidation and judgmental qualities he'd known in his father;

- a student whose fear of the homophobia he'd be sure to face in the corporate world kept him in the "closet" via procrastination. If he didn't graduate, he wouldn't have to mingle with co-workers who might expose his status as a gay man, something his brother had shamed him for since age six when he was caught dressing up in his older sister's clothes.

As with these and many other cases of procrastination, flaws in early parenting styles can create the conditions for procrastination in the child's later life. For example, researchers such as Gordon Flett and his colleagues, as well as Joseph Ferrari and his associates, have discussed the finding that procrastination is associated with exposure to overcontrolling and authoritarian parents. What children need is appropriate limits and parents who are consistently constructive in giving guidelines for appropriate behavior. Otherwise, the roots of procrastination may very well take hold.

* * * *

Childhood Neglect

We all want to believe that we were not "neglected" as children. Visions of starving babies in filthy tenements arise when we think of the nearly three million reported cases of child neglect and abuse that were confirmed during 1994, according to a Child Welfare League of America fact book discussed in a recent *National Association of Social Workers News* article. (And that's not counting all those cases that go unreported, let alone the fact that parents in a 1995 Gallup poll admitted to 16 times the officially reported amount of child physical abuse and 10 times the amount of officially reported child sexual abuse.) Yet even subtle forms of neglect can bring problems in later life. Check off any statements below that may apply to you.

_____ One or both of my primary caretakers was usually depressed.

_____ Right after my birth, my mother had postpartum depression.

_____ My mother usually had postpartum depression after she gave birth to each of my siblings.

_____ My mother became withdrawn and apathetic toward me whenever she had her period (my mother may have suffered from premenstrual syndrome).

_____ I felt very lonely as a child.

_____ I was often hungry as a child.

_____ I was embarrassed by:

    _____my hygiene.

    _____my clothing.

    _____my house.

    _____my parents.

_____ We didn't have enough money in our family because one or both of my parents had trouble with:

    _____ the Great Depression in the 1930s.

    _____ getting a job.

    _____ keeping a job.

    _____ gambling.

    _____ alcohol.

    _____ drugs.

    _____ sexual addiction.

    _____ other addictions: _____.

    _____ other problems: _____.

_____ I was not offered any guidance regarding my future.

_____ My parents/caretakers did not attend my school functions, such as plays, sports events, awards banquets or Parents' Day.

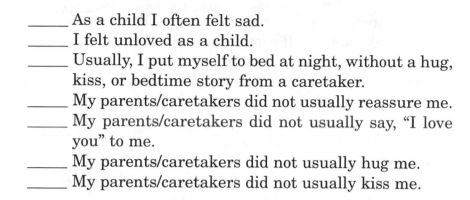

_____ As a child I often felt sad.

_____ I felt unloved as a child.

_____ Usually, I put myself to bed at night, without a hug, kiss, or bedtime story from a caretaker.

_____ My parents/caretakers did not usually reassure me.

_____ My parents/caretakers did not usually say, "I love you" to me.

_____ My parents/caretakers did not usually hug me.

_____ My parents/caretakers did not usually kiss me.

Notice that these less obvious factors in childhood neglect are relatively common, yet the result is often procrastination due to residual shame.

How often do we put off a certain task simply because it is boring? Instead we want instant gratification. I have worked with numerous men and women who come up with wonderful ideas but don't have the patience to sit down and write up their ideas. Thus, the projects never get started, or finished. In these cases, the clients usually had basic needs for love, affection or food that were not met during childhood. As adults they prefer to engage only in activities that provide immediate gratification, since these individuals cannot tolerate delayed gratification—they've had enough of that already, thank you.

Although childhood neglect is a common source of procrastination and shame, it is often difficult to identify, since, by definition, the nature of neglect can be rather nebulous. How would a child know what he or she was missing if the child never had it in the first place?

It may seem implausible, but infants and children can sense, on some level, when they are being neglected. They may not show it outwardly, and, in fact, children may defend their parents against accusations of neglect or even abuse. On a deeper level, however, these children are hurting inside, and feelings of loss and shame begin to seep into their foundation of self-esteem.

One client spoke of his early years as a time of painful abandonment. There was no affection from Keith's mother, who said she wished "he had never been born." As Keith explored his childhood, he recalled the feelings of "emptiness" that never seemed to end. He recalled being told that he was "bad" and believed it. The only relief from this vast chasm of neglect came from a neighbor, a vivacious mother of two, who occasionally baby-sat for Keith. Whenever he went to her house, she baked cookies. Thus, as an adult, whenever Keith delayed a chore, he would turn to fresh-baked cookies instead. However, once Keith released these old emotions of loss, grief and shame, he was gradually able to increase the length of solitude necessary for task completion, without the assistance of food.

* * *

Another client, a woman in her late 30s, had a severe case of writer's block, which she saw as a personal defect rather than as an unconscious form of procrastination. Although Marcia had always been aware that her hard-working father had been (and still was) aloof and dismissive, she had never acknowledged or released the feelings of loss and shame she had felt as a toddler.

Through various techniques, particularly therapeutic writing, Marcia was able to release the tears and feelings of shame she had felt when her father came home from the factory each day and walked right past her, as though she didn't exist. This feeling of being invisible only diffused her sense of self. Thus, any attempt to draw on her inner self caused Marcia to literally draw a blank. However, once she began to heal from this sense of loss, Marcia became a more prolific writer.

* * *

Another client, a self-described "jack-of-all-trades," had procrastinated for years in terms of "getting a real job." Although Isabel was adept at many tasks and talented in many ways, she had never chosen a profession and suffered under the constant fear of financial chaos.

During art therapy sessions, Isabel soon became aware that her anger toward her parents, who had failed to provide her with any guidance whatsoever, was lurking behind her indecision regarding her choice of a career. Her sense of shame that she wasn't "good enough at any one thing" had been an outgrowth of her feeling that she must not have deserved any guidance in one specific direction from her parents, since their neglect had engendered in Isabel a sense of not being worthy. However, Isabel began working toward focusing her career options once she realized that it had been her parents' ongoing depression rather than lack of love for her that had generated the parents' apathy toward her in the first place.

I have seen similar cases where, once the client becomes aware that he or she was not responsible for a caretaker's withdrawal of love, the healing process can begin. How many of us had "moody" mothers who may actually have had severe premenstrual syndrome that went undiagnosed in a time when PMS was not recognized as a valid issue? (See chapter 8 for more information on current treatments for PMS.) In my current work with women who have PMS, I have seen women who are excellent mothers for 20 or 25 days a month, but who can become quite depressive, self-absorbed and neglectful—and at times even emotionally abusive—to their children during the premenstrual phase (days 14 to 28 in a 28-day cycle, with day 1 being the first day of menstruation). It may be difficult to determine if PMS was what made your mother so moody, but it's certainly worth investigating via the techniques offered in chapters 6 and 8.

As with so many other cases of procrastination, once the original source of shame has been identified and worked through, the client is then freed up to forge a different path in life, one that is not being controlled by the issues of the past. Indeed, researchers such as Juliet Hopkins, as well as Mary Main and her associates, have discussed the finding that once early childhood rejection is understood to be a function of the flawed parent—not of the self—then the possibility of repeating such a flawed pattern with one's own children is greatly reduced.

* * * *

Childhood Abuse

Though you may be initially turned off by the term "child abuse," it's important that you check off any items on the following pages that pertain to your childhood. Keep in mind that what may have appeared normal to you may have damaged your self-esteem. Reading novels such as Lisa Shea's *Hula,* Kaye Gibbons's *Ellen Foster,* Russell Banks's *Success Stories* or Amy Bloom's short stories, "Light Breaks Where No Sun Shines" and "When the Year Grows Old" in *Come to Me,* may be helpful in getting you to feel empathy for the adolescent narrators who are suffering from the neglect and abuse they take for granted as part of life.

Remember, once we discover that the flaws in our upbringing rather than flaws in us are what cause feelings of rejection, shame and low self-esteem, we are much less likely to repeat these patterns with our own children. Thus, we have everything to gain and much to lose. At worst we'll find out our parents weren't perfect—a painful but not surprising fact.

Keep in mind that many people repress memories of their childhood pain. The right brain is more than happy to store away all those feelings and events we'd rather not deal with. For example, in a recent national survey of psychologists, Shirley Feldman-Summers and Kenneth Pope found that 24 percent of the therapists said they themselves had been abused as children, and of that 24 percent, 40 percent reported periods of time when they had forgotten about the abuse. However, of those who had forgotten the abuse, half had actual corroboration of the abuse.

Remember, much of what was considered "normal" 20 years ago is now known to damage a child's self-esteem, thereby generating shame. A very simple and nonthreatening book for determining if you suffered any childhood neglect or abuse is *Outgrowing the Pain,* by Eliana Gil. If your caretakers were in any way abusive, chances are it was because they themselves were abused as children. They are simply following "tradition," raising you the way they were raised.

By responding to the items below, you are making a courageous choice to break this chain of transgenerational flawed parenting.

_____ I was emotionally abused as a child.

_____ I was verbally abused as a child.

_____ I was publicly humiliated as a child by:

    _____ a parent or caretaker.

    _____ a grandparent or other relative.

    _____ a sibling.

_____ someone outside the family, such as a baby-sitter, school bully, neighbor or teacher.

_____ other persons.

_____ Physical discipline occurred more than once a year in my childhood household.

_____ I was forced to listen to or watch a sibling or parent being beaten or harmed by a parent.

_____ I was physically disciplined by my caretakers via:

     _____ a slap in the face.

     _____ a punch in the face.

     _____ use of a belt, switch, paddle or other object.

     _____ pinching or biting.

     _____ physical torture.

     _____ other means.

_____ As a result of physical discipline, I had bruises, welts, bleeding or cuts.

_____ During physical discipline from a parent or care-taker, I was partially or fully nude.

_____ When I was a child or a teenager, comments about my breasts, buttocks or genital area were made by:

     _____ adult family members.

     _____ adult family friends.

     _____ adult neighbors.

     _____ baby-sitters.

     _____ older children.

     _____ children who were intimidating to me.

_____ Someone touched me or made me touch them in sexual areas when I was a child.

_____ I was molested as a child.

_____ As a child, I was exposed to pornography by an adult, by a child who was more than two years older than me or by a child who was intimidating to me.

_____ As a child or teen, I was the victim of an exhibitionist.

_____ As a child or teen, I experienced coercive sex (I allowed or did things even though I didn't really want to).

_____ I was assaulted by someone's mouth, hand, penis or foreign object.

_____ As a child or teen, I was sexually harassed by a teacher or employer.

_____ I was sexually abused as a child.

_____ During my childhood or teen years, I felt very uncomfortable when I was touched by:

_____ my mother.

_____ my father.

_____ a certain caretaker.

_____ a grandparent.

_____ a certain relative: cousin, uncle, aunt.

_____ certain older children or adults outside of the family.

As is apparent from this list, there are several types of child abuse: emotional, verbal, physical and sexual. Evidence suggests that the perpetrators of such abuse, whether family members or not, are usually repeating experiences that they had endured during their first two years of life, even though these experiences are not available to their conscious memory. Their impoverished self-esteem and strong need to be loved often lead them into young and immature marriages. Later they turn to their children to meet their needs. Of course, youngsters cannot meet these needs or make up for the childhood emotional wounds of their caretakers. Thus, the adult becomes frustrated, takes it out on the child, and the cycle of abuse and shame continues.

We now have the opportunity to break this vicious cycle. If we don't, chances are that this cycle of negative caretaking of our children will continue. Otherwise, particularly among those survivors of more severe physical or sexual abuse, we will continue to see problems with post-traumatic stress disorder (PTSD) in these individuals. PTSD is characterized by such symptoms as recurring nightmares, unexplained outbursts of anger, difficulty in concentrating and constant states of anxiety. Just hearing this list of symptoms, it is not surprising that researchers such as Ferrari and his colleagues have discussed the finding that persons suffering from PTSD are more likely to exhibit higher levels of procrastination behaviors.

One client of mine developed a severe case of procrastination regarding his academic work. Eventually, he became aware that the roots of his problem were due to shame from early verbal and emotional abuse. Harold's father had constantly called him "stupid," thereby creating in Harold a lack of confidence in his academic pursuits. The resulting procrastination was due to fear of poor grades and their accompanying public humiliation.

Furthermore, Harold's mother had developed a pattern of what Dr. Patricia Love has called "emotional incest" in her book entitled The Emotional Incest Syndrome: What to Do When a Parent's Love Rules Your Life. *Harold's mother, who also endured verbal abuse and infidelity from Harold's father, constantly used her son as a sounding board for all of her problems. She also smothered Harold with hugs, whether he wanted them or not. The mother would take Harold with her wherever she went, rarely letting him out of her sight, and would protest if he tried to study or to spend any time with his friends. By creating in effect a role reversal with her son, in which Harold was the parent listening to her problems and providing her with the reassurance of affection, she was thereby using her child to meet her own emotional needs for attention and affection. During adolescence, Harold finally rebelled.*

Because of this "emotional incest" with his mother, Harold was terrified of being engulfed in intimate relationships. So he had none. He spent many lonely nights allegedly studying for his B.A. in History. In reality, he smoked countless cigarettes as he watched television, unopened books at his side. Being alone with his studies was intolerable, since Harold had spent his entire childhood virtually bonded to his mother (who of course disapproved of his being alone to study).

Although Harold was terrified of being in a relationship with a woman, he simultaneously craved the affection that can only be supplied by another person in an intimate way. Thus, to avoid these painful feelings of fear and loneliness, he used nicotine and the constant drone of television to anesthetize himself against such pain.

When Harold tried to study in public places, the reassuring presence of others would initially make him more optimistic. However, his father's insults would soon start replaying in his head, and Harold would once again feel hopeless and ashamed. However, through art therapy and therapeutic writing, Harold began to release his rage toward his parents, as well as his longstanding problems with procrastination.

Unfortunately, verbal and emotional abuse are not the only types of abuse that many children endure. Physical and sexual abuse are problems that are finally coming to the public's attention, even though they have existed for years.

In her book entitled *Breaking Down the Wall of Silence,* Alice Miller focuses upon the fact that beating children is seen in many cultures as a perfectly normal "tradition." To this day, many people try to justify hitting a child by saying, "My father beat me, and I turned out all right." Of course, this is much easier than saying, "My father beat me, and I carry a great deal of rage and shame as a result, which makes me act out my anger on my own children."

Instead, most people who were abused as children must automatically repress their feelings of anger, hurt and shame. They begin to "identify with the aggressor" in order to survive and justify what has happened to them. For example, Miller cites the fact that currently, there are 74 million women alive today who have undergone clitoridectomies, the surgical removal of the woman's clitoris at the age of 12, with or without anesthesia. This brutal procedure, which limits a woman's sexual pleasure for life, is performed because it is "tradition" in certain cultures. What is even worse is the fact that the women who perform this brutal act were the victims of this procedure themselves. One woman whose daughter actually died from this procedure stated that the clitoridectomy was still justified, since without it her daughter would never have been able to get a husband.

In *Breaking Down the Wall of Silence* (pp. 76, 91), Miller points out that Westerners are appalled by this tradition, but that we should also be appalled by our own commonly held belief that "severity and discipline aimed at inducing a child's obedience results in the creation of a responsible and caring human being."

Miller states that in 1987, more than half of all parents in what was then West Germany believed that beating a child was an appropriate way to teach a lesson. Throughout history, according to Miller, such beliefs have legitimized acting out one's childhood pain onto others. The logic runs like this, even to the extremes of ritual abuse, the horrors of human sacrifice and the Nazi regime of Hitler (who was beaten regularly as a child). The logic runs something like this:

If I inflict on others what was once inflicted on me, I don't have to feel the pain that memory would bring. If I skillfully dress everything up with ideology or religion and keep telling the lies which those around me have learned to believe in, then many people will follow me. If I can also—like Hitler— employ the talents of an actor and take on the allure of the threatening father, the father that nearly everyone totally believed and feared in childhood, then I can find countless helpers for every possible crime, the more absurd, the easier.

We are only now becoming aware of how damaging such abuse can be. Our caretakers most likely were not aware of Jan Hunt's "Ten Reasons Not to Hit Your Kids (as cited in Miller's *Breaking Down The Wall of Silence*). According to Hunt, hitting children:

- increases the child's use of violence;
- induces fear rather than respect;
- fails to teach the child appropriate problem-solving;
- may cause sexual and physical problems in adulthood.

In other words, spanking a child on the buttocks, which is an erogenous zone during early childhood, can lead to associating pain and sexual pleasure. It can also lead to back pain in adulthood as a result of repeated jarring of the spinal column.

Though we would rather not believe that these horrors exist, they do. Physical abuse is unfortunately still a reality in our world today—and so is sexual abuse.

Freud's development of the Oedipal theory and its matching Electra complex have helped keep us in the dark about the true nature of such abuse. Freud knew that his hypnotized female clients were not having sexual fantasies about their fathers, but were instead describing their actual memories of sexual abuse.

In Christine Courtois's excellent book, *Healing the Incest Wound,* she includes a discussion of Freud's purposeful attempts to hide the high levels of incest he was seeing in his clients. Unfortunately, Freud's fraudulent theory that the child desires sex with the parent of the opposite gender is not only a classic model of the "blame-the-victim" mentality, but it is still taught today in most university psychology departments!

So is it any wonder that many psychotherapists don't routinely ask about childhood sexual abuse? Is it any wonder that many clients will not routinely disclose sexual abuse experiences unless they are asked directly?

When Marilyn Stinson and Susan Hendrick investigated this problem in a recent study, they found that once the therapists did ask directly about sexual abuse, approximately one-third of the students coming for therapy at a university counseling center reported that they had been sexually abused. On the other hand, of those who were not asked directly about any history of sexual abuse, only 8 percent actually reported the abuse voluntarily. This implies that many abuse survivors go untreated—an alarming notion, considering the fact that childhood physical or sexual abuse has been found to be related to later problems with depression in adulthood, according to many researchers such as Antonia Bifulco and her associates.

So it should come as no surprise that the public's level of denial regarding sexual abuse has remained particularly high. Yet a variety of research projects have found an epidemic: sexual abuse rates of 20 to 45 percent for women and 10 to 18 percent for men.

Among the first to report these epidemic levels was Diana Russell in her research report *The Secret Trauma,* in which she described a prevalence rate of 25 percent for girls who were sexually molested before the age of 14 and 31 percent for girls who were sexually molested by the age of 18. Frank Bolton reported in his book *Males at Risk* that most studies such as those done by David Finkelhor and his colleagues indicate that approximately 15 percent of boys are sexually molested as children. But these statistics represent only the tip of the iceberg when you consider, for example, the rest of Russell's research results: Only 5 percent of the sexual abuse cases in her study were ever reported, and only 1 percent of the sexual abuse cases resulted in conviction. Unfortunately, the shame emanating from such prevalent cases of abuse can often create the most severe cases of procrastination.

What is even perhaps more alarming is the fact that, according to research cited by such experts as Carol Bohmer, Andrea Parrot and Peggy Reeves Sanday, many of these children will be revictimized as adults in the form of acquaintance rape or relationship violence—both of which can aggravate one's sense of shame.

Unfortunately, because survivors of childhood abuse often feel the behavior is "normal," they become easy targets for emotional, physical or sexual abuse in later life. This can lead to a pattern of constant revictimization. The victim believes that he or she is damaged merchandise and deserves no better. In a recent report, Lisa Goodman noted that 21 to 34 percent of adult women in the U.S. are physically attacked by intimate adult partners, and 14 to 25 percent of adult women are raped.

Many people do not understand that individuals who are abused as adults are often unconsciously fighting residual battles of childhood shame. And as long as these survivors remain locked in this cycle of confusion, they are not likely to discover the underlying shame that has triggered a lifetime of procrastination and unhappiness.

I have worked with numerous survivors of childhood physical and sexual abuse who have been victimized again as adults. Their problems with shame and procrastination worsen after these later attacks. They often have eating disorders as a mask for their shame. Their obsessive thoughts about food make it difficult to concentrate on academic work or their job, and procrastination becomes a normal pattern of avoidance. They are also prone to engaging in substance abuse, which of course numbs them, but also leads to further delaying tactics—it's certainly much more difficult to write a term paper with a hangover.

Acting out sexually is another problem among sexual abuse survivors, as they try to win the old battle for control once and for all. If these individuals become "sex addicts," they will use sexual activity, either alone or with others, not only to block out childhood anger and hurt, but also to avoid their daily chores at work or at school.

Survivors of both physical and sexual abuse feel a deep sense of humiliation and often blame themselves. Sadly, they judge themselves as if they were adults when the abuse occurred, forgetting that they were only children at the time.

> *I once worked with a very intelligent woman in her late 20s who was procrastinating regarding her last few classes in medical school. Alicia had recently married, and it soon became apparent that arguments with her spouse were a major source of distraction from her studies. When I asked Alicia to describe for me a typical argument, she said her husband was still upset about the way her father had slid his hands over her breasts at the Christmas dinner table— in clear view of her husband and the entire family.*
>
> *"My father's always done that," Alicia said to me. "I don't see what the big deal is."*

Clearly, this highly educated young woman had no idea that her father's behavior was inappropriate. She had been the victim of a very subtle form of "brainwashing" over the course of many years. This pattern is typical among sexual abuse survivors.

Usually, these individuals minimize the trauma, saying there was "no bleeding" or "no penetration." But when I ask them to imagine how they would feel if their children were beaten or forced to perform oral sex by an adult, they are outraged.

Even less obvious sexual abuse can engender shame. Imagine that, like one of my former clients, you have to sleep with your mother until you are 16 years old. You would feel used and ashamed, even if there was no explicit sexual activity. Such "covert" incest can be extremely damaging to one's self-esteem. Similar examples of "covert" sexual abuse include adults' comments about a child's breasts, buttocks or genitals; being exposed to pornography or family nudity as a child and/or adolescent; or being told about a parent's sex life.

If you suspect that your family was engaged in "covert" incest, or if you were sexually accosted by someone outside the family, by all means see a therapist who has experience with treating childhood abuse. Guidelines for choosing an appropriate therapist are discussed in chapter 6, or you may want to consult the guidelines offered in such classic texts as Ellen Bass's and Laura Davis's *The Courage to Heal* or Mike Lew's *Victims No Longer*.

Below is a partial list of symptoms based on what Courtois calls "disguised presentation" of sexual abuse in *Healing the Incest Wound*. A more detailed list of symptoms is available in E.S. Blume's *Secret Survivors*. Although these symptoms *may* indicate childhood sexual abuse, keep in mind that they may also be characteristic of other types of abuse.

_____ Compulsive-addictive behaviors
_____ Promiscuity
_____ Avoidance of sex
_____ Becoming overweight
_____ "Hiding" the body with slouched posture
_____ "Hiding" the body with baggy or unattractive clothes
_____ Preference for much older sexual partners
_____ Preference for much younger sexual partners
_____ Recurring nightmares
_____ Anxiety regarding going to sleep at night
_____ Large memory gaps regarding childhood
_____ Persistent, unexplained phobias (especially regarding bathrooms or bedrooms)

Women who have been sexually abused as children often marry physically or sexually abusive men. And even after the realization that the man is unhealthy and won't change, the woman may procrastinate for years before she seeks a divorce. She is so sure that she can change him—thereby proving that she is indeed worth loving and thereby negating all of the shame she feels from her childhood sexual abuse— that she often stays well beyond the point of no return.

Sexually abused men who marry emotionally abusive or castigating women also tend to procrastinate when it comes to getting to divorce court. (Books such as Laura Davis's *Allies in Healing* or Eliana Gil's *Outgrowing the Pain Together* can sometimes be helpful in situations when you are a nonabusive person in a close relationship with someone who was abused as a child.)

People who have been sexually abused as children are especially prone to procrastination since they are usually plagued by depression. Indeed, in a recent review of research on the physiological changes associated with childhood sexual abuse, Tori DeAngelis discussed the finding that the biochemical changes found in sexually abused girls mirrored changes that are associated with depression in studies of adults.

What I have seen in so many of these men and women who were abused as children is a tremendous fear of being in the public spotlight, as if the audience could somehow see all the way through to those hidden horrific childhood scenes stored away in their unconscious memories. However, until these clients become aware that they have been sexually abused during childhood, they simply see themselves as procrastinators who just "never hit the big time."

In these and many other cases of procrastination, as we continue to collide with other dysfunctional human beings, we must strive to discover the source of our inner residual pool of shame that propels us toward procrastination as protection. The next few chapters will offer further methods for uncovering these issues that are clamoring to come out under the red flag of procrastination—our clue to a better life.

5

Let Me
Count the Ways:
Discovering
Your Protective
Procrastination Masks

Shame can also be created by
the exposure of an unacceptable aspect
of the self to the self.

—Helen Block Lewis

In previous chapters, we discussed how unresolved shame can set up a pattern of procrastination as protection. In this chapter, we will begin identifying the protective masks that we may use to hide from our shame—masks that in turn aggravate our tendencies toward procrastination.

As we have seen in figures 1 and 2 in chapter 1, there are many layers of shame that can mask the original problems underlying procrastination.

There are also many, less obvious clinical symptoms of shame—symptoms discovered by experts on procrastination such as Joseph Ferrari—that can restrict the flow of your creative, productive and decision-making energies. For example, June Tangney and her associates have revealed a significant relationship between the concept of shame and such issues as self-esteem, self-consciousness, social anxiety and fear of negative evaluation. Other subtle clinical masks for shame are listed in table 2 on the following page. Identifying which of these may be underlying your pattern of procrastination is an essential prerequisite to utilizing the techniques offered in chapter 6 for releasing shame and ending procrastination.

TABLE 2
Protective Procrastination Masks

Anger

Anxiety

Assertiveness Problems

Co-dependency

Depression

Evaluation Anxiety

Fear of Failure

Fear of Intimacy

Fear of Rejection

Fear of Success

Perfectionism

Powerlessness

Shame

Anger

Anger is a shame-based dynamic that contributes to procrastination by blocking the energies needed for decision-making, creativity and productivity. Let's see what your gut-level reactions are when assessing your own thoughts and feelings about anger in general. First use your dominant hand, then your nondominant hand.

Dominant Hand

When I think of anger, I think _____

_____.

When I think of anger, I feel _____

_____.

Nondominant Hand

When I think of anger, I think _____

_____.

When I think of anger, I feel _____

_____.

Are there any differences between the way you think and the way that you feel about anger? Are there any differences between the responses from your dominant and nondominant hands?

Anger, whether conscious or unconscious, not only masks and protects you from the deeper feeling of shame, but it also stifles your ability to think clearly. I have worked with many clients whose anger and resentment toward their life partners appeared to be the obvious source of their delay in finding a job. These individuals were able to get back at their loved ones for perceived or real offenses in the relationship by not working. So how does all this relate to shame?

Essentially, it is the shame-based person who will take his or her anger to such an extreme, in spite of the fact that the unemployed procrastinator suffers just as much from the lack of income in the household. Although most of us would probably enjoy some time off work, we don't usually choose to stay off the job for months or years at a time, unless we can afford to do so. But if the procrastinator's anger is tapping into a pre-existing pool of shame, then the anger is often magnified. After all, what is so difficult about directly expressing your resentment and anger toward your loved ones in order to resolve the situation? Why go so far as to make yourself suffer as well from the financial deficit in the household?

More often than not, this anger is mirroring an earlier siege of anger that no doubt went unexpressed or unresolved. Perhaps you are afraid of directly expressing anger because you have experienced the rage of someone else all too often, either as a child or as an adult. Or perhaps you have a great deal of anger and have no appropriate outlet for it. Either way, putting things off is a way of not dealing with your anger.

> *One client had a difficult time with anger not only because he was filled with it, but also because he feared it. Jacob, a man in his 20s, experienced a great deal of anger whenever he tried to work on his novel. What bothered him most about writing was that he had to do it alone. However, once he discovered that as a child he'd been banished to his room for days at a time, Jacob was able to release the pent-up rage he'd been forbidden to express. He also learned that by expressing his anger in therapy in appropriate ways, he was not mirroring the verbal and physical rage of his father. Eventually, Jacob was able to tolerate longer periods of solitude in order to write his novel.*

Other cases of procrastination that are rooted in anger often involve a type of passive-aggressive behavior. In other words:

1. Who will be upset if I procrastinate? _____
   _____.

2. Is this the only way I can show my anger toward the person(s)? _____
   _____.

3. What would happen if I expressed my anger directly at the person(s)? _____
_____.

4. Am I willing to face those consequences? _____
_____.

These questions usually elicit some troubling answers. Suppose you cannot express anger because you may be fired from your job, your spouse may leave you, or you may even experience emotional or physical abuse. If this is the case, then you must be cautious so as to protect your finances, your self-esteem, or possibly your physical safety. But if you don't express your anger directly, you may find yourself—consciously or unconsciously—in a state of perpetual procrastination, an indirect way of showing your anger. As long as you continue to procrastinate, you end up suffering the accompanying anxiety. In other words, your abusers, whether past or present, are still perpetuating your self-abuse, only this time you are your own perpetrator. Although it is difficult, you must let go of the anger to break this cycle.

There are other ways to release anger besides giving it directly back to its rightful owner. After all, if I hand you an apple, does that mean you have to carry it around with you for the rest of your life? Of course not.

Anger is no different. If someone hurts you or inflicts his or her anger on you, you don't have to carry that anger around with you for the rest of your life any more than you have to carry around that apple—which of course is going to rot anyway, just as your anger will coalesce into bitterness.

Instead, you can release anger—that person's and yours—by writing about it (you don't have to send the letter to your abuser), punching a pillow, expressing your rage in a mirror, or using the shouting/breathing technique described in chapter 3. What's important is releasing your wrath. It is not important to change the other person. Chances are that other person isn't going to change. But you can release your anger, even if it's only into thin air, to free yourself from the prison of procrastination.

If our anger turns to rage, then we are likely to fall into what Thomas Scheff and others have called the "shame-rage" spiral. In other words, when the shame is too great to bear, we quickly spiral into rage in order to mask our true feelings of humiliation. If we were raised with so-called "rage-aholics," then we were victimized by our caretakers' residual pool of shame as well. And it is this residual pool of shame that once again is the source of procrastination patterns that prevent us from living our lives to the fullest.

* * * *

Anxiety

Anxiety is another mask for shame and will usually aggravate a case of procrastination considerably. Let's see how you feel about this overwhelming feeling in terms of your responses to the items below.

Dominant Hand

When I think of anxiety, I think _____
_____.

When I think of anxiety, I feel _____
_____.

Nondominant Hand

When I think of anxiety, I think _____
_____.

When I think of anxiety, I feel _____
_____.

Bear in mind your responses to these statements as we explore the notion that any threat to your life or to your self-esteem can trigger anxiety. Just as a tiger coming at you in the jungle will trigger the classic "flight or fight" response, so will threats to your self-esteem. Virtually any shame-based issues can trigger a tremendous amount of anxiety, or perhaps just enough to keep you jumping—away from achievement, decision-making or success. Anxiety also contributes to procrastination by interfering with your ability to think clearly. So much energy is needed to control your anxiety that other thoughts cannot receive your full attention.

Obviously, we all face threats to our self-esteem on a daily basis, at home, on the job, or on the street. We may be able to handle most of these, such as an insult, a bad review from a supervisor, or a racist, sexist or homophobic slur. However, protracted procrastination sets in when such "normal" daily events tap into our earlier pools of shame.

I have worked with numerous clients whose unresolved and sometimes repressed childhood memories were so threatening that they would do almost anything to avoid being alone. For them, being alone, without the distraction of others, made it difficult to block out painful feelings. Although many of these clients were holding at bay terrible memories of abuse, others were simply trying to evade that inner child who had been told that he or she was "stupid," "bad" or "ugly" by a shaming caretaker.

The anxiety arising from such shame is often enough to keep many procrastinators from working on tasks that require solitude. For some people, bringing projects to a library or café can help reduce the anxiety of being alone. Sometimes having a pet nearby can be a source of comfort until the original source of anxiety can be discovered, worked through and released. So-called "pet therapy" has proved to be successful in working with a variety of disorders, particularly anxiety and depression.

But remember this: Anxiety is nothing to be afraid of. It is simply a signal from your body that something is threatening you or your self-esteem. Anxiety can be seen as a signal to help you sort out your problems by raising pertinent questions such as:

- In which situations do you become anxious? _____
  _____.

- With which people do you become anxious? _____
  _____.

- Whom do those anxiety-provoking individuals remind you of? _____
  _____.

- Which tasks does your anxiety lead you to delay?
  _____
  _____.

The answers to these questions may help you to get in touch with earlier life issues that may have set up this automatic response of anxiety whenever anyone or anything threatens to tap into that pool of pre-existing shame.

In essence, anxiety can help you to face the very life issues that perhaps you've come here to learn from. As you begin to work through these shame-based issues, you'll no doubt start to see that anxiety is simply a stop sign—not a roadblock—reminding you to slow down, look both ways and proceed with caution. You don't want to be hit broadside by those earlier shame-based issues that are triggering your anxiety and subsequent procrastination about a current decision or task. You just want to slow down long enough to see them. And then you can move on.

* * * *

Assertiveness Problems

As with other factors related to procrastination, lack of assertiveness emanates from a sense of shame. It is as if we feel on some level that we don't deserve to have our needs met. Let's check in to see how you feel about this issue.

Dominant Hand

When I think of assertiveness, I think _____
_____.

When I think of assertiveness, I feel _____
_____.

Nondominant Hand

When I think of assertiveness, I think _____
_____.

When I think of assertiveness, I feel _____
_____.

Did you hesitate in responding to these items? Are you more assertive at work than at home? Are you more outspoken with strangers than with close friends or family? Is it easier to ask for what you need than to say "no" to someone else's need?

Any time we take a stand for ourselves, we risk being attacked by others. And to be attacked by someone else means that this person just might become angry enough to leave you. When I ask, "What stops you from finishing your project?" or "What stops you from making that important decision?", I am not surprised when I hear a response like, "Joan will get angry!" or "I might get Bob upset!"

If we allow ourselves to be controlled by the needs of others, then we become trapped in a pattern of procrastination that protects us from ever having to be assertive regarding our own needs. Thus we are exempt—or so we think—from being rejected. Of course we can thereby avoid feeling the shame associated with rejection.

But the reality is that others will soon sense our resentment and we may get rejected anyway, just for being who we are. For example, if you are a painter or musician or writer and your significant other is not supportive of your endeavors, then he or she may not be accepting you for who you are—you are being rejected implicitly. If you deny yourself the time you need to work on your projects, then you are denying your self-expression and rejecting your selfhood as well.

Such was the case of a young woman with whom I worked several years ago.

> *Heather's husband was so threatened by her desire to be a musician that she would become blocked every time she tried to write lyrics. Her husband had been hurt deeply by the infidelity of his previous wife, and he was afraid that Heather would be unfaithful to him if she ever went on tour. Although Heather reassured him constantly, she didn't feel comfortable testing her husband's limits, since he was the primary breadwinner and she still had one more year of college.*
>
> *Once Heather began to see that her lack of assertiveness was rooted in childhood issues relating to the unintentional deprivation she had suffered as one of nine children in a large, guilt-driven family, she began to work on her assertiveness skills. She started to realize that her lack of assertiveness was rooted in a sense of shame at having any needs in the first place. She began to see that it was not wrong to expect others to take an interest in her ideas, nor*

was it wrong or shameful to spend time expressing herself when others felt she should be meeting their needs instead of her own.

As part of her treatment, Heather began to experiment with two images. By imagining that she was surrounded by an invisible force field, she was able to maintain a sense of boundaries when negotiating a new relationship with her husband. When he became angry, she would imagine a mirrored coating on the outside of the force field so that by keeping silent, she could simply mirror back to him his own childish antics. It didn't take long before Heather's husband began to realize he could no longer engage her in verbal battle, let alone to realize how ridiculous he appeared waging such a war all by himself. Gradually, as Heather felt more comfortable, she was able to express herself in a more assertive way, and she began to spend more time—guilt-free—pursuing her dream while maintaining a healthier relationship with her husband.

Another client whose lack of assertiveness contributed to her problems with procrastination was aware of the fact that she had the right to be assertive. However, her general style of relating to people was one of passivity, since she feared being seen as too aggressive.

Elizabeth's issues related primarily to her weight problem. She thought her children would be deprived of proper nutrition if she cooked low-fat foods and would be deprived of her attention if she went to the gym. However, when I asked Elizabeth what she would do if her daughter was diagnosed as diabetic and had to have a special diet, she agreed that she would cook foods that would be suitable for her daughter's needs. When I asked, "What stops you from doing the same thing for yourself?" Elizabeth started to cry.

She began to detail the way she'd felt as a child: unworthy and unloved. Raised by a gruff, aggressive father and a highly passive mother, Elizabeth had learned to identify with her mother's meek behavior as a way of avoiding the wrath of her father. She had also vowed that she would never become loud or aggressive like her father. Thus, with her own children, she had swung the pendulum in the other direction and was overly accommodating to their needs.

Once Elizabeth understood that her children needed a healthy, assertive mother, and once she believed she had the right to feel good in her own body (even if it meant saying no to her children now and then), she made the time to exercise and started cooking healthier foods. The more assertive she became, the less ashamed she was for having needs in the first place. And the more shame she released, the less she procrastinated when it came to taking care of herself.

* * * *

Co-dependency

Although the word "co-dependency" has been used in countless ways, the basic concept deals with habitually putting your needs aside to meet the needs of others, often at the expense of your own comfort, health, safety or self-esteem. Co-dependency is closely related to lack of assertiveness. However, a co-dependent person not only has trouble saying no, but also will tend to volunteer his or her time without even being asked. Let's see how the two sides of our brains feel about this.

Dominant Hand

When I think of co-dependency, I think _____

_____.

When I think of co-dependency, I feel _____

_____.

Nondominant Hand

When I think of co-dependency, I think _____

_____.

When I think of co-dependency, I feel _____

_____.

In scanning your answers you may have noticed a pattern that involves some degree of guilt. Obviously, such a behavior pattern can wreak havoc on the time management schedules we all try to implement on January 1 of every year. Often we feel that we should entertain our loved ones constantly. Rather than dividing our time between relationship maintenance and the tasks we need to accomplish, we spend the bulk of our time with others, putting in face time, but resenting every minute of it.

What keeps us from meeting our own needs to accomplish certain tasks and goals? Is it true that our loved ones would absolutely wither up and die if we weren't there for them 24 hours a day, eight days a week? Of course not—but that doesn't stop us from being prey to that nagging guilty feeling that we are being "selfish" if we take time out for ourselves to accomplish tasks, engage in exercise, or simply rest so that we won't end up procrastinating into our coffee cup during the next day's alleged work.

Work is another place where co-dependency rears its ugly head. Some of us feel that we must meet the needs of our co-workers and/or employers, and perpetually find ourselves staying late each night, thereby negating the possibility of getting out for that walk or jog before nightfall, even if we had the energy left to exercise. Our well-being gets relegated to second place and the cycle of procrastination continues.

One client was so caught up in meeting the needs of his employer and his ailing parents that he had gained an enormous amount of weight. Food had become his only source of pleasure. William had no social life in terms of friendships or dating. Though it was not required, he felt that to please his employer, he had to finish certain projects at work before he could go home each night. William stayed until 8 or 9 P.M., then went home to cook and clean for his parents.

Exhausted and frustrated, William would delay exercising. Instead, he ate huge portions of food just before collapsing into bed.

When William initially came to me for weight loss counseling, he had no idea that it was co-dependency that had restricted his life. Once he began to see that early childhood messages about his self-worth were no longer needed, he was able to take charge of his own life, start a program of self-care and hire a part-time home nurse to help care for his parents.

The source of all co-dependency is shame. We feel that we don't deserve to have our needs met, that the needs of others are more important. Where did we learn such unhealthy notions? Who taught us always to put others first? Did we perhaps take that message too literally? Isn't it okay to take care of ourselves, too?

At my workshops on procrastination and stress, I remind people that it's okay to be a little bit more "self-ish." After all, the word "selfish" simply means "pertaining to the self." What's so bad and shameful about your "self" that it must be neglected so that other people's "selves" can benefit?

As long as we don't take it to extremes, being "self-ish" instead of co-dependent is often the antidote to procrastination in and of itself, since procrastination often is our veiled attempt at showing resentment because we don't "have" (translation: make) enough time for relaxation and fun. After all, why would your inner child want to clean up his or her room full of strewn clothes (translation: office full of paperwork) when he or she hasn't been allowed to go outside on a Saturday and just play—for years? Is it any wonder that inner child keeps tugging at your shirt-sleeve until you pay some attention to him or her and let the child go out to play (translation: take some time off to relax)?

So why do we feel that we must meet the needs of everyone this side of the Mississippi before we can meet our own needs? Why are we so terrified of being called "selfish" just because we happen to take care of our own needs, too? Again, as with all the other dynamics of procrastination, this pattern of co-dependency is rooted in shame. Since, on some level, we feel that we aren't good enough or adequate as human beings, we have learned to put others first; surely our needs cannot be as important as their needs. Since we are ashamed of the fact that we have needs in the first place, we tend to deny them, saying things like, "Oh, I don't mind helping out, I really didn't have anything important to do tonight." If that allegedly "unimportant" activity you didn't really have to do tonight involves something you wanted to do, then it *is* an important activity.

If I haven't convinced you to examine the source of your co-dependency, or at least to buy a book on co-dependency such as Melody Beattie's *Beyond Co-dependency* or Charles Whitfield's *Co-dependence: Healing the Human Condition,* then perhaps I can appeal to your co-dependent side to stop all this co-dependency! Remember, even though you think that you are helping others by meeting their needs at the expense of your own, if you are draining your own battery, you won't be able to charge up anyone else's, either. Why do you think that airline personnel tell you on every flight to put your own oxygen mask on first—before your child's—in the event of an emergency? Considering how quickly you're going to need oxygen in a cabin that is no longer pressurized and airtight—your mask should be on within the first seven seconds, the child's within the first 10 seconds (it won't work so well in reverse!)—in this situation, *not* being co-dependent can literally save your life as well as the other person's!

Keep in mind that small children can appreciate, and even benefit from your need to take care of yourself. It really is okay to stop procrastinating when it comes to self-care. If a child knows that the primary caretaker needs a "nap time," the child can learn to respect and accept it.

In the case of children who cannot appreciate this need, it's still important, for their sake as well as yours, that you take time out for yourself. For example, I have presented workshops on stress management to parents with severely disabled children. These parents often resist the idea of taking time out for themselves. However, when I asked what they are trying to give to their children (some of whom cannot speak or hear or comprehend language), "love" was the universal answer.

Yet how can these parents transmit the idea of "love" to their disabled children when their facial expressions register exhaustion, irritation or anger? The child picks up these nonverbal signs. In essence, by not taking care of yourself, you are preventing yourself from giving a child the love you'd like to give.

Think about it: If you're at work on Monday at 2:00 P.M. and you're feeling tired, you think, "Oh, I can't wait to get through this day." But if it's Friday and you know you have the "reward time" of two weekend days off, if you feel tired at 2:00, you think, "Only three more hours—I can get through this." Similarly, if you've decided to stop procrastinating about taking care of yourself—you finally called the

Inner Child Abuse Hotline on yourself—and you know you have your own time off to exercise tomorrow morning, somehow, taking care of a dependent child doesn't seem quite so taxing today. Your child will sense that you are content and relaxed, and your child will absorb the love you're trying to transmit—along with a healthy message about lifelong self-care. (If you need further information and encouragement on this issue, you may want to pick up Donna Albrecht's book entitled *Raising a Child Who Has a Physical Disability*.)

Other individuals often get caught in the waters of co-dependency due to a form of "survivor guilt." It is as if they see others around them—perhaps other family members, friends or colleagues who are worse off in some ways—and this leads these co-dependent individuals into thinking that they, too, must suffer. They must give up their goals and dreams—or even a night or two at the gym—so they won't feel guilty for feeling better than their loved ones. But if you really stop and think about it, what good does it do for others who are still in the perpetual turbulence at the base of the waterfall if you jump in there with them? Wouldn't it give those others something to strive for if they can see that you have made it out of the turbulence and into the calmer waters of health? In other words, if you decide to stop procrastinating regarding your exercise program or getting your real estate license, maybe your spouse or other loved ones will, too.

No matter how you look at it, taking charge of your life, rather than trying to take charge of others' lives, is part of the reason you are here. If you don't allow yourself to live, then you don't allow yourself to learn. And whether you adhere to an Eastern philosophy that encourages you to work out all those kinks in your "karma," or a Western philosophy that advises learning how to practice goodwill—

even goodwill toward the "temple" of your body—learning is what it's all about.

* * * *

Depression

Even the word "depression" sounds depressing, doesn't it? Whether we are thinking in terms of mild, chronic feelings of sadness or severe, acute suicidal tendencies, this isn't a word we want in our daily vocabularies. Let's see what your gut-level responses are to this highly charged word.

Dominant Hand

When I think of depression, I think _____
_____.

When I think of depression, I feel _____
_____.

Nondominant Hand

When I think of depression, I think _____
_____.

When I think of depression, I feel _____
_____.

As you glance over your responses to the word "depression," keep in mind there are many reasons people get depressed. Anger turned inward upon the self; a negative view of the self, the world and the future; and physiological reactions are some explanations. However, it does not necessarily take a major depressive episode to create a severe case of procrastination. Sometimes a milder case of depression, known as "dysthymia," can sap your motivation.

Dysthymia feels like a low-grade fever—you kind of get used to it after a while, just as you might notice that you never need a sweater due to your low-grade fever, even though everyone else seems to feel a chill in the air.

According to experts such as Donald Klein and Paul Wender, an average of one in seven people (one in five for women and one in ten for men) will suffer from depression at some point during their lifetimes. That's about 30 million people in the U.S. at any given point in time. Yet most people refuse to acknowledge the signs of depression, let alone take antidepressants, even though such medications are not addictive (as opposed to many of the older anti-anxiety drugs like Valium or Librium).

Perhaps only therapists can see the true value of getting help for depression. In a recent survey of psychotherapists conducted by Kenneth Pope and Barbara Tabachnik, 84 percent of the therapists who responded reported that they had been in therapy, and of those in therapy, 61 percent had gone for the treatment of depression.

According to some experts such as Wendy Hoblitzelle, Nancy Morrison and June Tangney, depression is closely related to feelings of shame, and researchers have even found that some people have a stronger physiological tendency toward shame as well as depression. For those of you who have had your share of depression and its second cousin, shame, what I am about to say won't seem all that unfamiliar—which is good, because once you know what the problem is, you're on your way to resolving it.

Depression feels like a dim gray cloud, forever threatening to rain, but more often than not just hanging there, oppressing you with its weight, its meaninglessness and its perpetual presence dampening what's left of your enthusiasm for life. You wake up in the morning—if you can grope your way through the grogginess you experience at the edge of this cloud—and the last thing you want to do is get out of bed. Your eyes feel heavier than they used to do, as do your body and the weight of your thoughts.

You think, *I have to go to work / wake up the kids / start the day's activities / all of the above.* Simultaneously, another thought rushes in: *I don't care.* If you are able to, you drag yourself up, aware of the oppressive feel of the day already, just minutes out of your fitful sleep. And that's another thing. You'd really like to get a decent night's sleep—you've either been sleeping too much or too little, waking up at odd hours of the night, sometimes in the midst of an upsetting dream, sometimes not.

Then there's the feeling that you no longer own your appetite. Food can become aversive—repulsive to the taste buds, a further weight upon the stomach, a burden to the psyche when you haven't the energy to face the clerk at McDonald's, to call for a delivery, let alone to cook. Or perhaps your appetite has turned into a Godzilla, controlling you and your workday, insisting upon raising your levels of mood-enhancing brain chemicals (such as serotonin and endorphins) with loads of white flour, sugar and high-fat foods (e.g., doughnuts, chocolate, cookies, breads). Any excuse will do, including "because I felt like it." Some people may experience vascillations in appetite, from voracious to nonexistent, and similar fluctuations may occur in terms of sleep—anywhere from falling asleep throughout the day to developing insomnia.

Loss of interest in sex and other pleasurable activities—such as creative hobbies, exercise, sports, reading, going to the theater—is also a clinical symptom of depression. This apathy in turn creates further problems in our personal relationships—let alone problems at work in terms of our procrastination—which in turn deepen the depression.

Although antidepressants can truly help to lift the mood state of many individuals long enough to get them back on

track, many people resist taking such medication, prefer-
ring instead the Great American Self-Reliance Method of
Getting Through Life, living by the old motto of "paddling
your own canoe." But without antidepressants, many individuals will resort to some of the compulsive or addictive
behaviors discussed in chapter 7 in order to achieve a temporary lift in their levels of serotonin, dopamine, norepinephrine or endorphins. That's not exactly "paddling your
own canoe," either. And, as you'll see in chapter 7, although
such methods of escape will initially elicit an antidepressant effect in the body, they will eventually have the reverse
effect on levels of neurotransmitters and actually worsen
the depression in the long run.

Many people don't realize that taking antidepressant
medication is like getting a jump start in your car on a cold
winter morning. You try and try to jump-start the engine
with a neighbor's car, but it won't take. So you resign yourself to unhitching the battery, taking it to a nearby service
station and letting them plug it into their battery charger
for several hours. Once this is accomplished and your battery is installed again, your car will continue to recharge the
battery as long as you keep the vehicle running.

Similarly, at the start of every depressing day that you
have to endure, your brain must pump up an awful lot of
serotonin, dopamine, norepinephrine, endorphins and other
such mood-regulating neurotransmitters just to get you out
of bed each morning. After a while, your body basically
becomes immune to the effects of its own neurotransmitters.
And once your levels of serotonin, dopamine or other necessary neurotransmitters are too low, you can't seem to get
yourself charged up about life anymore. No matter how hard
you try, your energy remains depleted.

But antidepressants can help. For example, many of the
newer breed of antidepressants are SSRI's, or selective

serotonin re-uptake inhibitors. In other words, when serotonin jumps the gap from one neuron to the next in your brain, these medications inhibit neurons from re-uptaking the serotonin, so that your body has a longer time to experience the full effects of its own serotonin as it lounges between neurons. All that the antidepressant medication does is to recharge your battery, to allow your system to benefit from feeling its own serotonin, so that eventually your system will begin recharging itself and you'll no longer need the medication.

Once you are feeling better, you'll have the strength to face the painful feelings you've held so long inside, you'll start to make the changes necessary to improve your attitude and your life, and eventually, you'll begin to decrease the amount of the medication under the guidance of your psychiatrist. At that point, you'll find that you're no longer immune to the desired effects of your own neurotransmitters. As long as you continue to stay in charge of your own life, your energy and mood state will remain at the levels you need to feel good, to be productive and to be confident in decision-making. (However, some individuals, such as those with bipolar disorder—formerly known as manic-depression—must continue to take antidepressants for the entire life cycle, since their chemical imbalance is due to the natural state of their physiology, though situational factors can aggravate this imbalance further.)

* * * *

Evaluation Anxiety

Closely related to fear of failure, evaluation anxiety is often a more subtle mask for self-sabotage, emanating from a feeling of hidden shame. While fear of failure focuses upon our fear that we will fail, evaluation anxiety focuses upon our fear that others will perceive us as failures. Let's see what your ideas are regarding this common feature in the process of procrastination.

Dominant Hand

When I think of the concept of "evaluation anxiety," I think _____

_____.

When I think of the concept of "evaluation anxiety," I feel _____

_____.

Nondominant Hand

When I think of the concept of "evaluation anxiety," I think _____

_____.

When I think of the concept of "evaluation anxiety," I feel _____

_____.

Depending on your current level of self-esteem, your feelings about this issue could be a deciding factor in the age-old question, "to procrastinate or not to procrastinate."

This problem is quite common in the workplace as well as in other learning situations when we're evaluated by people who either don't understand or appreciate our work, or who disagree with us because it conflicts with their opinions.

One young man in his mid-20s had a severe case of procrastination regarding his doctoral dissertation. This is a common phenomenon, since many graduate students, teetering on the brink of professional status, view the dissertation as an integral part of their emerging identity.

Jeffrey realized that no matter what he wrote, his advisor, who was also the department head, would attack his work until Jeffrey caved in and espoused the advisor's views. This alone could cause a delay in finishing the task, but Jeffrey's residual feelings about his childhood served to aggravate the situation.

In Jeffrey's family of origin, the only source of approval came from getting good grades. Without this achievement, there was no attention or affection. Thus, Jeffrey strove for excellence and had attained it—until meeting this particular advisor. Now he faced the prospect of a lower grade, which meant loss of approval and lowered self-esteem, if he didn't sacrifice his integrity.

To complicate matters further, Jeffrey's father (a janitor) had never attended college and often spoke of "those uppity types." Thus, Jeffrey was given the dual message that he should get high marks, while at the same time maintaining the family's simple values. Thus, no matter how his advisor evaluated him, Jeffrey still faced an internal dilemma: If he did poorly, his self-esteem would suffer, and he would incur the disapproval of his father and risk tapping into his pool of pre-existing shame from early childhood. If Jeffrey wanted a positive evaluation, he would have to compromise the integrity of his ideas, yet still face the prospect of his father's disapproval for becoming "one of those uppity types."

Once Jeffrey was able to develop a stronger sense of self by letting go of the confusing image his father had designed for him, Jeffrey was able to complete his dissertation. He realized that no matter how his advisor evaluated him, it didn't really matter, since the dissertation was only a paper he had to write, not the cornerstone of his identity. Jeffrey also realized that he was free to write the paper he'd truly wanted to write in the first place—it just wouldn't be his dissertation. But it might become the subject of his first professional article, an article where his name would be followed by the Ph.D. he had worked so hard to attain.

* * * *

Fear of Failure

Everyone can recognize this all-time favorite. Even if we deny the fact that we may experience fear of failure, we don't usually begrudge ourselves the right to experience fear of failure—it's obviously an inherent factor whenever we face the prospect of success. When the fear of failure taps into that pre-existing pool of unconscious shame, procrastination can become a major problem. Let's see how this issue may be affecting you.

Dominant Hand

When I think of the concept of "fear of failure," I think

_____

_____.

When I think of the concept of "fear of failure," I feel

_____

_____.

Nondominant Hand

When I think of the concept of "fear of failure," I think

_____

_____.

When I think of the concept of "fear of failure," I feel

_____

_____.

Your answers to the above items probably indicate that you're right at home with what is perhaps the most common reason cited for procrastination: "If I don't try it, then I can't fail."

> *This fear of failure was a major factor in the case of a young man who had delayed his training as a visual artist. Although Aaron was highly talented, he would put off his major assignments, then frantically try to pull his act together at the last minute. He was so afraid of failure and facing the notion that perhaps he wasn't as talented as his teachers seemed to think, that he tried to guarantee failure.*
>
> *However, if Aaron failed, he could always point to his procrastination as the culprit—rather than to a possible lack of talent—by saying, "I could have done better if I'd had more time."*
>
> *Once Aaron was able to release his underlying sense of shame and low self-worth stemming from his relationship with an absentee alcoholic mother, he was finally able to accept himself as a talented artist, instead of seeing himself through a shamebased lens as "damaged goods."*

* * * *

Fear of Intimacy

Just as we are bound to fail at times, since we are imperfect beings by definition, we are also bound to get hurt at times by engaging in close relationships. On the other hand, if we don't risk love, we will never experience the positive benefits of being in a warm relationship. Let's take a look at how you feel about this underlying trigger for procrastination.

Dominant Hand

When I think of the concept of "fear of intimacy," I think _____
_____.

When I think of the concept of "fear of intimacy," I feel

_____
_____.

Nondominant Hand

When I think of the concept of "fear of intimacy," I think _____
_____.

When I think of the concept of "fear of intimacy," I feel

_____
_____.

As you have probably noticed with previous examples, this protective mask is often quite difficult to recognize. That doesn't change the fact that most of us experience fear of intimacy to some degree.

Angela, a 27-year-old attorney, came for counseling. She felt lonely and depressed and found herself constantly putting things off at work. While her new job did not require working weekends, Angela never seemed to get her work done by Friday. So she would put in eight or nine hours on the weekend. During that time she would doodle, daydream and listen to a portable radio on her desk. Naturally, her social life suffered. Angela would avoid making plans with friends, and she would tell men that she was "too tired" to go out on Saturday nights because she had "worked all day."

Once Angela clearly examined her work patterns, she admitted that she could probably complete her regular work during the week. During our review of her college and high school years, it became apparent that Angela had consistently procrastinated and so had never developed close friendships or dated very much.

One day, when I asked Angela if she felt that she deserved the close companionship and love of others, she began to cry. Her tears soon led her down a path of self-discovery that she had been avoiding since the age of four when her parents had divorced. Angela stated that she had always missed her father terribly, and had never recovered from the hurt of his abandonment. She also felt angry that her mother, a very astute attorney herself, had never permitted any sort of visitation or custody arrangements in the divorce agreement.

During a photohistory session, Angela became quite upset at certain early photographs of herself with her father, and soon began to have very uncomfortable feelings about him. Then, during an "indirect interview" with her mother, Angela found out that the reason for the divorce was due to her father's incestuous behavior toward her. Though she was quite upset about this discovery, Angela eventually began to understand why she had always felt so depressed and why she had unconsciously structured her life to avoid being close to anyone.

As she worked through her anger with her mother and father, Angela began to work more effectively at the office, leaving herself ample time on the weekends to develop closer social ties with women as well as with men.

This example clearly illustrates how previous negative experiences with relationships can make us fearful of ever trying again. Any form of neglect or abuse can establish the fear of being close to another person. However, once we recognize these early experiences, we can begin to develop a new attitude that includes love, respect and feelings of accomplishment.

* * * *

Fear of Rejection

All's fair in love, war and procrastination until you bring up the idea of rejection. While evaluation anxiety (others will judge us harshly) and fear of failure (we will judge ourselves harshly) involve our performance at certain tasks or activities, rejection involves a direct hit on our self and our self-expression.

For many of us, procrastination is a way to avoid the potential for disapproval and possible rejection. Let's get some deeper insight on this issue by responding to the items that follow.

Dominant Hand

When I think of rejection, I think _____
_____.

When I think of rejection, I feel _____
_____.

Nondominant Hand

When I think of rejection, I think _____
_____.

When I think of rejection, I feel _____
_____.

Rejection feels like a sudden slap in the face. When your decisions or talents carry a strong possibility that someone will reject you, procrastination steps in to protect you. It's certainly easier to procrastinate than to face any of these possibilities:

_____ My kids will reject me if I initiate a divorce.
_____ My kids will reject me if I start dating again.
_____ My family will reject me if I choose a certain career.
_____ My family will reject me if I write a book that displeases them.
_____ Someone I love will reject me if the book I'm writing in honor of them isn't a bestseller.

Obviously, this is only a partial list of possible situations in which we may be personally rejected by using our creativity or making a decision. And these examples relate primarily to personal rejection, rather than professional rejection. All you have to do is scan the pages of André Bernard's *Rotten Rejections,* a collection of rejection letters sent to famous authors before they were famous, and you can get a feel for how much people can hurt you professionally when they've never even met you. Rejection, since it taps directly into shame, is clearly a potent force in generating protracted cases of procrastination. If we have a history of previous rejection—whether personal or professional—we are much more likely to allow the threat of renewed rejection to keep us locked in the prison of procrastination.

* * * *

Fear of Success

The flip side of failure is success, which can be a lot more intimidating than we think. Let's check your responses to the statements below to see how this factors into your tomorrow trap.

Dominant Hand

When I think of the concept of "fear of success," I think _____

_____.

When I think of the concept of "fear of success," I feel _____

_____.

Nondominant Hand

When I think of the concept of "fear of success," I think _____

_____.

When I think of the concept of "fear of success," I feel _____

_____.

You may find you're not afraid of success at all, or that you are truly intimidated by the prospect of success—there's not much room in between. More often than not, we are afraid of the *consequences* of success. The list below is only a partial list of issues that may contribute to that fear.

1. Whom will I outshine if I succeed? _____

_____.

2. Is that permitted? _____

_____.

3. Who will be left behind if I succeed? _____

_____.

4. Is that a separation I am prepared to deal with? _____

_____.

5. Am I afraid of the imposter syndrome—the notion that if I succeed, once I'm in the limelight, others will find out that I'm not as good as I appear? _____

_____.

6. Once I'm in the spotlight, I'm afraid that others will find out about _____

_____

or begin to suspect _____

_____,

as if they'll see all the way through me, and they'll realize that _____

_____.

Regardless of how many of these issues seem to be preventing you from succeeding, they have one thing in common: They are all based in shame. A case example will illustrate.

Norman, a man in his late 30s, had been procrastinating regarding his writing career for many years. Upon closer scrutiny, it became clear that as the youngest child in a family of seven (all of his siblings were much older), Norman had not only been neglected emotionally, but he was also the family's scapegoat. Norman always seemed to get blamed, and shamed, for anything that went wrong in the family. Eventually he revealed that his mother had said his birth had prevented her from obtaining the divorce she wanted. As a result, she called Norman "the loser." The other family members had followed suit.

Even though he was a talented writer, Norman had been taught "not to get too big for his britches." His fear of success was a direct outgrowth of this internalized self-image left over from childhood. However, once he was able to release his anger and hurt regarding this early childhood programming, Norman began to ease himself into the writing career he'd always dreamed of.

* * * *

Perfectionism

Although perfectionism may appear as an obvious source of procrastination, what is not always so clear is the origin of such perfectionism.

In your family, did everything have to be done "the right way"? Did you get punished for making mistakes? Were mistakes not acceptable? Were you taught that no matter what you did, it wouldn't be good enough, since it came from you? Let's take a glance inside to see how the two sides of your brain respond to this protective mask in many a procrastinator's life.

Dominant Hand

When I think of perfectionism, I think _____
_____.

When I think of perfectionism, I feel _____
_____.

Nondominant Hand

When I think of perfectionism, I think _____
_____.

When I think of perfectionism, I feel _____
_____.

As you examine your answers to the statements above, observe once again whether there are differences in the way you feel versus the way you think about perfectionism. Most of us feel that we should be striving for perfection, even though we don't like the pressure it puts on us.

I have worked with many clients who wore their self-avowed perfectionism like a badge of honor, protecting them from any criticism. When questioned they could say, "I try to do everything perfectly—at least I'm trying."

This attitude is a set-up for procrastination. The translation sounds like: "I admit I'm not perfect, and that may mean I'm inadequate, but as long as I cling to my high standards, I have a right to exist."

Most of us wither under the criticism of others. When we are alone, we are even harder on ourselves. Each project takes longer to start or to finish; we fear that we'll miss our self-imposed standard of perfection.

After all, if our statements, decisions, behaviors and performances—all that emanates from us—must be perfect, then we are by definition setting ourselves up for failure. Since we are, as mere human beings, inherently flawed, we'll never be able to achieve perfection. But this inability to achieve perfection makes sense, regardless of whether you apply a Western spiritual perspective—which decrees that we aren't supposed to be as perfect as God—or an Eastern spiritual perspective which implies that we are here to learn, not to be perfect (or at least, not until we reach moksha or "nirvana"; and if such beliefs are valid, by then we wouldn't even be in bodies anymore, so what difference would it make!).

No matter what our spiritual beliefs, until we get to that point in our spiritual development, most of us yearn for such perfection. We are impatient with the learning process we must experience in life, especially since our mistakes are often the only learning tools that we have. We are so ashamed of being human that we become immobilized.

This morbid fear of criticism and imperfection is prevalent among the shame-based writers I have treated for perfectionistic patterns and procrastination. It is as if the writer has transferred the power to shame him- or herself from the original source of childhood shame to the reading audience. Whether the reader is a teacher, editor, publisher, or just someone who bought the book, it doesn't seem to matter—these people all have tremendous power over the shame-based writer who has yet to reach nirvana, literarily or spiritually.

There is often the assumption that somehow this reading audience will see all the way back to the author's first draft (also known as the obligatory "shitty first draft," according to Anne Lamott in her marvelous book on writing entitled *Bird by Bird*), so there is a great deal of fear in writing that necessarily quite imperfect first draft. It is as if the author fears that by seeing all the way back into this lousy first draft, the reader will also see all the way back to the author's lousy childhood and its accompanying painful overflow of shame.

Regardless of your profession, the perennial problem of perfectionism is a direct outgrowth of shame and a direct precursor to procrastination. When we say, "I can't start the project because I'm so afraid it won't be perfect," what we are really saying is, "I won't start the project because I'm not perfect." We are saying that we will not take the chance of being who we really are because that would mean having to face the shame instilled in us as children.

One client, a highly talented graphic artist who worked for a prestigious advertising agency, lived under the fear of being fired. Sue's work was so good that she received the highest of accolades from her employers and colleagues, no matter how long she took to finish a project.

Yet Sue was convinced that at any moment she would be "found out." Thus, each project took longer to complete. She was convinced that it had to be absolutely perfect. She was sure that her work was inadequate, and that sooner or later someone would see that.

Once we began to explore her past, Sue saw that her mother's disapproval during childhood had a negative impact on Sue's self-image. Nothing Sue did as a child was given approval unless it was exactly the way her mother would have done it. Since the child was not an adult who could anticipate her mother's preferences, let alone the mother's verbal rage when Sue did not perform adequately, then as a child Sue was always doomed to failure and left striving for perfection, hoping for the long-awaited approval she so desperately needed.

In therapy, Sue began to see that she had transferred the fear of her mother's disapproval to her employers. That surprising discovery led her to dismantle her system of perfectionism—one step at a time.

The real beauty of giving up the quest for perfection means that you get to live again. As Anne Lamott puts it so well in *Bird by Bird* (p. 28):

I think perfectionism is based on the obsessive belief that if you run carefully enough, hitting each stepping-stone just right, you won't have to die. The truth is that you will die anyway and a lot of people who aren't even looking at their feet are going to do a whole lot better than you, and have a lot more fun while they're doing it.

* * * *

Powerlessness

Feeling powerless is one of the most pervasive elements that you'll find in the tomorrow trap. We feel powerless over the task at hand—and powerless over our habit of procrastination, as if it has taken on a life of its own. The decision or task seems so big that we cannot even try to take it on. And so procrastination rolls in like a cold front, taking over our lives like a winter storm that provides us with genuine "snow days" to legitimately skip school or work. However, the guilt-free moments we experience on a genuine "snow day" somehow elude us when it comes to procrastination. Let's see what your brain has to say about this mask for deeper issues of shame.

Dominant Hand

When I think of powerlessness, I think _____

_____.

When I think of powerlessness, I feel _____

_____.

Nondominant Hand

When I think of powerlessness, I think _____

_____.

When I think of powerlessness, I feel _____

_____.

Taking note of your responses above, ask yourself how frequently you end up feeling powerless—and in which situations. Regardless of your answers, you'll probably find that being powerless keeps you in the victim role. It is as if you are still lying helplessly within the boundaries of the white chalk outline drawn around your body at the scene of the crime. Until you empower yourself to get up, you will remain a victim rather than becoming a survivor—let alone becoming a "thriver," as experts such as Paul Hansen and Adrienne Crowder would recommend. Getting up and out of this powerless role can be accomplished by some people through the use of contingency management—breaking the task down into manageable steps and self-administering rewards for each step completed. But how many of us refuse to try such a system, or try it and simply end up procrastinating on these smaller tasks as well?

Most of the people who come to see me for treatment regarding procrastination exhibit this sense of powerlessness. They feel as if they have no control over their habit of procrastination, which is often described as being outside of them. Technically speaking, of course, we are the ones who perform the behaviors that then become "habit." Eventually such habits—procrastination, smoking, overeating—seem to take on lives of their own.

Why do we continue to engage in such habits when they are clearly self-destructive?

Habits provide us with a sense of security, a "sameness" that makes us feel safe in a world of chaos. If we grew up in a chaotic environment, then we probably became accustomed to it, regardless of how destructive it may have been. Even children who have been beaten will cling to their abusers when human services caseworkers try to remove the children from their dysfunctional homes.

So through the habit of procrastination, we continue to re-create that familiar feeling of being surrounded by chaos. Not only does this provide a sense of security via that feeling of "sameness," but it also provides a convenient way to avoid our true feelings and deeper problems. For if we are always frantically trying to make up for our procrastination, then we never have the time to sit down long enough to feel anything. Thus, we can successfully avoid any emotion that could possibly tap into that pre-existing pool of shame we work so hard to ignore.

Many procrastinators claim they like working at the last minute under a tight deadline. It makes them feel important, especially when others offer attention and sympathy. Some procrastinators may have become addicted or at least accustomed to that adrenaline rush they may have felt as children growing up in a chaotic environment, in which they never knew what would happen next. Forever on guard, they became accustomed to living with a high state of anxiety and andrenaline, both of which can be triggered quite readily via the habit of procrastination. (Obviously, other biochemical imbalances may also cause this craving for excitement, such as bipolar disorder or attention-deficit/hyperactivity disorder—genetic issues that may also generate shame throughout the life cycle, as discussed in chapter 8.)

For example, I can recall one day when I was trying to make the deadline for turning in a chapter of my master's thesis—a "psychoautobiographical" analysis of Kurt Vonnegut's novels—to my advisor in the English department. Since I would be driving right by the Laundromat on the way to the university, I had planned on doing my laundry that day as well. Accustomed to chaos and a frenetic pace of life since early childhood, this seemed like a perfectly normal plan of action to me. Well, as you may have already guessed, sure enough, chaos ensued. Not only did the last available dryer break down on me, but so did my car. So between the shoddy maintenance job done by that particular Laundromat owner and a flat tire, I didn't graduate—again.

Now, could this have had something to do as well with my feelings of powerlessness in relation to my thesis advisor, who had been strongly suggesting that I change my topic to something less radical that would suit his preferences? After all, wouldn't he look bad, too, if I was held back one more semester? He had already had my teaching contract canceled for one semester to "give Miss Peterson more time to devote to her thesis," and I still hadn't caved in to his pressure for a more "mainstream" project. Certainly, on an unconscious level, I can see now that this whole scenario may have been at least in part a reaction to the powerlessness I felt inside. I knew my thesis idea was on target (in a post-graduation correspondence with Kurt Vonnegut, he told me I'd been correct), but I also knew that if I didn't change to a more conservative topic, my advisor would continue to pressure me, and I saw no real way out of my dilemma.

On some unconscious level, I must have felt victimized by this authority figure who had all the power. But at that point in my life, on a conscious level, I'd relegated those feelings of powerlessness to the likes of GE clothes dryers and Goodyear tires. It was my way of staying in the victim role I didn't even know I was in—my way of saying, "Can you believe all this happened to me?!" Since at that time I had no real awareness yet of the extent of my childhood neglect and abuse, I had no idea that I was unconsciously self-sabotaging in order to stay in the familiar and therefore "comfortable" victim role. Somewhere during that time of my life, I actually had six flat tires within two weeks. All four went flat *from different causes,* then two blew out again—and I suspect now that this was probably a cosmic nudge to get up off of that victim sidewalk and let some genuine tears wash away that chalk outline of my body!

Like other procrastinators, my sense of powerlessness prevailed also because of a transgenerational pattern of learned helplessness. As discussed earlier, such a pattern arises from the influence of caretakers who no longer feel that they are effective in solving problems, so they just don't bother to try. Being raised in such an environment can have a powerful impact on children, who may then grow up to think that procrastination is a completely normal mode of operation.

In families of origin such as mine, where one or more caretakers is a substance abuser, this pattern of helplessness emanates from the children's awareness that they are powerless over their caretaker's substance abuse and inappropriate behaviors. No matter how hard these children try to be "good," the caretaker still turns to drugs or alcohol rather than to the family for support and love. Thus, these children grow up feeling that it is pointless to try to be "good" at anything, since it won't get them the attention, respect and love they need anyway.

For others, feelings of powerlessness can arise as a replication of an abuse experience.

One client, a talented student, was frozen with shame when his teacher began reading his poetry aloud in class. Although it was chosen because it was so well-written, all Brian could feel was a sense of powerlessness as he reeled with reverberations of shame, listening to the thinly disguised details of his early physical abuse. While no one could have known that the poem was autobiographical, Brian was so ashamed that he never returned to class, and he developed a severe case of writer's block. However, once he was able to fully recall those early traumas, he slowly began to use the psycho-autobiographical writing techniques described in chapter 6. Eventually, Brian started writing again and enrolled back in college to finish his degree.

One other concept to keep in mind that may help you understand your sense of powerlessness involves what psychologists call "locus of control." This phrase refers to the way in which we view our portion of control over our lives versus what we feel is due to chance or to the control of others.

An internal locus of control implies that you feel as if you are pretty much in charge of your own life. You create your own success and take credit for it. You take responsibility for your failures and try to learn from them so that you won't repeat the same mistakes over and over.

An external locus of control implies that you do not feel as though you are in charge. If you succeed, it's by sheer luck. But if you fail, it's your fault. You may often feel that other people seem to have all the luck.

People who suffer from procrastination usually have an external locus of control. They feel as though other events "just get in the way" of completing tasks—as if they have no control over these events whatsoever. Sometimes this is true: You can't account for a bad case of the flu two days before a deadline. But the same flu wouldn't be nearly so problematic if the project was nearly finished anyway. So we do have some choice in the matter. However, when we procrastinate, we have left no room for adversity—and so any disruption feels like a stroke of bad luck rather than an everyday circumstance. As I said earlier, you can't go around blaming everything on Goodyear tires and GE dryers.

On the other hand, if we are still trapped in the cycle of shame from childhood, during which events were indeed controlled by our caretakers, then an external locus of control takes on new meaning. Suppose our caretakers did not praise us when we were successful, and instead they told us we "sure must have been lucky that day" to do so well. This is how we learn to feel ashamed of our perceived so- called inadequacies, and this is how we learn not to accept the fact that we can create and take credit for our successes. It is also how we learn to think that events are controlled by factors outside of us, and even if we had a vote, it wouldn't count.

In terms of competition, having an external locus of control can be particularly destructive and can lead to even greater levels of procrastination. Think about it: If the only way you can succeed is through sheer luck (which you cannot drum up on your own), and the only way you can fail is through your own inadequacy (rather than just having bad luck), then the odds are against you from the start. Why bother even trying to achieve something when you can do nothing to help yourself succeed and must guard relentlessly against your perceived propensity to fail? Again, procrastination comes to the rescue to protect you from any feelings of shame associated with potential failure. Such a world view tainted by feelings of powerlessness has kept many of us locked in the tomorrow trap for decades at a time.

* * * *

Shame

And without further ado, let's take a look at the culprit underlying all other culprits in the crime of procrastination: shame.

Dominant Hand

When I think of shame, I think _____
_____.

When I think of shame, I feel _____
_____.

Nondominant Hand

When I think of shame, I think _____
_____.

When I think of shame, I feel _____
_____.

No doubt, right about now you are feeling ashamed of being ashamed—even the word "shame" sounds uncomfortable. Well, join the club. It's a universal feeling and perhaps the most uncomfortable of all. But it's still a part of the human condition. And remember that procrastination is most likely to occur when we have an overwhelming backlog of shame from earlier events involving loss or humiliation.

Two types of shame may be involved here. The first relates to a previous experience of failure regarding a particular task.

For example, let's say that you're not good at math, and when you filled out your income tax return forms, you inadvertently created a $1,000 refund for yourself, when in actuality—according to the IRS calculations you received four months later, long after you'd spent the money—you actually owed the IRS $400. Just thinking about having to pay back that $1,400 mistake—the source of a major argument with your spouse—may be enough to elicit an "I'll start it tomorrow" attitude when it comes to this year's tax return. Why would you want to face a stimulus that you now associate with shame and embarrassment?

This type of embarrassment may turn into a more protracted case of procrastination if you already have a backlog of deeper shame from childhood issues of deprivation, neglect or abuse. Keep in mind that a certain type and amount of healthy shame—emanating from our imperfect behaviors that we know are inappropriate, such as damaging a friend's car—will not usually trigger problems with severe procrastination. But when the normal level of healthy shame—which can be envisioned, just like other emotions, as being at the heart level—has risen to the eyelid level due to an influx of unhealthy shame from negative life experiences, just one more drop of shame can create an onslaught of tears that may seem inexplicable and definitely beyond the level of intensity warranted by the situation. I have seen this pattern repeatedly during my work with clients suffering from severe procrastination.

Take the case of a young reporter who could not bring himself to look for a job after he had been fired. John delayed his search for another news reporting position for over a year.

I asked about the reasons for his termination from his previous job at a small newspaper. His eyes welled up as he detailed the humiliation he had felt at the hands of his direct supervisor, a person with whom John had had many quarrels whenever he tried to run an article with a liberal viewpoint. In a last- ditch effort to discredit John, the supervisor had tampered with the young reporter's article before it went to press, changing the names of important community leaders without John's knowledge.

As a result, John had not only been fired, but he also felt a deep sense of shame as a member of the community of writers and reporters by whom he felt he would ultimately be judged.

Upon closer scrutiny, John's year-long bout with procrastination in getting another job was part of a pattern. A similar situation where he had felt publicly humiliated occurred during high school.

As John explored his problem over the course of several sessions, he began to see how both his newspaper supervisor and his high school advisor reminded him of his father—a man who had perpetually criticized John in front of the entire family regarding his radical ideas. This resemblance had triggered John into arguing with his supervisor and with his high school advisor. Eventually John began to see that it was the effect of public humiliation that had silenced him.

During the process of photohistory, John recalled an even more traumatic public humiliation. While his parents were out of the country on a business trip, an uncle had beaten John severely, in the nude, at the age of nine. This traumatic event was aggravated by the fact that the uncle had assaulted his dignity in front of three other cousins. As John tearfully recounted this incident, he began to recognize the fact that any type of public humiliation had automatically tapped into the shame he felt regarding this public beating.

> *Once John released his feelings of hurt, anger and shame toward his uncle and toward himself, he was able to return to his profession with a renewed sense of pride and commitment.*

＊ ＊ ＊ ＊

Writer's Block: A Special Case of Unconscious Procrastination

And speaking of this particular profession, I'd like to say a few words about writer's block, which, as I have said, I consider to be an unconscious form of procrastination. I once met my favorite poet, Denise Levertov, and when I asked her, "What gives one the right to write?" she knew exactly what I meant.

She replied: "Is there something that will go unsaid if you don't write?"

"Of course," I answered.

"Well, then, you simply *must* write," she said.

Her words were a source of great inspiration to me, but it took some deeper levels of healing before I could put her words into practice when it came to writing fiction.

Writing can be a virulent source of procrastination because it means self-exposure, which entails the possibility of shame. The written word cannot be retracted, so the risk of public exposure is heightened. Indeed, researchers such as Kaye Bennett and Steven Rhodes have found that such problems with "writing apprehension"—anxiety about one's level of writing skill—are often what is underlying many cases of procrastination even in business and industry.

For most writers, the concept of writer's block has always held some connotation of shame. To have writer's block often suggests that one is somehow inadequate, inept or a lousy writer. Even though recent research by such experts as Mike Rose indicates that it is usually the more skilled writers who suffer from writer's block, most writers won't admit to it, and if they do, they won't call it "writer's block," but rather, the "incubation" phase of a creative project. However, when it comes to staring at a blank page, there's a big difference between incubation and incarceration.

This distinction is crucial in understanding the concept of writer's block. Regardless of how we label it, the inability to complete a writing project entails much frustration. Experienced writers realize that often a true incubation period *is* necessary, and at these times, it is appropriate to turn one's mind to other tasks or even to other writing projects, and to allow the unconscious mind to do its work undisturbed—it will let you know when it's ready to cooperate with that silly conscious part of you that turns on the computer or picks up the pen.

But what if it's not a case of the incubation phase in a creative project? What if we just cannot bring ourselves to sit down at all, to deal with even the peripheral tasks involved in a writing project? Others begin to ask how the project is going, and no matter how socially acceptable our answer is to such inquiries, we stand there with doleful eyes trying to evade our own sense of shame.

When this sense of shame enters the picture, we usually have a true case of writer's block. (Remember: the experienced writer feels no shame when in the doldrums of the writing process and knows that incubation is a natural and necessary part of the creative process.) This is because writer's block—or any form of creative blockage—often occurs even in the face of an otherwise potentially successful project. In other words, we already have an original idea and perhaps some notes, a library research plan, or pages of dialogue and other such ammunition—either on paper or in our heads—but for whatever reason, we cannot bring ourselves to shoot. It is as if we are paralyzed. Although scraps of paper filled with potent notions may abound in our cars, homes and jacket pockets, we cannot seem to start, continue or finish a given project. And for some writers, this happens again and again.

The frustration in not writing is perhaps matched in intensity only by the desire to write. Even though attempts may be made to sit down at the computer or with a tablet of paper, the unconscious shame lurking just below the surface may be just too threatening to tap into.

Remember: Our creativity and our deeper, often more painful—and usually repressed—feelings and memories both reside in the right side of the brain, so for many people, it's simply less threatening to just stay away from those minefields. Unfortunately, by avoiding our creativity, we also avoid our own potential—until we drum up the courage to face and release some of our shame-based issues via the right-brain techniques explored in this book.

In some ways, you may have already stumbled naturally upon some of these right-brain techniques, such as using writing as a way to vent your feelings. For example, during an interview in 1992 with poet/editor Gerald Costanzo, I was impressed with the way he, unlike many others, has been able to drum up the courage to face some old shame-based issues. In spite of the fact that he was mistreated as a child, Costanzo has still managed to write excellent poetry, receive literary awards and direct the prestigious Carnegie Mellon University Press, even though, as he told me, he felt as a child the way he did in the last line of one of his poems, entitled "The Smallest Thing on Earth": "Your life is more fragile than water in the hands of a bucket brigade." He added:

I feel about myself much the way I did when I was five years old. Life was something of a struggle. Even then I felt burdened and defenseless. I've tried to outgrow those feelings.

Although he has been able to use humor to cope with the aftereffects of his childhood, Costanzo still has trouble occasionally with individuals who remind him of his father.

Any relationship I get into, whether it is professional or personal, which involves a personality like my father's still gives me great difficulty. I have low tolerance for the short-tempered bully, the verbally abusive . . . and in these situations a part of me reverts to being five and feeling defenseless, and another part of me just won't allow it anymore. In recent years I've learned more subtle, less confrontational, ways of responding.

Interestingly enough, Costanzo reports two different reactions to dealing with people who remind him of his father. These two reactions correspond easily to those that would be typical of the two sides of the brain—the right side holding the emotional memories of the defenseless five-year-old, and the left side presenting the appropriate reaction of an adult defending himself against an inappropriate, rageful bully.

However, unlike others who may experience emotional or intellectual paralysis in the face of such a bully, Costanzo has turned to the process of writing to cope. In discussing a former employer who had reminded Costanzo of his father, he said that although he wanted the employer's approval, he knew it wouldn't be forthcoming.

I dealt with it by writing . . . I just wrote. . . . It seems that writing was always, for me, a way of dealing with frustration. It would calm me; make me sit in the same place for a long time, which is usually difficult to do when one is frustrated. Usually something successful would result. I would never allow the frustration to become self-destructive, though I know several others for whom it causes writer's block.

What do we make of Costanzo's words? First, it's obvious that even successful individuals have many of the same problems we do. Second, we don't have to give in to such ghosts in our unconscious—but we do need to deal with them at some point in time, in some way. Apparently, Costanzo has done just that to some degree, and has an awareness that many people do not in terms of understanding what makes his own psyche work for or against him. He also has intuitively been drawn to the use of writing in order to cope with these demons of the past that often rise up when we least expect them. In the next chapter, we'll explore a detailed approach to writing as a therapeutic technique to eradicate procrastination, as well as other techniques that can help us to access the right side of the brain, where our pools of residual shame have accumulated over the years.

After reviewing the various protective masks for shame that can trigger our problems with procrastination, we now have diagnosed ourselves as being perhaps perfectionistic, angry, anxious, powerless, co-dependent or trapped by fears of intimacy—or, if we're really lucky, all of the above. So let's take a look in the next chapter to see just exactly how we can begin to discover the underlying feelings related to events that have forced us to wear these clinical masks for shame as a form of protection for so many years. As we will soon see, facing these old feelings without a mask gives us a much better chance to stare them down—and find our way out of the tomorrow trap, once and for all.

6

Doing the Right Thing: The Whole-Brain Approach to Ending Procrastination

Writers get a nice break in one way,
at least: They can treat their
mental illnesses every day.

—Kurt Vonnegut

Throughout this book we have been using nondominant handwriting to access the right side of your brain. No doubt it has produced some surprising reactions to feelings or thoughts you didn't know were there. In this chapter, we will explore other right-brain techniques as a way of escaping from the tomorrow trap. We can also combine these techniques with some traditional left-brain methods and physiological approaches to regulating brain biochemistry. In essence, if we are going to escape from the clutches of the tomorrow trap, we are better off knowing as many approaches as possible that will tap into any and all areas of the brain. So without further ado, let's take a look at some of these techniques. Feel free to pick and choose among them, selecting those that are more appealing to you at this point in time.

Self-Interview

After performing the exercises in the previous chapter, you are probably aware of which protective masks you have been using to conceal your problems with procrastination. This exercise will help you to conceptualize these masks into a more coherent pattern, almost as if you were conducting your own first interview in a psychotherapy session. This "self-interview" contains some questions that would normally be asked by a psychotherapist. Asking the right questions is crucial in determining the underlying issues associated with your particular pattern of procrastination.

1. What is your primary symptom?

   _____

   _____.

   (For example: I would like to become an artist, but I get anxious whenever I try to draw or paint, so I usually procrastinate.)

2. What would happen if you didn't procrastinate?

   _____

   _____.

   (For example: I might make a fool of myself. Or, if by some miracle I became successful, I'd be terrified that eventually I'd fail, and everyone would find out I'm not really that talented.)

3. What does it feel like when you try to perform the task you've put off?

   _____

   _____.

   (For example: I feel inadequate, like a grade school kid. Who would ever want to see my work anyway?)

4. When did you first notice this problem?

   _____

   _____.

(For example: It started when I was about nine, and my art teachers told me I had potential, but I didn't believe them.)

5. What was happening at that point in your life?

_____

_____

_____.

(For example: Nothing much, really. My parents had just been divorced, and that's about it.)

6. How did this event affect your life?

_____

_____

_____.

(For example: Well, I didn't have to listen to my parents fight anymore. My mother moved us into a smaller apartment, and all of a sudden, we never seemed to have enough money. I always felt embarrassed at school when I didn't have money for lunch.)

7. What caused this event to happen?

_____

_____

_____.

(For example: My father kept having affairs, and they'd fight.)

8. What other side-effects occurred as a result of this event?

_____

_____.

(For example: I'd wake up in the middle of the night with nightmares.)

9. How does your procrastination affect your life now?

_____

_____.

(For example: Well, I usually feel guilty whenever I think about how I'm running my life. I'm stuck in this dead-end job, and I'm

always spending all of my spare money on art supplies that I never use, so I never go out to socialize or anything because I never have the money. My life is pretty boring, really.)

10. Other than not fulfilling your goals, what is missing from your life as a result of your procrastination?

_____

_____.

(For example: I don't really have the quality of life I'd like. I don't have any close relationships.)

11. Do you think you deserve to have these missing elements in your life?

_____

_____.

(For example: Well, I'd like to get married someday and live in a decent house instead of this crummy apartment.)

12. What's the payoff? What would you have to face if you didn't procrastinate?

_____

_____.

(For example: I guess I don't have to risk being hurt by others. And I guess I don't have to face the fact that on some level, I don't think I deserve to have a higher quality of life. I can just blame everything on my procrastination problem.)

Although only you can know what your answers are to the 12 questions, let's take some of the hypothetical answers I've supplied in parentheses to determine what the dynamics would be, so you can model the analysis of your own answers after them.

Look again at the list of protective masks in table 2 of chapter 5. With the above example, you can identify several shame-based dynamics. This person has many sources of shame and is afraid of failure, success and intimacy. His or her fear of public exposure—which may tap into a pre-existing pool of could stem from a variety of events.

Loss of love from a parent, guardian or primary caretaker almost always triggers shame. Because the parents fought and subsequently divorced, the child would internalize such continual conflict as something he or she had caused by being "bad." The client's shame regarding the loss of regular contact with his or her father may also have contributed to problems with creativity, which began right after the divorce. Shame regarding the lower standard of living after the divorce could also lead the client to avoid public attention.

The client's observations of the parents' unhealthy relationship would also contribute to his or her avoidance of intimate relationships. Notice, too, how the client has also managed to re-create the deprived environment in which he or she grew up: a low quality of life in a "crummy apartment." Though the client states that he or she would like an upgrade in lifestyle, the client manages to maintain the "sameness" of his or her home life as a child. Thus, procrastination protects this client from having to face up to and work through his or her fears of failure, success and intimacy.

* * * *

Dialoguing

As you can see from your responses to the self-interview, asking the right questions is more important than drumming up answers to rote questions. Since most of us may not know what to ask, our unconscious minds can do the talking for us. I have worked with numerous clients who, when left in the Writer's Floe—the colorful room I use for the treatment of writing anxiety and separation anxiety—were able to discover what was bothering them by writing with both their right and left hands.

Here is a conversation that my right hand had with my left hand one day when I felt frustrated over my procrastination regarding the writing process. (My right hand is dominant.)

Right hand: *Okay, so what's going on? I'm sick of being blocked and I want out.*

Left hand: *I hate this room. It's boring. I hate this ugly brown desk. Just looking at it makes me want to run away. I hate that painting. And it's too dark in here. I need the daylight. I need to go outside.*

Right hand: *But this room is just for writing. I set it up with all my books and the computer, and I got that painting because the woman has purple hair. It's just an office. What's the big deal?*

Left hand: *There's too much green on the painting. I hate brown. Everything was brown in their house. I hate it. I just want to go outside. There's not enough light. It's too dark.*

At this point I recognized what the problem was. Unconsciously, in decorating my writing area, I had re-created some of the negative elements from my childhood. My grandparents' house, where I was abused on a regular basis, was decorated primarily in drab green tones with heavy brown accent pieces. And my parents' home—which wasn't a safe place for me, either—was always dark, with curtains drawn against the outside world.

So it's no wonder that the primarily green painting, brown desk and darkened atmosphere in my writing studio was keeping my inner, creative self at bay. Needless to say, I took down the painting, got rid of the desk and its matching brown chair, and replaced them with light gray furniture and a bright purple tablecloth. My current studio has one wall that is all windows, and when weather permits, I take the laptop outside and enjoy the daylight even more.

I have noticed similar dynamics with my clients whose work entails finding a "nest." Many of these talented individuals have unwittingly re-created the dynamics of their childhood abuse, often through colors, patterns overuse of clutter to re-create feelings of chaos, and by keeping photos of their undiscovered abusers nearby. Sometimes just by having a dialogue between your two hands (your adult self and your inner self), you can discover why you avoid that wonderful "nest" you spent so much time creating.

Although it is often best to ask open-ended questions with one hand and then answer them with the other, sometimes a more structured approach can be helpful as well. Many potential sources of information can be tapped by allowing your right and left hands to "converse" using the roles listed below.

Dominant Hand	Nondominant Hand
Your productive side	Your procrastinating side
Adult self	Inner child
Your proud self	Your ashamed self
Someone who shamed you	You (at that time)

At my workshops on procrastination, I have found that most people find it easier to write when they are given a stem. Try the following fill-in-the blank tasks below, using extra paper if you need more space. Be sure to switch from the dominant to the nondominant hand for the second part of each dialogue. If you get stuck, switch hands and try each role with the opposite hand again.

Dialogue Between Productive and Procrastinating Selves:

Productive Self: _____
_____
_____
_____.

Procrastinating Self: _____
_____
_____
_____.

Dialogue Between Adult Self and Inner Child:

Adult Self: _____
_____
_____
_____.

Inner Child: _____
_____
_____
_____.

Dialogue Between Proud and Shameful Selves:

Proud Self: _____
_____
_____
_____.

Ashamed Self: _____
_____
_____
_____.

As you read over your responses, do you detect a tone of judgment or compassion? Are you kicking yourself while you're already down? Do you find that you are divided against yourself? Or are you able to understand your own fears and foibles?

If one side of you is responding with harsh judgment, it may be the internalized voice of someone significant who had shamed you in the past. Let's take a look at that aspect of the problem.

Dialogue Between Shamer and Shamee:

Person who shamed you: _____

_____

_____

_____.

You: _____

_____

_____

_____.

Is there judgment or compassion in either of these two voices? These may be clues to deeper issues that must be resolved in order to break through the walls of procrastination. Whether or not your issues are related to fear of intimacy, fear of success, fear of failure, or any other dynamics related to procrastination, keep in mind that all of these elements are masks for the deeper problem of shame.

In order to eradicate procrastination from your life, it is necessary to ferret out the original sources of your shame. Although the techniques outlined above may assist in this process, we will now explore several others that may allow you to explore even deeper.

* * * *

Photohistory

This technique, also called "phototherapy," can provide a rich introduction into the dynamics of your childhood years. When I ask clients to bring in photos from their early life, some bring in four or five huge family albums, while others present me with only a handful of tattered photos. But no matter what is presented during a photohistory, it is always meaningful in some way. So grab your family photos and listen up.

Often, the array of photos selected proves to be meaningful. Perhaps one significant relative is missing, or appears in every photo. Sometimes clients bring in photos that are sexually suggestive without even realizing that such postures are inappropriate in a family photo. Any of the following aspects of your photographs may provide important clues for further exploration.

_____ Significant person missing in most or all of the photos

_____ Significant person appearing next to client in most or all photos

_____ Significant person suddenly disappears from chronology of photos

_____ Certain people never adjacent to client (mother, father)

_____ Certain people never touching the client (mother, father)

_____ Certain people always holding tightly onto client

_____ Certain people always holding tightly onto each other

_____ Certain people never together (mother and father)

_____ Client's body veers away from certain person

_____ Client appears distressed in photos with certain person

_____ Suggestive poses of client or other family members (note who was taking the photograph)

_____ Very little or no smiling

_____ Hurt, angry or humiliated expressions on client's face

_____ Hurt, angry or humiliated expressions on faces of client's caretakers

_____ Other signs of shame in client or caretakers:

    _____ frozen facial features

    _____ false smiling

    _____ gaze aversion

    _____ hand covering part or all of face

    _____ blushing

    _____ forehead wrinkled transversely or vertically

    _____ biting, turning in or licking the lips

    _____ biting the tongue

_____ Holiday pictures consisting of a very large number of gifts under the Christmas tree, without people

_____ Pictures of family dinner table at a celebration, without people

_____ Incongruent facial expressions:

    _____ left side of face does not match right side

    _____ lower portion of face does not match upper portion

_____ Client has uncomfortable emotional reaction to certain people or items in some photographs

In conducting a photohistory, it's the entire collection of photographs and your response to them that is important. Be careful not to over-interpret one photograph, unless your reaction to that one photograph is very intense. Look for patterns. If one particular photograph elicits a strong response, pay attention to your gut instincts. Chances are there's something in that photo that can help you to discover important feelings or events related to your past.

The clues listed on the previous pages can be vital in determining not only the nature of the shame one carries around, but also the approximate age at which the event occurred. For example, I will often see happy baby pictures of a client up to a certain age. Then, perhaps at age two or five or ten, the client appears depressed in most every photo: lifeless, glassy eyes; a grim, forced smile; tension around the eyes or mouth. Some clients appear angry, with narrowed eyes and clenched fists. Others suggest a feeling of shame and a need for protection: hands clasped in front of the stomach or groin, shoulders hunched, toes turned inward, downcast eyes. I ask the client what life was like at that particular age or just before that age. Nine times out of ten, there is a significant shaming event that occurred around that time period—perceived or real abandonment, neglect, abuse, or public humiliation of some kind.

Sometimes clients will balk at the notion that these facial expressions indicate anger, shame or depression in the photos. At that point, I usually bring out a photo of a truly joyful baby: eyes sparkling with glee and curiosity, and a genuine, gurgly smile. Then I compare this photo with the client's photos, filled with wounded expressions.

If that doesn't work, I cover up the left side of the face in the client's photograph, then the right, to show the client that there may be two completely different expressions. One is the public side that usually appears to be happy, content or strong, and the other is the private side, masking the barely suppressed feelings of hurt, anger, shame or despair. Sometimes this discrepancy is more obvious when the top part of the face is covered, revealing that the smile below is really a grimace, or when the bottom part of the photo is covered, revealing eyes that are clearly enraged, wounded or distrustful.

Together, the entire face may appear relatively benign. But when you compartmentalize features—the eyes, mouth, or the left and right sides of the face—you can often discern which emotions may also be internalized within the client. (Check your caretakers' faces for similar trends.)

For example, the photograph on the following page, taken of me as a toddler, appears to be a benign shot of a baby playing outside in the summertime. However, if you cover the right side of the photo, you can see the other side of my face is clearly sad. If you cover up everything but the eye on the left side of the photo, you'll note the downturned eyelid and the apprehensive upturn of the eyebrow. If you cover the left side of the photo, you can see that the other side of my face is frozen into a glassy, dissociative stare—a clear sign of masked childhood pain. Similarly, if you cover up the bottom half of my face, you'll see that my eyes are tense, afraid, and guarded—not sure what's going to happen next. And if you cover up the top half of the face, you'll see that my mouth is strained, with lips partly turned down, nothing near a smile.

This phenomenon of facial compartmentalization is due partly to the fact that the left side of the face is usually more expressive, because it is controlled by the right side of the brain (dominant for the perception and expression of emotion). However, since the negative of a given photograph may be reversed, it is important to note any discrepancy in expression between the two sides of the face. You cannot always be sure which side of the face in the printed photo is truly the right or left side.

Figure 3. The Author, 1955

Sorting the photos can also be helpful. Sometimes I find that the photos where the client appears relaxed or happy are taken with a pet, a doll, or with friends—not with family. Other times it's helpful to sort the photos into those that contain certain people, facial expressions or trends in body language. Some clients have discovered their memories of early childhood neglect or abuse at the hands of people in the photographs just by looking at the abusers' haunting facial expressions. Even an inanimate object, such as an old desk or a bed, can trigger memories that might otherwise remain repressed. They can be released by tapping into the sensory-emotional memory system of the right brain, where childhood memories and more emotional memories are more likely to be stored.

Additionally, our negative memories of a given person or event are much more likely to be stored in the right brain, while our positive memories of the same person or event are stored in the language-based left brain. Positive memories are more likely to be discussed, given a verbal label and, therefore, filed in the language zone of the left brain. This is why we can repress painful memories so readily—until some sensory or emotional cue taps into our non-language-oriented right brain. All it takes is the right visual image, smell, sound, taste or touch. Suddenly, we feel uncomfortable, flooded with disconcerting emotions that seem to appear from nowhere. Therapists dealing with such sensory cues often call them "triggers" for memory recall.

This division of duty and memory recall between the two sides of the brain is further enhanced by the fact that the *corpus callosum*—the bridge of brain matter between the right and left sides of the brain—is immature in children until the age of 10. Since the *corpus callosum* is responsible for communication between the two sides of the brain, the retrieval of memories that occurred before the age of 10 involves a different process than the retrieval of later memories.

In other words, for events prior to age 10 or so, we usually have two completely separate memories of the same childhood experience. The positive one is available through language via the left brain, but the negative one is trapped in the sensory-emotional recesses of the right brain, unlikely to be recovered unless the correct sensory or emotional cue is presented. Simply talking about a given memory usually isn't enough, whereas the smell of fresh-cut lawns, the texture of suede boots, or seeing a photograph or movie can trigger a negative emotional memory in the right brain. (See Marsha Sinetar's book *Reel Power* for an interesting discussion of film as a modality for spiritual/emotional growth.)

Suppose at age six, a young girl's uncle says, "I like your party dress." The left brain will recall *what* was said, while the right brain will recall the *way* it was said. Thus, the left brain simply recalls an ordinary compliment about a new dress, while the right brain may recall the lust in the uncle's eye, the knowing smirk of his lips and the clutch of his hand around her waist.

Another example might be what a mother says to her child who wants to be an artist: "That's a nice drawing." The left brain recalls a compliment, while the right brain may recall the grim line of the mother's angry lips, the glare in her eyes and the enraged tone of her voice with a child who is distracting her once again from what the mother considers to be a more important task. If this were a chronic experience, shame would begin to occur, and the roots of procrastination would be set in motion.

Aside from the use of sensory cues to trigger memories in the right side of the brain, photographs can provide other pertinent clues regarding the shame-based roots of procrastination. If a family member is suddenly absent from the sequence of photos, it's important to ask why. Was there an argument, a job transfer, a death? Does the client appear more relaxed or sad in the photos after this person is gone? Was the missing person the primary source of the client's love and approval? If so, did anyone else try to replenish that source of love?

If someone is always at the client's side, does that suggest a loving caretaker or an emotionally smothering caretaker? Look closely at the body language. Does the child seem to welcome the physical contact, or are the child's head, trunk, arms or legs consistently or frequently veering away in all the photos with that particular person? Compare the photo with ones that contain the client with other caretakers or adults.

If the photos with one parent indicate love and attention to the child, compare them against photos with the other parent. Does the child seem equally at ease with both caretakers, or does one of them appear stilted, awkward, or clearly uncomfortable holding the child? How does this pattern compare with the child's body language and facial expressions around other adults, family members, siblings, or neighbors?

Suppose there simply are no pictures of one of the child's

primary caretakers. Does the consistent absence of the father in the photos indicate an absentee father, or perhaps one who would never under any circumstances relinquish his controlling role as the family patriarch/photographer? Or does the absence of the mother in any and all photos suggest the mother's avoidance of the camera due to body shame, as a result of some unresolved issues in her past that may have suppressed her ability to love the child unconditionally?

Does the client seem concerned that certain caretakers or other individuals are never adjacent to the client? I have worked with numerous clients who were finally able to acknowledge the maternal or paternal neglect they had suffered as children, once they had seen a few pictures worth far more than a thousand words. Similarly, many clients have discovered covert sexual abuse by acknowledging how uncomfortable they were when being asked to pose in suggestive positions by the photographer, who may have been a family member, a neighbor, an older child, or perhaps a "friend" of the family.

Another issue that often arises during photohistories is the fact that many dysfunctional families are prone to taking pictures of inanimate objects rather than people. I have worked with far too many clients whose "family" albums were composed of photos detailing scenes from family vacations that contained nothing but scenery—or scenes from holiday or family celebrations that contained nothing but gifts, cakes or a fully loaded dinner table, without any people. These pictures are expected to provide mute testimony regarding the family's goodness: "Look how well we have provided for our children!" It is the facade that is important enough to be photographed, not the family members.

During photohistories, I have noticed that many clients' family albums also contain copies of grade-school report cards, written assignments and drawings from the client's childhood. These, too, can provide valuable clues about behavior problems, thoughts or feelings at the time.

For example, when I look over the photos and my writings during one of the time periods of my life when I should have been happy and proud of my achievements, I'm amazed at the obvious features of shame that were so prevalent. There I was, valedictorian of my undergraduate class, recipient of several scholarly and literary awards by age 20, walking around with a 3.9 grade point average, and feeling perfectly lousy about myself without any clue as to why.

The three photographs on the following page clearly illustrate my emotional—or should I say, unemotional—state at that time of my life. The toll of procrastination—and all of its underpinnings—is clearly there, and you don't have to be an expert in photohistory or psychotherapy to see it: the frozen face, glassy dissociative eyes, tentative grimace of a smile, downcast eyes in the universal sign of shame, gaze aversion—hardly the appearance of someone joyously enraptured about life, academic success and the future. All you have to do is look at the three photos taken nearly 20 years later (p. 216) and you'll be saying the same thing I do every time I see these blasts from the past: *Who was that alien occupying my body?*

At that time in my life—1975—I tended to look at my intellect and life in general as a burden. Most of my poetry was indicative of my dilemma—but lacking the insight I have now about my patterns of academic workaholism and procrastination regarding my desire to write fiction. Although I had received a poetry award from the university literary magazine where the three poems that follow were published, these poems all foreshadowed the imminent shutdown of my creativity. Shortly after they were written, I suffered a bout of writer's block regarding fiction writing that lasted 10 years—a serious case of unconscious procrastination.

It was as if my creative writing was getting just a little too close to the truth—I even suffered simultaneously from a "reader's block," but only when I tried to read fiction. On some deeper level, I was unable to tolerate any kind of emotion on paper. In *Writing the Blockbuster Novel*, Albert Zuckerman's comments (p. 12) provide an eerie echo of those years in my life:

> *A novel is emotion. A novelist's true lode, his font of inspiration, if you will, is in the feelings, passions, sufferings and ecstasies that he himself has experienced and that, in the process of writing, he transmutes through his characters.*

Figure 4. Photo Montage

The author, 1975 . . .

. . . and 1991

Photos by Scherley Busch

In the first poem, "English Major" I toyed with the idea of mental retardation as a way out, exchanging my burdensome intelligence for that of a child with Down's syndrome. I saw my high I.Q. as an albatross I was being forced to wear as I floundered in a sea of depression and procrastination. I simply resented my intelligence for prodding me to do intellectual work I hadn't the emotional energy to do.

English Major

Doing 50 on the expressway,
I think of Joseph Conrad
and his critics.
I think of James Joyce
and his critics.
I think of how nice it would be
not to be educated any longer.
Quit.
How it would be,
my evenings free,
the empty bookshelves—
and the mind purified
by the fast.

The ramp curves
onto a sidestreet
like it did yesterday.
Glancing ahead,
I see a child

playing at the grass and
almost wish
until I note the
slanting eyes,
the thick-tongued smile.

—Fall, 1975

This second poem explores my fears about what might be underlying the academic workaholism/fiction writing procrastination continuum in which I lived, and my desire to write about that underlying pain.

Leakage

A soft Italian music,
that music seeping into my room
from the apartment below.
It makes me
think of what might be
missing,
after all the books are taken down
from my shelves,
after my last cactus has died, and
the yellow curtains have been swept aside:
my bare windows,
my naked, empty windows
with no sun;

I try not to hear it but it's
getting in at the pages,
getting into my plants they're
so feeble and wilting it's
come through my windows,
my bare and empty windows.
I must sing.

—*Spring, 1976*

This third poem illustrates the fear that my writing would be insubstantial—a likely prospect unless one has access to the full range of emotional experience. On some level, I knew that was something I'd been avoiding for years.

Hint

she comes to me slowly,
cupping a poem-bowl
in her hands.
i drink soup,
straight out the bowl,
slowly savoring its texture,
a window at the side of my head.
i am yet hungry,
i am not full.
"where is the meat,
my dear?"
they will ask you.
critics ravenous,
where is the meat?

—*Fall, 1974*

From what I know now about my childhood, it's pretty scary to see how much of it was just beneath the surface 20 years ago. At the time I was completely unaware of it. As a good friend of mine said, "A little repression goes a long way." Although I didn't know then precisely why I was procrastinating regarding my career as a writer, I was afraid to bump into those "ghosts in the unconscious," as John Gardner calls them in his foreword to Dorothea Brande's classic book, *Becoming a Writer.* For me, at that time in my life, imagination was just a little too close to memory. The right side of my brain was simply off limits. But now that I've been there and back, I'm glad to have full access to all of me.

It is clear that the use of photohistory, with or without one's earlier writings, can be valuable in learning which sources of shame may be triggering your procrastination. For further information on the use of phototherapy to discover shame-based issues, Judy Weiser's book *PhotoTherapy Techniques: Exploring the Secrets of Personal Snapshots and Family Albums* is an excellent resource, as is the chapter on "Video Studies of the Shame-Rage Spiral" by Suzanne Retzinger in Helen Block Lewis's text, *The Role of Shame in Symptom Formation.*

One last note on this powerful technique for accessing the right side of the brain: Keep in mind that it is also important to scan the photos of one's parents, grandparents and other extended family members. Notice if there is a pattern of weight problems, hopeless or grim expressions, angry or glassy eyes, compartmentalized facial expressions, or other signs of shame. If so, using the indirect interview discussed in the next section may help to provide clues as to how this shame was transmitted to your caretakers and on to you.

* * * *

Indirect Interview

Sometimes people can look at family photos and see the pain in everyone's faces, but not understand why. At this point, you might try what I call the "indirect interview" to find out just why your parents, grandparents and extended family members or neighbors were so depressed or shame-based. Just as Christine Courtois, in her book *Healing the Incest Wound,* recommends the avoidance of such terms as "incest" or "sexual abuse" when therapists are assessing for such problems, so, too, is it best to avoid these emotionally charged phrases when you are making queries about your own childhood. Whether you choose to interview your original caretakers or someone who knew them, this indirect approach is much less likely to engender resistance in your interviewees.

The questions you will be asking are designed to give you a clearer picture of family life during your first few years. If your caretakers were not as loving as you might have needed them to be, sometimes learning the reason why can help. It is especially important to recognize that any shame you may have felt as a child was not warranted—your caretakers had their own problems that may have kept them from loving you properly. You may have been denied their love not because you were unworthy but for of a variety of reasons you probably don't even know existed.

On the pages that follow are questions that you might ask of your childhood caretakers, relatives, neighbors, or friends of the family. What you are looking for is any dynamic or event that may have triggered a loss of love and a sense of shame in you or in your caretakers. Refer back to chapter 4 for a detailed list of events that could have triggered that shame—anything from perceived physical flaws to unintentional neglect or actual abuse.

Besides being indirect, so as not to trigger defensiveness or alarm in your interviewee, these questions are also open-ended, requiring more than just a yes or no response. Bear in mind that this is not an exhaustive list. You may devise some of your own questions based on your particular need for information (especially after reviewing your responses to the queries in chapter 4), or you may consult books such as *The Inner Child Workbook* by Cathryn Taylor, *Homecoming* by John Bradshaw, or *The Artist's Way* by Julia Cameron, to help generate other questions you may want to ask. Colin Murray Parkes's excellent chapter on bereavement in his book, *Attachment Across the Life Cycle,* also offers a list of potentially damaging life events that can trigger problems in children as well.

Keep in mind that you needn't ask all of the questions listed; sometimes one or two answers will give you enough clues to understand the problem. If your caretakers are unavailable for comment, you might pose some of these questions to someone who knew your family while you were growing up, or who knew your caretakers when they were children.

Although some of these questions cannot be answered by anyone other than the individual concerned, for those that can be addressed by someone else, simply replace "you" in the question with "my mother," "my father," "my grandmother," etc. If no one is available to answer any such questions, you may want to consult books such as *Unpuzzling Your Past: A Basic Guide to Genealogy* by Emily Anne Croom, in order to sort out your family's history and get a feel for how their lives may have been affected by war, natural disaster or changing times.

Indirect questions to ask regarding the caretaker's childhood experiences include:

• What was it like when you were growing up?
• What was your family like?

- What was it like living in a large/small/average-sized family?
- Tell me what it was like to live during the Great Depression in the 1930s.
- Tell me about life in your hometown when you were growing up.
- What was it like in grade school back then?
- What kinds of games did you play?
- What was it like to be a boy back then?
- What was it like to be a girl back then?
- What kinds of family activities did you do for fun?
- What kinds of things did you talk about with your mother when you were growing up?
- What kinds of things did you talk about with your father when you were growing up?
- What kinds of things did you talk about with your grandmother when you were growing up?
- What kinds of things did you talk about with your grandfather when you were growing up?
- Who were your most favorite and least favorite relatives when you were a child?

As you listen to your interviewee's responses, keep in mind that these are perfectly normal and legitimate questions for someone to ask. If your caretaker wants to know why you are asking one or more of these questions, simply say, "Just curious." Take note of his or her emotions, body language, choice of words, and willingness to answer your questions. Does he or she get tense, defensive, irritable or angry? If so, it's likely that you've tapped into his or her pre-existing pool of shame that is somehow related to the perfectly normal topic you are trying to discuss.

Does the caretaker's body language change? If so, does the person become more relaxed, allowing a slow smile to emerge as he or she begins to reminisce about happier times? Or does the person exhibit signs of shame and resistance via gaze aversion, a frown, biting of the lip, abruptly crossing the arms or legs, covering the mouth or face with a hand, or a grim smile? If so—no matter what the person's words are saying, such as "Oh, I had a wonderful childhood"—it is likely that shame is not far from the surface of his or her memories of the events in question.

Researchers such as Mary Main have found that people who resist discussing their childhood years are more likely to have a negative, insecure attachment with their own children. As she was interviewing parents about their own histories, Main found that those who had created insecure bonds with their own children were unable to stay focused on the questions asked, were unable to access early memories, and exhibited contradictions as well as "slips of the tongue" when discussing their own childhood histories. In comparison, parents who had healthy bonds with their children did not have these disruptive features during interviews about their own childhood years.

Along with noting the relative level of cooperation and coherence in the responses to your indirect interview, note the words used to answer the questions. If they all sound too good to be true (like "perfect childhood," "no problems at all," "we could talk about anything as a family"), then you've either bumped into one of the few who really did have a pretty decent childhood, or you've come up against a wall of denial.

Everyone's had something happen, even if it's just a broken leg. But if that broken leg kept the person's cast-bound mother from adequately caring for the person as an infant, or if that broken leg kept the person's father from ever playing baseball again, resulting in years of taunting as a failure by this same-said father who'd expected another Babe Ruth to come forth and live his baseball dreams for him, then shame can again enter the picture. So when someone uses absolute terms—"never a problem," "always attentive"—you have to wonder what is lurking in his or her inner pool of shame. Whether it's the Loch Ness monster or a threatening mass of what appears to be innocuous seaweed, shame is usually not far from the surface.

Finally, does the interviewee seem to bristle or shut down when you start asking these questions, offering cryptic responses or no response at all? Does the person have no recall of his or her childhood? Large blocks of such "lost" time usually indicate repression. If a traumatic event or a painful set of circumstances has been repressed, then the unconscious mind behaves like a cautious surgeon who removes not only the cancerous tumor, but also the surrounding tissue. Although the repressed event or circumstances may have occurred over the course of an hour or several years, the unconscious mind represses not only the event, but possibly an entire decade of time surrounding it—until such time that the individual is ready and willing to recall and work through the painful emotions associated with the repressed material.

Thus, it may be true that your caretaker does not recall his or her childhood years. Or it could be that the caretaker does recall, but after an abrupt response, quickly changes the subject because he or she is reluctant to discuss such events that are tapping into painful emotions.

In asking the next set of questions below, you may find that your caretakers also try to avoid discussing your childhood experiences. Or, if the caretaker witnessed or perpetrated abuse on you, he or she may have repressed such painful events about your childhood as well.

Indirect questions to ask childhood caretakers regarding your childhood experiences include:

- I've always wondered what my birth was like. Tell me what was happening in your lives at the time, and how it all changed when I was born.
- How did my birth affect your job?
- What kind of work were you doing?
- What was I like as a toddler?
- What was our family life like when I was a toddler?
- What kind of accidents did I have as a child?
- What kind of health problems or hospital stays did I have as an infant or toddler?
- How did I react to being in the hospital?
- Where did we live when I was a small child?
- What kinds of things were going on in your career when I was first born/a toddler/in grade school?
- What were your friends like when I was a baby?
- What did you do for fun when you were raising me?
- Did you have help raising me?
- Who was our main baby-sitter?
- Did we have any other baby-sitters?
- Did you have any problems when I was a baby?

This is just a sample of possible questions for an indirect interview. You may have others. Notice again your interviewee's emotions, body language and choice of words.

For example, in response to the first question regarding your birth, an honest, healthy response might be, "Giving birth isn't exactly a joy in the physical department, but we were so happy to have you that it didn't matter. We had to shuffle things around quite a bit—a baby changes your entire life—but you made it all worth it."

On the other hand, a negative response might be, "The delivery was awful. I hope I never have to go through that again. All of a sudden I didn't have time to do anything. Your father started losing money at work because you kept both of us up all night. He nearly lost his job."

The first response gives an honest but loving description, while the second focuses only on the negative aspects of childbirth and its aftermath. When this attitude is still so strong years later, it suggests a lack of healthy parenting or unconditional love. Instead, it fosters a sense of guilt that you were even born.

If you hear a long list of minor accidents that you had as a child, keep in mind that children who are "accident-prone" are often the victims of abuse or neglect. Unless there is a physiological problem that affects the child's sense of balance or other psychomotor skills, the child might be so preoccupied and anxious regarding ongoing abuse that he or she cannot pay attention to surroundings and so becomes "accident-prone." In other cases the child may be self-destructive. Clumsiness becomes an unconscious way of punishing the self for perceived inadequacy.

As you attempt to discern the tone of your childhood, take note of the type of jobs your parents had. Did they like their work, or did they come home disgruntled and ill-equipped to provide affection? Did one or both work late? If so, who took care of you? Did you have numerous baby-sitters? Were any of those baby-sitters "fired" abruptly? If so, why?

Regardless of the responses you may get from this indirect interview, the temptation to minimize is ever-present. You may find yourself thinking, "So what's the big deal—my divorced mother worked two jobs and my cranky old grandparents screamed at us a lot. It could have been worse."

It's certainly true that the effects of such verbal abuse could have been made a lot worse by physical or sexual abuse, but is that what you say to a two-year-old getting screamed at in the middle of the mall? Do you go up to a seven-year-old boy at the school football field and tell him he shouldn't feel upset or ashamed of his father's raging behaviors over his inadequate performance because "after all, he could be sexually abusing you—you ought to be grateful it's only verbal abuse"? Of course not!

If you still find yourself minimizing, imagine those same grandparents—or any other adult—screaming at your nephew or niece, your own child, or any other child of whom you are fond. Imagine the child's reaction—and also your reaction to seeing this child getting verbally abused. Then see yourself standing next to that child, getting screamed at along with that child, and you'll probably feel once again the confusion, shame and rage you may have felt—and quickly repressed—as a child. The next step in the process of healing is to release this type of shame that unfortunately is still a common experience in most cultures today.

* * * *

Psychoautobiographical Writing

Just thinking about "working through" shame is painful to most of us. Shame is such an intolerable emotion—why would we want to enter voluntarily that murky pool of pain? The answer is obvious: If we don't enter it voluntarily, it will inevitably well up like a tidal wave and engulf us when we least expect it. So let's take a look at another method for riding this tidal wave to shore without getting caught in the undertow.

The best way to dispel shame is to talk about it. This is why 12-Step programs are so popular and successful for so many people. These groups offer an open forum where individuals can release their feelings without fear of judgment or retaliation. Likewise, in group therapy a person can discuss painful memories without fear that others will run screaming from the room.

If you are reluctant to face the reactions of others but want to start releasing your pain and shame, it may be helpful to start with an even less judgmental listener—a good old-fashioned blank sheet of paper. Writing has been considered therapeutic by many theorists and researchers. What could be more nonjudgmental than an empty piece of paper?

The work of James Pennebaker, most notably discussed in his recent book entitled *Opening Up: The Healing Power of Confiding in Others,* in particular has supported the idea that writing about trauma is not only psychologically therapeutic, but it also helps to prevent medical illness. Pennebaker has conducted numerous studies in which he asked subjects to write about their most shameful experiences. What he found consistently across all of his studies was the fact that subjects who "confessed" these traumatic experiences felt more relaxed and made significantly fewer trips to the student health center in subsequent months as compared with students who did not write about their shame-based experiences.

In other words, writing about shame not only improved the subjects' state of mind, but also enhanced their physical health. Pennebaker's work supports that of many others who are working in the area of psychoneuroimmunology, where numerous studies have indicated that stress and depression will deplete the body's resources and suppress the immune system, while expressing emotions can enhance the functioning of the immune system. Books such as *The Type C Connection* by Lydia Temoshok and Henry Dreher also offer evidence to suggest that letting go of negative emotions can improve your chances for optimum health.

Obviously, in Pennebaker's studies, it is clear that the subjects could not write about their shameful experiences unless they had remembered them. Thus, if you did not remember or were not aware of the source of your shame, the earlier writing exercises and checklists in this book may have been helpful in allowing you to zero in on the source of shame that has triggered your procrastination. Once you have discovered the source of your pain, therapeutic writing can then offer you an outlet for gradually exploring your emotions more fully, but in a safe, graduated way. Even if you have no idea of the source of your shame, Stage One of the technique that I'm about to describe may help you to discover potential sources of shame. Even successful writers have used writing as a form of therapy. For example, in a 1974 interview, author Kurt Vonnegut said, "Writers get a nice break in one way, at least: they can treat their mental illnesses every day."

Years later, in *Palm Sunday* (p. 322), Vonnegut describes how writing helped him to maintain his sanity during a particularly difficult time of his life:

> *I had left home, and was spending most of my time counting flowers on the wall and watching Captain Kangaroo in a tiny apartment on East Fifty-fourth Street. My friend with the gambling sickness had just cleaned out my bank account and my son had gone insane in British Columbia. . . . What saved my life? Pieces of paper eight and a half inches wide and eleven inches long.*

Similarly, in a recent *Publisher's Weekly* interview (pp. 50, 51) regarding her painful childhood experiences, novelist Connie May Fowler stated:

> *Writing a novel turns it into art, not gossip . . . I battle with depression, but the writing helps me through that. The writing gives me balance . . . . I write to reaffirm the past.*

Unlike these established writers, many of us are afraid of writing directly about our feelings, so I have devised a five-stage system of therapeutic writing based on the principles of dramatic effect used by fiction writers. I call this technique "psychoautobiographical writing" (PABW).

Essentially, the client is asked to write about his or her life experiences in a fictionalized form, beginning in third person, past tense, to create a distance between the writer and the painful subject matter. (Example: "She felt the slap of his hand across her face.") As the writer progresses, he or she will move to Stage Five writing, which is in first person, present tense, without any distance from the painful subject matter. (Example: "I feel the slap of his hand across my face.")

In PABW, the writer is intentionally disconnecting from the pain in order to approach the task of working through it. **However, if you have been diagnosed as suffering from post-traumatic stress disorder, or if you suspect that you may have suffered a severe traumatic experience (such as severe physical abuse, sexual abuse, or the witnessing of a rape or murder), it is essential that you seek out the help of a qualified therapist prior to engaging in PABW, since this technique can trigger strong emotions. Similarly, if you have been diagnosed with dissociative identity disorder (multiple personality disorder) or any other dissociative disorder, *do not* engage in PABW without the approval and assistance of a qualified therapist, since this type of writing entails intentional dissociation of the self from painful material.**

With these caveats in mind, let's look at table 3 (p. 233), which shows the primary differences between PABW and simple fiction writing. Fiction writers are aware that the use of various changes in persona, point of view and verb tense can alter the dramatic impact of their stories. In PABW, these same techniques are used to gradually increase the therapeutic effect of your writings as you explore your past. Although this would appear to be a language-based technique (one that taps into the left side of the brain), if you write with your nondominant hand, you can easily turn PABW into a method of accessing the deeper emotional states in the right brain.

Note that there are five levels of PABW. Stage One is an exploratory mode that involves the most distance from any potential traumatic material. This is especially useful if you are unaware of the source of your shame. Essentially, you allow yourself to free-associate and write a scene in third person, past tense, regarding an anonymous character who, for example, goes to a shopping mall and encounters a stressful situation. If you get stuck, feel free to switch hands and let the other side of your brain take over for a while.

Here is an example of Stage One writing:

> *Sally went to the mall even though she hated the way everybody looked at each other. She headed straight for Macy's to see what they had on sale. All through the mall men kept looking at her. She felt awkward and embarrassed about her clothes and her body. She always felt fat. She hated the way all the thin clerks looked at her while she shopped, and she was always worried that men could see into the dressing room through those slatted doors.*

This Stage One story, though it seems general enough, indicates a fair amount of body shame and fear of men. It could be used for further exploration.

Let's say you realized after writing the above paragraph that you've always been afraid of men, especially since you were an adolescent. Moreover, that's the same time you also started hating your body. The only other significant event at

TABLE 3
Differences Between Fiction Writing and the Five Stages
of Psychoautobiographical Writing

Fiction Writing	5-Stage Psychoautobiographical Writing				
	1	2	3	4	5
Purpose:					
Create art	Access facts	Access thoughts	Access feelings	Release feelings	Release feelings
Topic:					
Any	Any	Person talking about someone else with your problem	Person talking about his/her problem that is identical to yours	You talking about your problem	You talking about your problem
Persona:					
Fictional	Fictional	Fictional	Fictional	Yourself	Yourself
Point of View:					
Any	3rd person	3rd person	3rd person	2nd person	1st person
Verb Tense:					
Any	Past	Past	Past	Present	Present

that time was your parents' divorce. In the next stage of PABW, you'll use third person, past tense again. Since you know you'll be writing about something painful that is close to you, let your fictional character Sally speak not about herself but about someone else. This will enable you to approach your pain from a distance. For example:

> *After the divorce, Sally didn't like going to her father's house. It always made her think of that scene in that old '60s movie* Peyton Place, *when the young girl had to make dinner for her father. In the movie, the girl always seemed sad, and the father always seemed angry or something. Then one day he attacked her.*

Suppose this Stage Two writing triggered in you some flashback material related to sexual abuse that happened after your parents' divorce. In order to work through this abuse, you may gradually approach the feelings through Stage Three writing, in which you have a bit less distance from the traumatic material via writing about a fictional character in third person, past tense. That persona then discusses his or her own life, rather than the problems of another person. For example:

> *Sally hated going to her father's house after the divorce. He never liked to take her out anywhere fun. Her mother would leave her there every other weekend, and Sally would be bored without her friends and normal activities to keep her busy. Her father only liked to watch TV with her. He would make her sit right next to him on the couch, and he would touch her in places that she knew were wrong. Then he'd make her touch him, too.*

In this piece of writing, you no longer have the distanced perspective of being two people away from the painful material; you are closer to feeling what you need to feel in order to heal. In Stages Four and Five, the material is approached even more closely, by switching to second and first person points of view in present tense, which will eliminate your emotional distance and, in turn, elicit more feelings of shame that must be released in order to work through the painful experience.

For example, a Stage Four paragraph might read this way:

> *It's bad enough when your parents get divorced, but then you have to spend weekends with your father and he gives you the creeps when he touches you like that. You feel dirty. All you want to do is take a million showers. You can't tell your friends about it because they'd never believe you, and your mother would just kill you if she knew. You feel awful all the time, and you know there's nothing you can do about it.*

Switching from "she/he" to "you" has a powerful impact, as does the use of present verb tense—as if the event is happening here and now. That is precisely the point of Stage Four and Five writings—to make you feel as if it *is* happening right now, so you can relate to what you felt then and finally release those emotions in a safe way. Stage Five writing is even more focused on shame release since you finally come to "own" your feelings of pain by writing about it in first person. For example:

> *Ever since the divorce, I can't stand to be near my father. I can't stand the feel of his hand on my shoulder because I know what is going to happen next. It makes me sick to think of what he does to me—I can't even begin to describe it. I hate him for what he does to me.*

Notice how this Stage Five paragraph denotes a sense of disgust and anger, which will in turn lead to a healthy

release of shame. The Stage Four writing served as a prelude to this, with its focus on shame in the form of helplessness. But by becoming angry and by "owning" the
experience with all its charged-up feelings, you empower
yourself to release it once and for all.

Obviously, an individual who has a shame-based writer's
block due to incest would find it much easier to write the
Stage One paragraph example than the Stage Five paragraph. The difference between "she" and "I" becomes clear,
as does the contrast between the pain of a young woman in
the distant past versus your pain about something that
really happened and is affecting you now. Even under hypnosis, clients will often speak in third person as they try to
describe painful traumatic events they have endured: "I can
see the girl—her father is touching her in a bad way."
Indeed, one Holocaust survivor, as described by Joan
Borysenko in her book on spiritual optimism, *Fire in the
Soul,* at first could only write about his concentration camp
experiences in third person, but once he had healed from the
trauma of these experiences, he was finally able to write in
first person.

If I sense that a writer's block client has a strong autobiographical element in his or her fictional characters, I'll ask
the writer to choose one and to let that character feel the
pain for the client, on paper, as a prelude to a therapeutic
release. Essentially, Stage One writing is close to fiction
writing, except that the purpose is not to create art
(although many of my clients have saved their healing writings for use in future books).

The idea behind PABW is to use a fictional context to dis-
sociate oneself initially from potentially explosive and
painful material that may arise during the writing. Once
you have entered your own unconscious mind, the paths of
imagination (fiction writing) and memory (PABW writing)

may begin to merge, and repressed details may emerge. The type of writing done in Stages One, Two and Three is similar to self-hypnosis. However, the writing done in Stages Four and Five is more likely to resemble deeper hypnotherapy, where feelings arise and are released as a result of the writer "owning" the story by using first person.

Since this type of writing can obviously be viewed as threatening, I have encouraged my clients to use the Writer's Floe in my office—that small but very solid isle of stability amid the sea of confusion created by shame and procrastination—the first time that they attempt to write in a psychoautobiographical manner.

As stated before, the room contains no telephone, no books, no distractions of any kind. Instead, it is filled with every color of paper, pen, pencil, crayon and Magic Marker (they don't call them that for nothing!) you could imagine. The room is decorated in bright but soothing colors, with a couch for those who prefer to be comfortable and a small desk for the more studious writers who prefer to plug in their laptop computers in the spike protector provided (I often joke that it helps with emotional surges as well). Needless to say, I was certainly pleased upon learning that James Pennebaker's research on the therapeutic value of expressing one's feelings indicated that people are more likely to self-disclose if the setting is unique!

Writing about your feelings in a safe place can bring great relief as well as lead you to a point where you can be more empathic with your younger self who experienced those old hurts. Often when clients are too ashamed to attend group therapy, they can still get some of the benefits of "shared experience" by creating a fictional character with whom they can identify. This serves as a stepping stone to being able to feel for oneself with true compassion—and without judgment.

If you find that you experience sufficient relief from your pain and shame through this technique so that your procrastination has been eliminated, then the next few sections of this chapter may not be necessary for you. However, in his numerous studies on the effectiveness of writing as a release of negative experiences, Pennebaker noted that some participants may have a tendency to mis-perceive situations that they are writing about, and so may need the help of another person in interpreting their writings. In my experience, I have noticed that people often judge themselves harshly—even though the blank sheet of paper remains neutral. For this reason, it may be helpful to seek validation of your ideas by reading about similar experiences of others, by meeting those with comparable problems, or by seeing a qualified psychotherapist.

* * * *

Self-Help Books

If you end up with a bad case of "psychoautobiographical writer's block," sometimes reading a good book can help. Just as reading a novel often helps to tweak the creativity of the novelist with a temporary bout of "writer's block," reading a self-help book can often trigger emotions or ideas about procrastination-inducing life experiences that are blocked from your conscious memory. This is true especially if the self-help book contains detailed, sensory descriptions of others' experiences that may then tap into any memories stored in the sensory-oriented right side of your brain.

Numerous books regarding all of the clinical issues dis-cussed here are listed in the References for Further Reading can also check *The Authoritative Guide to Self-Help Books* by John Santrock, to get an idea of which books were recommended in a national survey of 500 therapists.

* * * *

Reading Fiction As Therapy

If you are uncomfortable reading self-help books and prefer an approach that is less direct and less didactic, you might try reading some of the works of fiction I've asked some of my clients to read. These are especially helpful to some people, since works of fiction are even more likely to contain detailed descriptions of sensory experiences to which the right side of your brain may respond. In some ways, a good novel can hit the right side of the brain with the same impact of a full-screen movie. Though such novels or movies may not have been intended to produce a therapeutic effect, they very well can.

The first week the film version of Terry McMillan's novel *Waiting to Exhale* was released, I had three clients say they wept constantly after watching it (the movie dealt with four women and their struggles to find men to love). In all three cases, the central issue arose from repressed feelings of loss and abandonment stemming from the clients' own life experiences. Seeing the movie helped to tap into the right side of the clients' brains, thereby releasing old emotions that had been previously blocked.

Some successful writers have even acknowledged that their fiction was written as a form of self-healing. For example, in a recent newspaper interview, Russell Banks stated quite clearly that much of his fiction writing was for therapeutic purposes:

> *Coming from a background that is broken and dismembered as mine was, you quickly learn how to put things back together again, even if only in your imagination. . . . Writing was a . . . psychological necessity.*

As you might expect, some of Banks's work can be used as powerful tools in accessing the emotional lode stored up in the right side of our brains. For example, Banks's short story "Queen for a Day," in *Success Stories,* provides a poignant account of a divorced 1950s family from a male adolescent's point of view, as the young man tries to justify why his abandoned mother should be allowed on TV as "queen for a day."

Other fiction writers' works provide a similar avenue of right-brain access, such as J.D. Salinger's classic *Catcher in the Rye,* a novel that offers Holden Caulfield's response to the effects of shallow parenting and fraternity-style sexual assault. Amy Bloom's story "Where No Light Shines," in *Come to Me,* paints a touching portrait of a young girl who willingly accepts the fact that she is being used sexually by an adult, but who craves his attention, since she gets none from her overly critical mother and aloof father. And haunting portraits of childhood neglect and abuse are portrayed unforgettably in Kaye Gibbons's *Ellen Foster,* Lisa Shea's *Hula,* Dorothy Allison's *Bastard Out of Carolina,* and Connie May Fowler's *Sugar Cage, River of Hidden Dreams* and *Before Women Had Wings.* These are just a few of the many psychological resources available to us in the world of literature (see References for Further Reading for a list of such works).

* * * *

12-Step Groups

Twelve-Step groups such as Alcoholics Anonymous, Co-dependents Anonymous, Sex Addicts Anonymous, Incest Survivors Anonymous and Debtors Anonymous, to name a few, have been a tremendous help to many people, especially during the early stages of recovery from shame-based issues that induce procrastination. Just listening to the detailed,

sensory-oriented stories of other individuals' shaming experiences can help trigger emotions in you that have remain
repressed for years. It is usually easier to cry for others than
for ourselves—another form of being in "third person"
rather than "first person." Even as you cry for others, you
cry for yourself as well. When you release your feelings, you
are in essence releasing the shame that underlies them.
Remember, the best treatment for shame is to talk about it.

However, some individuals have reported that the 12-
Step format has induced further shame, thereby impeding
the process of recovery. For example, in a recent discussion
of current research on drug addiction treatment strategies,
Lani Nelson-Zlupko and her colleagues found that many
female substance abusers do not respond well to the highly
confrontive, punitive approach of traditional drug treatment programs. Similarly, since the 12-Step format was
initially structured by men to meet the needs of men, some
women report that it is not effective for their needs.
Obviously, it is very important that you feel accepted and
supported rather than shamed in any form of therapy.
Behavioral and holistic alternatives to the 12-Step model
have sprouted increasingly over the years, such as Gershen
Kaufman's shame model for addictions discussed in *The
Psychology of Shame* and Deepak Chopra's holistic medicine model discussed in *Perfect Health.*

* * * *

Psychotherapy

If you feel that you need professional guidance, it may be
wise to seek psychotherapy, which can provide a mixture of
right-brain and left-brain techniques for shame release. If
you've been struggling with a problem for six months or

more without major symptom relief, then it's probably a good time to see a therapist.

After all, if you have a toothache, do you brave the pain for months, and then finally tie a string between your tooth and the nearest door, then slam it shut to yank out your tooth? Of course not. You consult a dentist, who will know what to do and have the skills and equipment to do it as painlessly as possible. If you have a serious legal problem, do you go into court alone and risk losing the suit by representing yourself? Of course not. You find yourself a good lawyer and let him or her handle it with all the knowledge and expertise he or she gleaned in law school. So if you have a serious personal problem that hasn't gone away by itself within six months, you can seek out an expert for that, too. (And you certainly don't have to wait six months before you decide to do so.) Some motivational experts—such as Marsha Sinetar, author of *To Build the Life You Want, Create the Work You Love*—have even stated that psychotherapy is a prerequisite for some individuals who seek to benefit from the advice offered in books on time management and motivation.

There is one main reason why getting into therapy can be at times the right course of action. It usually works, especially if you stick it out until you're "finished." Take note of a survey published in the November 1995 issue of *Consumer Reports*. This survey indicated that clients benefited very substantially from psychotherapy, especially from long-term therapy—a finding that was upheld in a recent review of this survey by Dr. Martin Seligman, the well-respected psychologist whose work on learned helplessness we have already discussed.

Therapy also can help in a physiological way. According to neuropsychologist Dr. R. Joseph, it's important to note the physiological changes that take place in the brain whenever we discuss an old event, behavior pattern or feeling. Every time you have a thought or a feeling, a biochemical change occurs in the brain. And every time you think a certain negative thought—or a positive one, for that matter—you reinforce that same neural pathway in your brain. Thus, by talking about a familiar negative pattern or experience in a different way with a therapist—or even with a friend—you can begin to establish new neural pathways in your brain, so that you don't automatically think the same negative thoughts, or feel the same fearful emotions, whenever you think of a negative event.

In looking for a qualified therapist, it's important to be selective. We tend to spend more time shopping for a new pair of shoes than we do shopping for a therapist who will be compatible with our needs. To start, check with your local branch of the American Psychological Association or the National Association of Social Workers.

Ask the therapist if he or she is familiar with some of the more well-known professional or self-help books regarding shame (*The Psychology of Shame* or any other professional books by Gershen Kaufman, Helen Block Lewis or Donald Nathanson, or self-help books such as *Healing the Shame That Binds You* by John Bradshaw or *Facing Shame* by Merle Fossum). Ask the therapist about his or her familiarity with books on adult children of alcoholics (*Adult Children of Alcoholics* by Janet Woititz), childhood neglect (*Homecoming* by John Bradshaw) and physical or sexual abuse (any books by David Finkelhor, *Healing the Incest Wound* by Christine Courtois, *The Courage to Heal Workbook* by Laura Davis). And ask the therapist about his or her familiarity with treating cases of protracted procrastination, and whether he or she has read books such as this one, or at least *Procrastination: What It Is, What To Do About It* by Jane Burka and Lenora Yuen, or *The Artist's Way* by Julia Cameron.

Don't be alarmed if the therapist is not aware of these books. There are newer ones coming out all the time, and your therapist may be more familiar with them than with the aforementioned list of classics in the field. If your therapist has not done any reading in these areas and you live in a rural or isolated area where your choice of therapists is limited, bring this book as well as any others to your first session, and ask the therapist if he or she would be willing to read one of these books and lead you through it. You may also find referrals from many of the resources listed in the References for Further Reading as well as in such books as Ellen Bass's and Laura Davis's *The Courage to Heal* or Mike Lew's *Victims No Longer* (a book on males who have endured sexual abuse).

Above all, do not give up trying to work with a qualified professional. Although most therapists will say that they are not familiar with formal "treatments for procrastination," most of them are trained sufficiently in child development to understand how your problems may have started. Encourage them to assist you in interpreting your photohistory, as well as in interpreting your psychoautobiographical writings. Be willing to allow your therapist to lead you through the Gestalt "empty chair" technique, in which you sit in one chair to talk with your "procrastinating self" and sit in another to talk with your "productive self." In so doing, you may find that you are truly at odds with yourself. Be open to the idea of group therapy. The more people you can express your shame to, the better.

One last word about a common reason people avoid the use of psychotherapy: "I can't afford it."

First, many insurance companies will cover the cost of some psychotherapy. Second, some private psychotherapists operate with a sliding fee scale, offering counseling at a lower fee to clients with limited funds. Third, most areas in this country have community mental health centers where you can be seen under a sliding fee scale, depending on your annual income. Fourth, consider group therapy, which is generally less expensive—and often more beneficial, since you get the feedback of five or 10 people instead of one. Above all, do not give up. Local hospitals and women's crisis centers sometimes offer free or low-cost counseling. Call your local mental health association for further information.

Whatever therapy may cost, you can probably find something in your budget that you can do without for at least a few months. Remember: Your self-esteem is far more important than a new pair of shoes or a carton of cigarettes.

* * * *

Hypnotherapy
Self-Hypnosis
Guided Imagery

I have grouped together these three therapeutic modalities for accessing the right side of the brain because at times there is a fine line among them. Let's take a look at each one, being keenly aware of when you need a licensed psychotherapist to assist you and when you don't. But first and foremost, remember that hypnosis—if conducted by a competent professional with appropriate training—is nothing to be afraid of because your unconscious mind will only allow you access to whatever information or feelings you can handle at that point in your life. I like to think it resembles a guardian angel of sorts, only allowing you passage to what you can safely absorb at any given time.

Hypnotherapy can release old memories or help you recall buried emotions. Make sure that whoever is conducting the session is a *licensed* mental health professional— such as a social worker, mental health counselor, marriage and family counselor, psychologist, psychiatric nurse, or psychiatrist —who has extra training in the field of clinical hypnosis. The most professional hypnosis training available is from the Ericksonian Society, the American Society of Clinical Hypnosis (and its state and regional branches), the Society for Clinical and Experimental Hypnosis, and graduate training programs at many colleges and universities. Don't be afraid to ask where the therapist received his or her training.

True hypnotherapy usually implies that you will be put into a state of trance, at which point the therapist will regress you back to an earlier time to help you to heal. Because of the nature of feelings that may arise during such a procedure, it is essential that the person conducting the hypnotherapy be competent. Using a "clinical hypnotist" or "licensed hypnotherapist" without a professional mental health license could put you in jeopardy. A "licensed hypnotist" may know how to put you into a trance and get you out, but this person may not have the skills to help you with the emotions that arise during the trance state.

Hypnotherapy is an incredibly powerful tool for accessing the right side of the brain. Even though you may not have any powerful memories the first time you are hypnotized, the lid on your unconscious mind has been loosened, thereby opening up the possibility that you might remember feelings spontaneously or in dreams.

The experience of hypnosis is somewhat like a "twilight" sleep—you're aware that you're sitting or lying on a couch in your therapist's office, listening to the sound of his or her voice. You may also be aware that you feel three years old, playing with a set of blocks when your father comes in and slaps you for making too much noise. The therapist can help you explore and express the feelings that come up in response to such recalled events, thereby allowing the right side of your brain to communicate openly with the left side of the brain, to absorb and integrate this material so that it no longer contaminates your present-day life.

Although I do not engage in formal hypnotherapy with all of my clients, there are some who may need to go beyond phototherapy and other techniques. That's when I may suggest hypnosis or guided imagery. While many experts would agree there is a fine line between guided imagery, self-hypnosis and hypnotherapy (although many will agree on the distinction between deep trance regressive hypnotherapy, as described above, and the practice of self-hypnosis for purposes of simple relaxation), the difference is usually one of formality. For some clients, a longer, formal induction helps them to relax, but for others, taking the time to count down from one to 10 just makes them more tense.

We may start out with a simple procedure, which is actually more of a guided-imagery technique used by many therapists, in which I'll ask the client to close his or her eyes and imagine a large number 3, followed by a number 2, then a number 1, and finally a large zero—which then turns into an oval mirror. When the client looks into this mirror, I'll say: "Imagine seeing yourself as a young child." Often, I'll ask the client to step into the mirror and talk or play with this "inner child," asking the child what it is that he or she needs the most. Usually, even without a long, formal trance induction that many people might expect, this guided-imagery exercise can tap into the lode of emotions in the right brain, and therapeutic results are usually evident.

On the other hand, some clients may prefer to do such an exercise alone, in the form of "self-hypnosis." In such cases, the client follows a script or a brief set of instructions, performs the exercise alone, and then reports back to the therapist with the result. Usually, those who use these techniques can gain empathy for that lost and lonely child who's been nagging for their attention when they've been "trying to get things done." The sudden appearance of such a needy young child in the psyche often helps to explain the basis of procrastination as a form of "holding out" until one's real needs are met.

If you're afraid of running into the "false memory syndrome," keep in mind that if you see a therapist with excellent clinical training in hypnosis, as well as ethical training from a university granting mental health degrees, this is very unlikely to happen. These professionals will not ask you leading questions that are inappropriate.

There is another reason why you are unlikely to experience any form of "false memory." Keep in mind that those who have sought to engage in research and have attempted to "plant" false memories in individuals' minds have by ethical constraint been limited to implanting non-traumatic memories. Because of the essential differences between traumatic and non-traumatic memories, we cannot really put much faith in such studies.

For example, at a recent conference offered by the American Society of Clinical Hypnosis, Drs. Sandra Wise and Richard Elmore offered a list of differences between traumatic and non-traumatic memories. This list included the fact that non-traumatic memories are easily distorted, while traumatic memories are impervious to change.

Similarly, at this same conference, Dr. Charles Mutter offered a list of the essential differences between real memories and false memories, which researchers are currently working on documenting in the laboratory. For example:

- Real memories have greater detail than false memories.
- Real memories are usually expressed from a child's viewpoint and in a child's words.
- False memories are told in a rote fashion with adult language.
- Real memories are usually the source of troubling symptoms.
- False memories do not produce symptoms that bother the client.

A simple example here may suffice. Try to recall the last time you were walking up and down the aisles in your local grocery store, selecting some food for the week. You can probably recall the overall look of the store as well as which vegetables you may have selected and where they were found. This is, of course, an example of non-traumatic memory. Now try to recall a time when someone truly hurt your feelings—or made you feel incredibly angry. Picture this person's facial expression, and your own, at the time of the painful event or situation. Feel the hurt or anger welling up inside of you. This is an example of a painful, but not exactly traumatic, memory. You can feel the difference between these unwanted negative feelings and the way you could so readily drum up the image of the grocery store in the previous image. Although this is a very simplistic example, it does illustrate the difference between memories drawn up from the left brain (usually non-traumatic) and memories drawn up from the right brain (usually more painful and less easily dismissed).

If you should ever decide to undergo hypnotherapy, a properly trained therapist will help you sort out fantasy from memory. However, it is important to remember that the only way to know for sure is through factual confirmation, which

is sometimes impossible. Unconscious memory is not necessarily an exact replica of your life. Images may be encoded in
the right brain like disjointed photographs rather than an
accurate videotape of your life. What is far more important
than factual accuracy are the feelings you may experience
during hypnosis, feelings which may have been sabotaging
and contaminating your current life. Once you have accessed
and released these feelings, you may find a great deal of
symptom relief and less procrastination in your life.

*I once worked with a young woman who always wanted
to be a dancer. Although Barbara had been given rave
reviews by her high school dance instructor, she had
delayed pursuing her career and, instead, had taken a
dead-end job as a receptionist. However, Barbara realized
during a photohistory session—filled with photo after
photo of her as a very depressive-looking child—that she'd
always felt too inadequate to pursue her dream. She'd
always had the feeling that she wasn't good enough and
would not succeed.*

*Although Barbara was able to talk about her feeling of
low self-worth, she was unable to really feel it and was
mystified about the source of her low self-esteem. Under
hypnosis, she saw a series of images of herself as a little
girl: in the kitchen, in the living room, in the family room,
in her bedroom. Each of these images seemed fairly benign
at first, but what gradually became significant, as I
watched the tears begin to flow from beneath Barbara's
closed eyelids, was the fact that she was always alone, yet
aware that her parents were in a nearby room.*

*Barbara's parents had not been verbally or physically
abusive to her—they just weren't interested in spending
time with her. Both parents, who were in their late 40s
when she was born as their only child, were tenured his-*

tory professors at a prestigious university, forever reading and writing in their shared studio, always discussing the latest theories about what really caused the French Revolution or the U.S. Civil War. They were highly intellectually oriented and apparently oblivious to the emotional needs of their child in the next room, a child they thought was enjoying the latest toys or books they'd purchased for her.

Since they didn't understand the emotional needs of their child, they just assumed she would be bored with their intellectual bantering and better off with her own books and toys. As a result, Barbara received very little verbal or physical affection during her childhood.

The result was a sense of low self-esteem. As an egocentric child, Barbara made the natural assumption that she must not be good enough to spend time with her parents. However, once she had released her grief and understood that her parents were simply unaware of her needs, Barbara was able to let go of the old image of herself as an unwanted, unworthy burden. She enrolled again in a local dance studio and, at the suggestion of her dance instructor, began seeking out an agent.

Thus you can see that hypnosis can be a powerful tool in releasing old feelings of shame that may be triggering problems with procrastination. Although the full exploration of this subject is beyond the scope of this book, if you would like more information on these issues, you may want to consult such works as *Discovering the Power of Self-Hypnosis* by Stanley Fisher, *Hypnosis: Questions & Answers,* by Bernie Zilbergeld and his associates, or *Clinical Hypnosis and Memory: Guidelines for Clinicians and for Forensic Hypnosis* by D. Corydon Hammond and his associates.

* * * *

Art Therapy

Although art therapy is best conducted under the guidance of a licensed mental health professional or art therapist, it is an exercise you can do by yourself as well. However, having an expert to guide you can save you time—as well as provide you with the appropriate psychological interpretations and support if you should encounter any uncomfortable emotions.

Obviously, if you draw with your nondominant hand, you are more likely to access hidden emotions or memories. Often when clients do not have photographs of themselves as children, I'll ask them to draw a picture of how they might have looked. This usually brings feelings to the surface. Or, if a client is disturbed by a certain image from a dream or from an old photo, I'll ask that person to sketch the image with the nondominant hand, choosing colors that match their emotions.

Sometimes a client is just plain angry or sad and doesn't know why. In those cases I ask the person to choose a color of crayon that reminds him or her of the current mood state, and doodle around (using only the nondominant hand) while we discuss the feeling, and what it means to hold back or express this feeling in front of others. Usually this will access other clues and will open doors for further exploration into the problem of procrastination.

On the next page is an example of art therapy from my own procrastination recovery process. As I recall, I was feeling terribly sad as well as angry about the painful childhood experiences I'd endured, and words just weren't enough. So out came my paints—at home, alone—and onto the page flew my feelings about the way my abusers had taken away the innocence of my childhood. Initially, I felt upset even while I was painting, but by the time I finished this flinging of my emotions onto the page, I felt much better. I realized that the darker colors in the center of the two "tornado" formations actually represented my creative spirit, which had, in spite of all the attempts to kill it, managed to spawn some solid "works of art," seen in the lower right corner of the drawing. Hence, the title, directed at my abusers, painted in tiny letters alongside the spewing winds of the tornadoes: *You Forgot Something.*

Figure 5. Art Therapy, "You Forgot Something"

Art therapy is also helpful when you use your nondominant hand to draw two images of yourself—one as a current procrastinator and one as a future non-procrastinator. With this technique, various signs may arise. Sometimes the first figure drawn has no clearly defined hands or feet, indicating a sense of powerlessness. Often, this first figure lacks a clear outline of the body, suggesting a diffuse sense of self and, perhaps, a lack of boundaries in relationships with other people. These clues from the right brain might lead to a discussion of how a person came to feel so powerless and to have such a blurred sense of self.

In contrast, the drawing of the more productive future self usually does not have these disruptive features and appears more well-defined. This pattern suggests a sense of strength and hope, thereby planting seeds of optimism that can begin sprouting even as the client may be feeling hopeless in the fight against procrastination.

Although a full explication of the techniques involved with art therapy is beyond the scope of this book, this modality can be a powerful one in accessing some of the underlying roots of shame-based procrastination that may lie dormant in the right side of the brain. For further information, you may wish to consult such books as *Art Therapy in Practice* by Marian Liebmann, *Art Therapy and Dramatherapy: Masks of the Soul* by Sue Jennings and Ase Minde, or *What Do You See? Phenomenology of Therapeutic Art Expression* by Mala Betensky.

* * * *

Alternative Medicine

In recent years, many forms of alternative medicine—medical practices based on Eastern rather than Western knowledge—have become more mainstream. They treat not only medical problems but also depression and emotional pain. These forms of alternative medicine are said to access the right and left sides of the brain and also the sensory "cellular" memory in different areas of the body (as Deepak Chopra so aptly explains in his bestselling book, *Quantum Healing: Exploring the Frontiers of Mind-Body Medicine*).

Although many will say that alternative medicine has a long way to go before the general public accepts its tenets, in 1992 Congress instructed the U.S. National Institutes of Health to establish an Office of Alternative Medicine to evaluate and help integrate new holistic approaches into mainstream medical practice. Books such as *Alternative Medicine: The Definitive Guide* have begun sprouting up in bookstores. And in a recent survey published in *The New England Journal of Medicine,* researchers found that in 1990, Americans consulted so-called "alternative" practitioners more often than they consulted physicians trained in traditional Western medicine. Articles in magazines such as *Time, Prevention* and *Consumer Reports* have highlighted the healing properties of alternative therapies as well.

The success of Dr. Deepak Chopra's many books on alternative approaches to healing is testimony that many Americans are turning to alternative medicine to cope with psychological as well as physical problems. In *Perfect Health,* Chopra discusses the three body types noted in traditional Ayurvedic medicine—kapha, pitta, and vata. Once you determine which is your body prototype, you can begin to influence your level of energy and productivity by choosing the appropriate foods, sleep patterns and time periods that might best suit your body's inborn tendencies.

Whether you choose Ayurvedic medicine, acupuncture, acupressure, spinal kinesiology, chiropractic, aromatherapy, yoga, meditation or any other form of alternative medicine to help with the symptoms of depression, shame or procrastination, it is important that you are comfortable using these as adjunct therapies to psychotherapy. For example, in chakra therapy, disturbances near the "root chakra"—an energy point near the base of the spine—are often viewed as indicative of problems with creativity and/or sexuality, a common pattern in procrastinators who have suffered some form of sexual abuse. Obviously, this information must be doled out cautiously to the client so as not to alarm him or her. Similarly, the use of therapeutic massage may be too overwhelming for the sexual abuse survivor, whose shame has been transferred to the body, and homeopathic remedies can at times produce overwhelming emotions in those who have been severely abused.

Thus, it is strongly suggested that you allow your psychotherapist and your alternative medicine practitioner to work as a "team" in your healing process, so that each knows what the other is doing and you can heal without any further traumatization. If you are being treated by a sensitive practitioner of alternative medicine as part of a team headed up by your psychotherapist, the results can be quite beneficial.

* * * *

Psychopharmacology

Although many people resist the notion of "taking drugs" to remedy psychological problems, it is important to remember that sometimes there is a physiological condition in the brain that must be treated. Books such as *The Good News About Depression* by Mark Gold and *Understanding Depression* by Donald Klein and Paul Wender go a long way in clearly describing the process of biochemical imbalance that can occur as a result of chronic psychological pain.

As we have already discovered, when it comes to procrastination, the problems of shame and its closely linked cousin—depression—are not far behind.

Experts such as June Tangney and her associates have indicated that there is research evidence to suggest a very strong correlation between shame and depression. And Nancy Morrison states that researchers have found that certain antidepressant medications called MAO inhibitors have helped to reduce shame in some individuals. Morrison also discusses evidence to suggest that some people may be more prone to shame than others, and this may be partly due to genetic biochemical factors.

Of course, psychotropic medication for depression—or shame—is not the answer for everyone. You may want to try some of the natural antidotes for depression that are discussed in Michael Norden's book, *Beyond Prozac.* But if your depression has not abated at least somewhat with the help of psychotherapy, alternative medicine, physical exercise (which raises endorphin levels), or some of the methods discussed in Norden's book, then taking antidepressant medication can be a welcome relief and can lead to the speedier recovery you deserve.

Contrary to popular belief, such medication will not cover up your problems or prevent you from dealing with them. Once the medication you need has been adjusted for type and dosage, you will have a "floor" on which to stand. Since you know that you won't slip any deeper into depression, you can afford to begin accessing the painful shame-based emotions of the past that are triggering your present-day procrastination. And once you begin to release some shame, with your lighter load it is more likely that you'll have the energy to tackle those tasks you've been putting off for so long—whether it's cleaning out a closet, writing a dissertation or starting to initiate a social life.

Once you have worked through your problems, your psychiatrist will gradually lower the dosage until you are weaned from it. However, for those with genetic or permanent biochemical imbalances, taking antidepressant medication for life must be seen in the same light as a diabetic taking insulin. Certainly there's no need for shame over taking care of your medical needs. For although such biochemical depression shows up strongly on the psychological level, it is based in the physical level.

If you take psychotropic medication, be sure to go to a qualified psychiatrist, not your family physician. A psychiatrist knows which psychotropic medications work best with which types of depressive symptoms. Some people eat or sleep too much, while others don't eat or sleep enough. Different antidepressants would be required to treat these opposite sets of symptoms. A psychiatrist will also be aware of possible side effects or interactions with other medications or conditions, unlike your family practitioner, who may simply prescribe the standard dosage without regard for your metabolism or tolerance for a specific type of antidepressant medication. People who are more sensitive to drugs may need a lower dosage, while others may have what is called a paradoxical reaction, where the medication has the opposite effect from its intended purpose. At times, taking less of a drug can have more of an effect, rather than the opposite. So if you are going to jump-start your system, be sure to do it with the appropriate guidance—we all know what happens when you hook up a positive cable to a negative one!

The temporary use of antidepressants can be, quite literally, a lifesaver. Although you may resist to the bitter end of your proverbial rope, you may come to the point that you know you deserve to feel better while working through your shame-based issues underlying your problems with procrastination. You certainly can't control people who neglected or mistreated you when you were a powerless child, but you can control the process of your recovery from that neglect or abuse. If not, it's likely that you might turn to one or more of the compulsive behaviors listed in the next chapter— habits that can and will temporarily raise the level of mood-regulating neurotransmitters that we all need to get by each day, let alone to fight depression. However, with chronic repetition, such compulsive behaviors eventually lead to further depression and the depletion of neurotransmitters, so that you cannot lead a productive, healthy and happy life. And you, my friend, deserve better than that.

7

Coffee and Doughnuts for Everyone: Compulsive Behaviors As Procrastination

*To be a good writer you have
to be absolutely lucid at every moment
of writing and in good health.*

—Gabriel Garcia Marquez

As you might expect, the role of physiological factors in procrastination is often overlooked. In this chapter, we'll examine the way in which deficits in brain neurotransmitters can trigger compulsive-avoidant habits that contribute to problems with procrastination. Many of us have habits we'd like to break, and yet no matter how self-destructive these habits are, we don't stop. And it isn't simply because we are "weak-willed."

Recent research indicates that there is usually a physiological component underlying compulsive behavior. In other words, if you are depressed or anxious, you may try to self-medicate through overindulgence in food, alcohol or other compulsive behaviors. In essence, you are trying to regulate the level of certain mood-affecting neurotransmitters in your brain. Remember our friends Uncle Serotonin, Cousin Dopamine and Aunt Norepinephrine? Well, here they are again, screaming about deficits in your neurotransmitter budget—deficits no doubt triggered by your interactions

263

with real-life aunts or uncles or whoever else helped to set up your base of shame in the first place.

What does all this have to do with procrastination? We are all human. No doubt every one of us has indulged in some of the compulsive behaviors described in this chapter. We may engage in them so much that we leave no time for productivity or creativity. Or we may use compulsive behaviors to avoid a decision. But whether your compulsive behaviors trigger your procrastination or your procrastination triggers your compulsive behaviors—or both—the underlying problem is still shame. Compulsive behaviors, such as procrastination, are simply a mask behind which we can hide from painful emotions.

As long as we hide behind these masks, trying to raise our levels of serotonin, dopamine or norepinephrine, we'll never face the underlying shame that triggered the depressive, anxious feelings that caused the depletion of those neurotransmitters in the first place. What a vicious cycle! Let's take a closer look at some of the more common avoidant behaviors and then explore some ways out of this layer of protection. Although the treatment of compulsive behaviors is beyond the scope of this book, suggestions for further exploration are in the References for Further Reading.

Compulsive Eating

With the onset of the Age of Oprah, this compulsive behavior, which plagues millions, finally has received a great deal of attention. Though many people overeat occasionally, the criteria for compulsive eating involves a certain level of chronic anxiety. Try to respond to the following questions as honestly as you can. Give your first gut-level response.

_____ I eat when I'm trying to avoid doing something.

_____ I eat when I'm trying to avoid making a decision.

_____ I eat very rapidly when I'm alone.

_____ I usually worry that someone else will eat my food.

_____ I worry that I won't have enough food.

_____ I constantly think about food.

_____ No matter how much I eat, I still feel empty inside.

_____ I usually overeat.

_____ When I eat, I feel desperate.

_____ When I eat, I feel out of control.

_____ Once I start eating, I can't stop.

If you answered "yes" to any of these questions, you may be using food to quell an inner hurricane of emotions growing out of the Sea of Shame. Put another way, you may be trying to use food to fill that emptiness inside where your self-esteem should be. Don't be alarmed; you are not alone. In a recent study of college women, researchers Laurie Mintz and Nancy Betz found that 61 percent had some form of eating-behavior problem such as compulsive eating, binging or purging when alone, or chronic dieting.

Our first association with affection or attention is usually food. Whether we are breast-fed or bottle-fed, someone has to be holding us, at least for the first few months. In later years, when we are suffering from the effects of low self-esteem, we are reminded of those early years when we craved physical touch. However, if we cannot get affection (or if we are afraid to reach out for it), then food is often seen as the next best thing.

Unfortunately, food works. It does quell anxiety and feelings of dysphoria. Foods that are high in white flour—such as breads, cookies and pastries—will release serotonin, the body's natural "Valium." Foods that are high in fat—such as chocolate or french fries—will release endorphins, the body's natural opiates. And foods that are high in sugar (who needs a list?) will release high levels of serotonin and, if combined with fat, high levels of endorphins in the body as well. So is it any wonder that we crave a chocolate doughnut—all white flour, fat and sugar—rather than a carrot stick in times of stress?

Indeed, according to nutritionist Debra Waterhouse in her book *Why Women Need Chocolate,* chocolate is an extremely pleasurable food for many reasons. It contains theobromine, a substance that increases alertness in much the same way that caffeine does. Chocolate also contains phenylethylamine, a chemical believed to be released in the brain when we fall in love. Considering the fact that procrastination tends to generate precisely the opposite effects—lethargy, downcast feelings and shame—it is not surprising that many people turn to mass quantities of chocolate to curb the pain of procrastination.

> *One client who suffered from severe procrastination also had a problem with compulsive eating and intense body shame. If Paul stopped eating, he reasoned, then he'd lose weight. If he lost weight, then he'd be more attractive to women, and he'd probably end up having an affair, since his marriage was miserable. If he had the affair, he'd probably get divorced, and that would mean he'd finally have to get a job.*
>
> *However, getting a job was terrifying to Paul. He feared success. If he was successful, he would threaten his mother, a woman who had the unfortunate habit of telling Paul as a child that he was conceited whenever he tried to discuss his successes in school or sports. Paul had learned not to anger his mother in this way, since she was his only*

resource for attention. He knew he could not turn to his father for support because his father was a rage-aholic who had beaten Paul frequently. Furthermore, Paul's uncle had molested him on numerous occasions.

As a young adult, Paul began to act out these shame-based experiences through compulsive sexual activity. But with the onset of the AIDS epidemic, he decided to marry to guarantee a constant source of sexual activity, though soon found that unsatisfactory—he missed the constant excitement of conquest and also feared being vulnerable if he became emotionally intimate with his wife. Gradually, he switched his addictive pattern to food. Paul lost job after job due to his fear of success and his lack of productivity, but his wife brought home a substantial salary, so he felt "safe," at least temporarily.

This case clearly illustrates the way that a problem with compulsive eating can mask not only shame but also other issues. Because of his dysfunctional childhood, Paul had developed patterns of compulsive eating and sexual activity, as well as procrastination regarding his job. He felt trapped and saw no way out until he began to recall and make sense of his traumatic early years. As Paul unraveled the story of his past, he began to see that his unresolved shame had caused his problems with food, and this gave him an excuse to hate his body, which in turn made him too embarrassed to go for job interviews. Once Paul began to assign his shame to its proper sources, he was on the road to recovery.

Until one discovers the original source of pain that triggers compulsive eating and, thus, procrastination, one cannot fully heal. This healing must be done in a compassionate atmosphere. Although I constantly tell clients who overeat that being overweight simply means that they have been wounded, they still carry a great deal of shame and depression about their weight. When they try on clothes that no longer fit, I ask them to say to themselves, "Gee, these clothes just won't fit over all of my bandages," rather than saying, "I'm just too fat to wear this."

Aside from psychological approaches to compulsive eating as procrastination, physiological interventions may prove to be helpful as well. Recent research indicates that compulsive eating is strongly linked with depression, and that antidepressant medication can be highly effective in treating this disorder.

Sometimes antidepressants can help to speed up this process because such medication can assist your body in overcoming its deficits in serotonin so you'll no longer crave foods that are high in sugar, fat and white flour.

Similarly, acupressure massage or acupuncture—which are often helpful for recovering drug addicts—may be effective in alleviating these neurotransmitter deficits. Many books are available to help overcome compulsive eating as well, including the aforementioned *Why Women Need Chocolate* by Debra Waterhouse, as well as *Making Peace with Food* by Susan Kano, *Feeding the Hungry Heart* by Jeneen Roth, *Fat Is a Feminist Issue* by Susie Orbach, *Emotional Eating* by Edward Abramson, and *You Can't Quit Till You Know What's Eating You* by Donna LeBlanc. But the best way to make sure that compulsive eating no longer aggravates your problems with procrastination is to face the underlying shame so that you will no longer need certain foods to quell the anxiety associated with those residual pools of shame from days past.

* * * *

Use of Caffeine

Like hot chocolate, a good cup of coffee can work wonders on a cold winter morning. You feel warmed and energized. Caffeine in any form releases dopamine, one of the neurotransmitters whose depletion can trigger depression. Dopamine acts as an energizer in the body. Thus, if you are holding onto old feelings from the past, even a mild depression can cause you to crave substances like coffee, tea or cola in order to self-regulate.

What does this have to do with procrastination? "I think I'll get a cup of coffee before I start." Does this sound familiar? Perhaps you use this as a distraction once you've already sat down to work. Although a cup of coffee can give you an energy boost, more than two cups a day can actually interfere with your concentration and performance. After your adrenal glands have been put on fast forward by caffeine, eventually your body is going to come down, leaving you feeling lethargic or exhausted. Thus, although you may drink countless cups of coffee, tea and/or cola in an effort to elevate those levels of dopamine, so long depleted by depression arising from unresolved shame, you may actually be impeding your ability to concentrate. This can lead to frustration, and your task then becomes associated with anxiety, and of course procrastination is not far behind. Additionally, overuse of caffeine has been related to anemia, which will definitely lead to a loss of energy and loss of productivity.

All this may not sound like much. But if you are truly addicted to caffeine and it is masking deeper feelings that have triggered your procrastination in the first place, then withdrawal can bring about some very unsettling results. On the other hand, maintaining a caffeine habit can keep you from feeling what you need to feel in order to heal from the underpinnings of procrastination.

I have worked with many procrastinating clients who knew exactly how to achieve higher levels of energy through simple dietary changes, but they still chose caffeine for its immediate, albeit unhealthy, burst of energy. After reading such books as *Boost Your Brain Power* (by Ellen Michaud, Russell Wild and the editors of *Prevention)* and *Life Extension* (by Durk Pearson and Sandy Shaw), these clients knew how to eat properly in order to have the high energy necessary for the performance of complex mental tasks. They knew that for high energy, it's important not only to maintain a healthy level of essential vitamins and minerals in the body, but it's also helpful to eat protein first and by itself, in order to give the brain a chance to release tyrosine, a precursor of energizing dopamine—before the tryptophan released by carbohydrates can trigger a surge of sleep-inducing serotonin. (Tryptophan will always win out over tyrosine if the brain is exposed simultaneously to carbohydrates and protein.)

Even so, these clients still chose the immediate route to dopamine via caffeine, in large amounts, all day long. They felt fortified, especially when spending long periods of time alone, writing or performing any other isolating task. And since most of them were more comfortable neglecting or abusing their bodies rather than nourishing and nurturing their bodies, using caffeine seemed like a natural choice to help them through the night—or day—when trying to deal with a long overdue project.

But when some of these clients finally chose to cut back on caffeine for health reasons, they were forced to confront feelings they hadn't known existed. They realized that they'd been chronically depressed most of their lives. Without the constant surge of dopamine, the feelings of hurt and fear made them suddenly feel vulnerable. They were no longer fortified via dopamine against the overwhelming residual feelings from unresolved issues during childhood and adulthood. But through self-help, therapy and antidepressant medication, they were able to stay on track and begin healing. Most of these clients report that now, when they have a cup of tea, coffee or a cola, they often don't finish it. They'll look over after an hour or so, or perhaps after a long day's work, and notice the half-empty cup or can adrift on a desk of paperwork.

The reality is that it's better not to need something so much that you fall apart when you can't have it. When I think of what I needed so much as a child but couldn't have—security, love and respect—I know that the only reason I didn't fall apart was because I kept myself glued together with a variety of compulsive behaviors. I can certainly think of healthier ways to stay alive, but I'm well past the point of judging myself for groping to stay alive via compulsive behaviors for so many years while carrying the tremendous weight of painful repressed memories and emotions.

As you learn other ways to cope with your inner shame, it is important to stop judging yourself for trying to survive. Try to remember to treat yourself with the compassion you might offer to a small child. You wouldn't smack a child for falling down when trying to learn how to walk, would you? Instead, you would applaud the child's efforts, even if he or she held onto a chair while trying to make that first step. And you wouldn't kick a sapling for not growing into a healthy oak tree overnight, but instead might lasso it to a tall pole to help it grow straight and strong. I'm not trying to say it's okay to abuse your body when trying to heal from past issues. I'm simply saying don't kick yourself while you're already down. Try to use the techniques offered in this book or offered by your therapist as replacements for that baby's chair and that young sapling's growing rod. All it

takes is a willingness to offer your inner self as much compassion as you normally would to someone else in distress.

* * * *

Use of Nicotine

Like caffeine, nicotine tends to go hand in hand with procrastination—pun intended. How many times have you lit
up rather than start your project? Again, though nicotine
may give you that boost of dopamine you need to "get
started" and remain energized, it may be keeping you from
facing the fact that you have a dopamine deficit in the first
place. This means that your unresolved feelings of shame
underlying your depression will remain repressed, keeping
locked away with them all the dynamics of your procrastination. In essence, using cigarettes to pump up your levels of
dopamine so that you can still feel well-defended against
your inner pain and shame amounts to yet another form of
procrastination in terms of the healing process.

*In the case of one client, I saw the combined use of nico-
tine and procrastination as a road to suicide. A young
woman, who had long since learned during childhood to
believe that she must take care of others before ever taking
care of herself, was under medical care for various problems.
Rosemary kept a vigilant watch over her cancer that was in
remission. Yet she continued to smoke as a way of coping.
And when I asked about her stress, she did not mention her
health problems but rather the problems of her friends and
neighbors. Rosemary was so involved with their problems,
and trying to solve them, that she "couldn't possibly think of
giving up smoking right now," even though her procrastination regarding this health problem could possibly kill her.*

If you want to stop smoking, numerous self-help books are available, such as Martin Katahn's *How to Quit Smoking Without Gaining Weight* or *How Women Can Finally Stop Smoking,* by Robert Klesges and Margaret DeBon (a book that explores why women may have more difficulty with nicotine withdrawal and weight gain, partly because of the menstrual cycle). What is essential is to determine whether or not nicotine is helping you to avoid dealing with any underlying feelings that may be fueling your problems with procrastination. And there's one sure way to find out: Give up smoking, at least temporarily, and see what happens. The feelings that may arise could be exactly what you've been looking for to help with your escape from procrastination prison.

* * * *

Use of Alcohol

Like nicotine, alcohol is a powerful drug that can conceal emotions that may be contributing to problems with procrastination. In a recent survey of 800 college students, Dennis Thombs and his associates found that "high-intensity drinkers" were most likely to use alcohol for two reasons. For women, the primary motivator was "emotional pain," and for men, it was "social facilitation." These researchers did not specify what made the women feel emotionally distressed and the men feel socially awkward, but suffice it to say that alcohol may be assisting many a shame-based procrastinator from coping with the effects of uncomfortable emotions and the discomfort of public exposure. Indeed, in reviewing some of the recent research on procrastination, Joseph Ferrari and his associates have noted a strong correlation between substance abuse and higher levels of procrastination.

We all know that alcohol, in small doses, can produce euphoria, but chronic heavy use depletes norepinephrine and serotonin levels in the brain. Thus it comes as no surprise that researchers such as Timothy Mueller and his associates have found that chronic alcohol use actually prevents people from recovering from depression, which is a shame-based trigger for procrastination. By continuing to drink alcohol, many people avoid dealing with issues of shame, and thus the platform of procrastination is bolstered once again.

But long before many procrastinators ever recognize their moody state as one of depression, they'll start using large amounts of alcohol to "have fun"—in other words, to dull their psychological pain. However, many individuals will unwittingly use alcohol to mimic the power of their former abusers—a clear pattern found in recent research conducted by Albert Ullman and Alan Orenstein. Instead of having a drink by choice, alcohol is used in an attempt to feel powerful—a compulsion driven by deep waves of powerlessness and shame.

I have seen this pattern of alcohol abuse again and again with clients suffering from protracted procrastination.

One client, a gifted writer, had used alcohol to dull her pain for several decades. Donna would basically soak her immense talent in alcohol and then wonder why it wouldn't dry out long enough to let herself write. Although it may seem obvious that Donna wasn't writing because of depression and substance abuse, she was truly perplexed about her condition. She had no awareness that she had been chronically depressed since the age of two, when she could first pinpoint her mother's rejection of her. Donna had simply grown accustomed to feeling dismal each morning, waiting for sleep or alcohol to take the pain away.

> *However, once Donna began to access her painful mem-*
> *ories and deal with the depth of her shame about being so*
> *"worthless," she was able, with the help of antidepressants,*
> *to stop her alcohol abuse, begin an active social life, and*
> *write the lovely stories that had been locked up inside of*
> *her for so many years. She can still have a drink or two*
> *with friends, but is vigilant about assessing her feelings if*
> *she starts to think about drinking alone. These days*
> *Donna does a good job of living her own full life, free from*
> *the procrastination that had protected her from her inner*
> *shame for so long.*

However, for the one person in 10 who develops a bio-chemical addiction to alcohol, other forms of assistance are usually necessary. (Kathleen Fitzgerald's book *Alcoholism: The Genetic Inheritance* explores this biochemical addiction issue and may be helpful in determining whether you are truly addicted to alcohol.) Besides seeking the assistance of a competently trained mental health professional, attending frequent meetings of Alcoholics Anonymous and/or Narcotics Anonymous can help individuals to maintain abstinence. Certain medications such as Antabuse, which causes aversive nausea if one uses alcohol, and Revia (naltrexone), which blocks the craving for alcohol and the pleasure of feeling high, can also help individuals to break their addiction to alcohol. And sometimes entering an addictions treatment center can be the first step in reclaiming a life that might otherwise remain adrift and bereft of meaning.

If you prefer to try to cope with these issues on an outpatient basis, it is usually best to consult a mental health professional to guide you through this process. It may also be helpful to start with such books as *Getting Started in AA* by "Hamilton B.," if you would like to start attending AA meetings but don't know what to expect. If you try attending

Alcoholics Anonymous and do not like the approach, you may want to read *When AA Doesn't Work for You* by Albert Ellis and Emmett Velten, which offers a "rational-emotive" therapy approach to overcoming alcohol abuse. A third alternative might be *The Small Book: A Revolutionary Alternative for Overcoming Alcohol and Drug Dependence* by Jack Trimpey.

In any event, it is essential that you are able to face the underlying issues that initially drove you to alcohol dependence, so as to uncover the deeper roots of procrastination that may have been plaguing you for more years than you deserve.

* * * *

Use of Other Drugs

We all know that most people who use drugs do so to feel "good." Drugs like cocaine and marijuana raise the body's level of dopamine, battling away those dreaded feelings of depression. Indeed, in some people, cocaine gives the same effect as tricyclic antidepressants. And research has suggested that levels of serotonin and norepinephrine are also affected by such drugs as cocaine and marijuana.

However, in larger amounts and with chronic use, both of these drugs can have a depressant affect. Cocaine actually begins to deplete the body's levels of serotonin, dopamine and norepinephrine; large doses of marijuana can also deplete levels of dopamine and serotonin. Thus, people who initially use these drugs to anesthetize themselves against buried feelings of shame and depression will often try to take more drugs for further relief, but with paradoxical results.

I have worked with many clients who have used marijuana compulsively, particularly writers who felt justified in its use because it made them more "creative." At a price, I'd say. You may be able to spill out chunks of seemingly creative ideas when you are high, but even if they do turn out to be relatively creative thoughts, what about the follow-through? Who is going to revise and edit those blurbs you were so proud of birthing when you were stoned? The problem is, marijuana doesn't come with muse-ijuana: You have to find that muse yourself. But with "amotivational syndrome"— the apathy that develops after long-term marijuana use— this can be pretty hard to do. Like other habits that help to fuel procrastination, the compulsive use of marijuana may appear to enhance creativity, but in reality it usually inhibits productivity in the long run.

And by helping you to avoid the "mundane" feeling of the day, chronic use of marijuana also keeps you anesthetized against the shame-based emotions you need to release in order to be free from procrastination once and for all. Because it may appear to temporarily lift your mood, marijuana can prevent you from dealing with a lifelong pattern of low-grade depression that may have inhibited your creativity and productivity for years.

Seeking the help of a qualified psychiatrist or acupuncture physician for antidepressant treatment, attending regular meetings of Narcotics Anonymous, learning how to meditate by reading such books as Joan Borysenko's *Minding the Body, Mending the Mind,* or finding alternative methods of relaxation through such books as *The Relaxation and Stress Reduction Workbook* by Martha Davis may prove to be helpful in providing you with other methods of coping with anxiety or other feelings that may be fueling your problems with procrastination.

* * * *

Compulsive Shopping/Spending/Gambling

Like other compulsive behaviors, those involving money, such as gambling or compulsive spending, can also induce an altered state of consciousness that can anesthetize individuals against feelings of shame that have triggered a pattern of procrastination. If the individual continues to shop or to spend money compulsively, he or she will continue to mask the shame-based issues that must be worked through in order to stop the cycle of procrastination and lead a healthier, productive life.

What is alarming, but not surprising, is that for many people, the compulsive use of money starts in childhood as a reaction to dysfunctional family issues. An article by Peter Freiberg in the American Psychological Association's monthly newspaper reported that researcher Durand Jacobs found that 75 percent of the children of problem gamblers had their first gambling experience before the age of 11 (compared with only 34 percent of subjects whose parents were not problem gamblers). Such a reliance on the compulsive use of money can obviously lead to serious problems, especially in terms of procrastination: It certainly isn't easy to pursue your life's goals when you are in a constant state of anxiety about where your next meal is coming from.

I have seen many clients whose financial stress brought them in for psychotherapy. However, it would soon become clear with most of these clients that compulsive spending was a contributing factor to their bankruptcy status. These individuals used compulsive spending as a way to mask their shame from childhood neglect and abuse. Many of them used their flashy new clothes and cars as status symbols to enhance their poor body images and waning self-esteem. For others, being in constant debt also offered a secondary pay-off in terms of "security": It kept them living in a constant state of chaos, which felt familiar, given their state of living during their dysfunctional childhoods.

For others, this false sense of "security" comes in the form of dependency as a necessity. In other words, since they are so far in debt, they can't afford to leave the homes of their families of origin, and thus they remain in the protected role of a financial dependent, accepting financial support in lieu of the emotional support they never received as children. Since they are not financially independent, they will procrastinate for years regarding career development, college and/or intimate relationships. They stay locked in this cycle of dependency, shame and procrastination—until they begin to unravel the mysteries of the past that have contributed to the pools of shame they've spent so many years avoiding.

For others, the dynamics underlying compulsive spending include fear of deprivation and co-dependency. For example, some individuals will use credit cards to buy excess groceries rather than do without certain high-priced items. If they want to go out to dinner, the movies or a club, it doesn't matter if they have the cash; they charge it. Because they felt deprived as children, they aren't about to deprive themselves of "life's little pleasures" as adults. By avoiding any feelings of deprivation, they are able to avoid the shame they felt as children, thereby postponing the recovery process from procrastination.

Other compulsive spenders have a particularly virulent form of co-dependency that helps to fuel their financial indebtedness. These individuals are certainly not averse to helping out with the financial crises of friends. They will allow others to put $2,000 purchases on their credit cards, and even though arrangements are often made for a repayment plan, you can guess where those "here and there" repayments end up, let alone who pays the interest on those $2,000 purchases. Other compulsive spenders will develop a pattern of sending money to friends or relatives who "need" it, because the compulsive spenders' need to feel good about themselves is often dependent on the approval of others. Although these compulsive spenders' intentions may be good in wanting to truly help others, by helping others in these ways, they are hurting themselves.

And each year, for Christmas, Easter, birthdays, Valentine's Day and any other holiday—any excuse will do—compulsive spenders will spend huge sums of money on gifts for loved ones, especially children. It is as if they are living through these children the childhood they never had—buying these children just what they themselves would have wanted at that age. They don't want these children to feel "deprived" in any way—it is as if by giving material goods to these children, these compulsive shoppers can somehow prevent themselves from having to feel the emotional deprivation they had felt as children.

For example, take a look (facing page) at the insight I gleaned by writing with my nondominant hand during my final compulsive Christmas experience. I had, of course, fooled myself into thinking that since I was buying less expensive gifts, it was fine to buy a large quantity of smaller gifts for the children of my siblings and close friends. However, these numerous gifts still cost money that I didn't have at the time, as well as time and energy and more money to wrap and mail them around the country. What I discovered by checking in with the right side of my brain was that I was still trying to make up for what my parents hadn't given to me (or my siblings) during childhood. In essence, I was acting like my mother, trying to patch up the holes in my self-esteem—and everyone else's, whether they needed it or not—with loads of brightly wrapped gifts. Each year, my mother would buy countless small gifts, then spend hours in self-avowed misery wrapping them. She'd dump them under the

Christmas tree as if these trinkets would make up for all that was missing the other 364 days of the year. Needless to say, it didn't work then and it doesn't work now.

Figure 6. Nondominant Handwriting

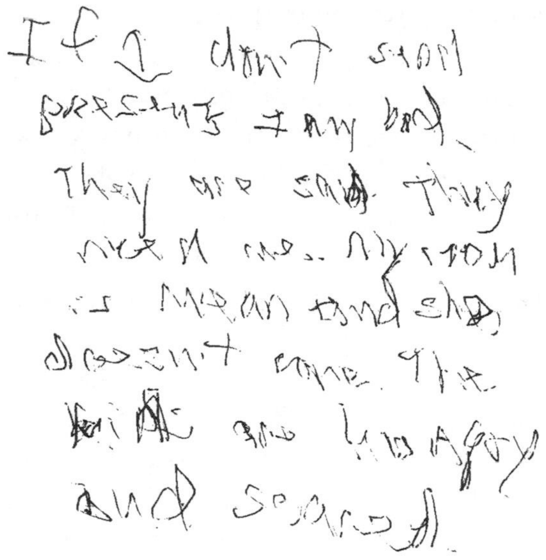

If I don't send presents I am bad. They are sad. They need me. My mom is mean and she doesn't care. The kids are hungry and scared.

As you can see, my attempt to cover up these feelings of shame ("I am bad") wasn't really working. I felt miserable, staying up late to wrap all of those gifts when I was exhausted, and the resentment was building. Something was wrong. When I checked in with the right side of my brain, I found the words you just read—a reminder that I needed to let go of this residual strand of co-dependency I'd carried since childhood. It simply wasn't my job to make up for the fact that my siblings ("the kids") were "hungry and scared" because my mother was too depressed to go grocery shopping and my father was too filled with rage to discipline his children with love instead of anger. As a child (and as an adult), I had placed myself in a caretaking position to my siblings, which made me feel exempt from being one of "the kids." Of course, I wasn't exempt at all. Confronting these old patterns and the accompanying painful feelings wasn't easy, but it certainly was worth it.

Many compulsive shoppers also spend a great deal of money on themselves, buying extravagant items they'll never use and don't need—items they could never afford if it weren't for that rich Uncle Visa or Aunt MasterCard. Other compulsive spenders will only spend small amounts of money on themselves, just for "little things." They will buy trinkets for themselves at every Dollarama sale at the local drugstore. Of course, they'll never spend the kind of money on themselves that they would spend on friends and family, but those little Dollarama gifts add up after a while—especially when you put them all on credit cards, year after year, while only making your "responsible" minimum payment each month on a Visa tab that starts to look like a Girl Scout convention receipt.

It is only after releasing childhood shame that such individuals are able to see that all these gifts for themselves and for others do not make them feel any better—except temporarily, just as those fleeting childhood moments of Christmas glee would dissipate into thin air as soon as the last piece of wrapping paper was crumpled and tossed under the dysfunctional family's tree. After facing the fact that they procrastinate because they now "don't have the money" to pursue their dreams, many compulsive spenders begin to see that compulsively spending money was just a mask for shame, a way to numb temporarily the feelings of stark pain they'd been hiding from all their lives. And though I know that many of these individuals have kept their commitments

to stop shopping compulsively—for others or for themselves—
I must say that each year at Christmas time I'm tempted to
start writing a book called *Co-dependent Some More!*

However, until then, you might want to consult such
books as *Overcoming Overspending* by Olivia Mellan and
Sherry Christie, or *How to Get Out of Debt, Stay Out of
Debt, and Live Prosperously* by Jerrold Mundis—or check
your local telephone directory for the nearest Debtors
Anonymous meeting.

* * * *

Television/Computer Addiction

Just as compulsive spending can mask the shame that
triggers procrastination, so, too, can the compulsive use of
television and computers offer an escape from the reali-
ties that must be faced in order to eradicate shame and
procrastination. Of course, a certain amount of time spent
watching entertaining or educational TV shows can offer
a healthy escape from the agitation of daily living.
Similarly, a game of computer solitaire can offer a much-
needed diversion.

However, when we turn to a TV or a VDT (video display
terminal) excessively or compulsively—especially if we are
delaying important tasks, or avoiding our partners—we
are most likely escaping from more than just commonplace
pressures. I have worked with numerous individuals
whose spouses or life partners spend every waking hour in
front of a TV or a VDT, even in the face of repeated
requests for more time together. Invariably, the underlying
factor involves, at least in part, a deep-seated fear of intimacy. It's much easier to spend time with a machine that
won't try to correct or reject you. As we've seen in previous

case examples, people who fear intimacy are reacting to earlier experiences in which they somehow suffered a loss of love. Thus, important tasks, as well as the growth of positive relationships, are put on hold.

Immersing yourself compulsively in any endeavor can lead to a numbing effect against the pain of shame, which in turn prevents recovery from procrastination. It short-circuits your decision-making capacity, productivity and creativity. A recent study by Patti Valkenburg and Tom van der Voort indicated that prolonged watching of television is associated with reduced creativity—a clear problem for individuals who compulsively use television to procrastinate regarding tasks requiring creativity. I have worked with a number of clients whose intense desire for the anesthetic effects of TV or a VDT has led them close to job loss or divorce. For others, procrastination regarding the development of their social lives has led to such loneliness that they are willing to spend hundreds of dollars each month to stay "connected" with others via the Internet or other online computer networks. If you're not sure whether you have crossed over into the realm of addiction, you may want to consult *Online Friendship, Chat-Room Romance and Cybersex* by Michael Adamse and Sheree Motta.

As with the compulsive behaviors of shopping or drug use, the immediate effect of on-screen addiction is instant gratification, but the long-term effect is a life lived alone and unfulfilled, surrounded by material objects, or hours of logged time, devoid of people and genuine accomplishments. Seeking therapy—particularly group therapy—can be the first step in sorting out just what has driven you into this state of frozen productivity.

* * * *

Compulsive Sex

In the age of AIDS, this mask for shame is perhaps the most dangerous, especially when combined with the diminished judgment that occurs with substance abuse. Many individuals use sex as part of an overall pattern of procrastination. Instead of studying or working, they might masturbate excessively, go "cruising" for sexual partners, or engage in compulsive sex with another person. The resulting reduction in anxiety does not, however, usually lead people back to a higher level of productivity. In other words, they don't exactly jump up out of bed to begin working on the procrastinated task. It's much more likely they'll have a cigarette, a drink, or something to eat—anything to prolong this avoidant high.

Of course, a good amount of healthy sexual activity (within the limits of safer sex) can calm the nerves and/or enhance feelings of intimacy. However, sexual addiction involves individuals who constantly crave the thrill of anonymity in casual sex or the release of endorphins in any type of sex just to get through the day or the week. These individuals are using compulsive sex as a mask for shame.

As I have discussed at length in my book chapter on "hidden populations" in *AIDS Prevention and Treatment: Hope, Humor and Healing,* it is likely that many of these individuals were sexually abused as children, and nearly all of them were physically abused or emotionally neglected. They use sex in an attempt to win the old battle against their abusers, as a way to control others, or to re-experience being controlled by others to understand how or why the childhood abuse occurred in the first place. I have worked with many procrastinators whose unresolved sexual abuse led to years of one-night stands. Needless to say, the level of productivity in these clients was severely restricted as a result of hangovers and loss of time spent in pursuit of emotional approval via sexual performance.

One client, a member of the 12-Step recovery group Sex and Love Addicts Anonymous, was surprised when I asked him how his SLAA group members felt about the risks of contracting HIV. "It never comes up," he said. Even though this level of denial may sound shocking—here is a group of people who openly admit they have problems with impulsive sex in the age of AIDS—I wasn't really all that surprised. Many people use a combination of sex, alcohol and drugs to dull psychological pain, long before they become aware of their childhood sexual abuse history. They tell themselves they enjoy the thrill of one-night stands, and they usually don't use condoms, even though they are dimly aware of the threat of syphilis, gonorrhea, chlamydia (a major cause of sterility), herpes (which can cause retardation or death in infants) and AIDS. It never occurs to them that they may have been abused as children and are simply trying to be in control of sex now. Instead, they think in terms of "going out to have a good time" or "getting wild." Considering the families of abusers many of them have been born into, they have no idea how true that old rock-and-roll song, "Born to be Wild," really is.

And it usually doesn't occur to these individuals that one-night stands are in any way interfering with creativity or productivity in terms of lost time and hangovers. It is all seen as just part of their routine, and still they constantly browbeat themselves because they can't ever seem to find the time to write or paint or be productive. Most of them don't think about the fact that alcohol is a depressant, that pot creates amotivational syndrome, or that the horror of HIV may be looming on the horizon of the next morning after. They are driven by a desire to use and to control others through sex, just as they were themselves probably used and controlled via sex as children. Such compulsive sexual behavior not only keeps individuals numbed, trapped in the vicious cycle of shame and procrastination, but it may also kill them. We live in a world where no one can afford to be "born to be wild" any longer.

Obviously, with such a dangerous pattern of living, psychotherapy can literally be a lifesaver in helping one to discover and to overcome the roots of sexual compulsivity, with an eventual by-product of increased productivity as yet another benefit of finally taking care of oneself. If you aren't sure whether your sexual patterns are compulsive, you may want to read any of the three books by Patrick Carnes on sexual compulsivity: *Out of the Shadows: Understanding Sexual Addiction, Contrary to Love,* or *Don't Call It Love.*

* * * *

Compulsive Exercise

Like compulsive sex, compulsive exercise can release large amounts of endorphins into a system depleted by depression, shame and procrastination. And, like sex, a certain amount of exercise is good. But it becomes destructive when we use it to avoid other problems. Rather than working on a project or sitting down to weigh the factors involved with an important decision, we may find ourselves literally running away.

However, since exercise is considered a positive element in our society, it may be difficult to tell when you've crossed over the line. In responding to the items below, try to give your first, gut-level response.

_____ I exercise more than one-and-a-half hours daily.
_____ I get extremely upset if I have to miss one day of
        exercise.

_____ I must complete my entire exercise routine every time I exercise.

_____ I never cancel my daily exercise routine for anyone or anything.

_____ My friends or family members complain frequently that my exercise interferes with things.

_____ I exercise even though it means I must neglect other very important tasks.

The more items on this list you checked off, the more likely it is that exercise has become a compulsive behavior for you. I have worked with many clients whose exercise was part of an eating disorder.

One young woman, a highly talented but procrastinating painter, was so terrified of gaining weight that she exercised for eight hours one day when the scale at the gym indicated she'd gained two pounds. Later that evening, Samantha found out that all the women in the gym had been upset until they had compared notes and realized that the scale had been off by two pounds.

In telling me about this mechanical error, Samantha was chagrined, but not horrified, that she'd nearly killed herself over two pounds. The fact that she had gone above the magic scale's number of 100 pounds tapped into her shame: She was no longer the "good little girl." This was so threatening that she was willing to risk her life to get back her size 5 shame mask. However, once Samantha began to understand that her shame was rooted in childhood events emanating from neglect and abuse, she was able to begin the process of recovery from compulsive exercise and from procrastination regarding her art.

In most other cases, compulsive exercise is usually not so life-threatening. But it may be keeping you from living a fuller life.

One client was so overwhelmed with life decisions that he began to exercise obsessively as a way of coping with the anxiety he felt about his career and his relationships. David soon began to realize that he was using exercise to avoid making any decisions that would break him away from his mother, who had always encouraged him to remain overly attached to her so that she would never be alone. He was her confidant and her comfort whenever she felt upset with her husband. David, who had just turned 21, felt that by getting on with his own life, he would be abandoning his mother. He was terrified that she would no longer love him if he spent time pursuing a career or any relationship.

Upon closer scrutiny of his feelings and his early years, David was able to recall that his mother would ignore him if he did not meet her demands for attention. He was abandoned by his mother every time he tried to make friends in the neighborhood or spend extra time in school activities. To avoid feeling that rejection, David had turned to compulsive exercise so he could avoid making friends, dating women, or developing a career that might take him away from his mother, who, in turn, might emotionally abandon him again. Once David realized that his mother needed him more than he needed her—that he held "the chips" in terms of their relationship—he set limits with his mother in a healthy way. David no longer has such high levels of anxiety about rejection, and the compulsive use of exercise has little appeal for him now.

In other cases, exercise is often used simply for its endorphin release by individuals who are so deeply depressed that they cannot live without the mood-elevating effects of sustained physical activity. Certainly, a healthy amount of exercise is beneficial, but when taken to an extreme, it usually means we are avoiding some painful underlying emotion. But no matter what the stated or implied purpose underlying excessive exercise, the real culprit underneath it all is shame. And this shame must be released in order to change the pattern of using exercise as a form of procrastination.

* * * *

Workaholism

In our society, work is viewed as a positive endeavor. As Gloria Steinem says in her marvelous book, *Revolution from Within: A Book of Self-Esteem* (p. 91), workaholism as a "drug of choice" is "the only one an addict is paid and praised for taking." But like exercise, too much of a good thing can lead to compulsive behavior and problems with procrastination. Most workaholics will protest by saying, "How can you say people are procrastinating when they work too much?"

The answer is quite clear: If you are working compulsively many hours of the day, every day, and are plagued with guilt if you don't, then we have to ask why. What keeps us from having a set schedule like everyone else, with time off for "good behavior"? We all know it's not healthy to spend the bulk of our time working, yet many of us continue to do just that. Or we spend hours of time intending to work, whittling the day away, neither working nor relaxing, and end up feeling the day has been wasted. What's stopping us from having the pendulum balanced between work and play?

Of course by now you know the answer: shame. We are ashamed of our imperfect work and spend all of our time trying to fix it; we are ashamed of our level of productivity and spend our time trying to produce more. It's as if we must work in order to justify our existence—as if we don't deserve to take time out and relax until we've accomplished just so much. Unfortunately, whatever we accomplish is never enough; it can never erase the shame we feel inside. Just as the anorexic promises to stop "dieting" when a certain weight is reached (but then keeps lowering the figure), workaholics say they'll stop when they've accomplished a goal or a project is finished. But then another goal or project pops up out of nowhere.

Procrastination dominates most every other area of the workaholic's life. The development of intimate relationships is postponed, time off for vacation is perennially delayed, and above all, the underlying shame that propels workaholism is never addressed. While the co-worker or spouse is forever saying things like, "When are you ever going to do X, Y or Z?" the workaholic feels completely justified in his or her procrastination regarding these issues, because the "work" that he or she considers most important is being addressed—but never finished. And the life of the workaholic, fueled by shame, is forever doomed to replicate hour after hour of unfulfilling effort.

> *One client had spent so much time working that he had begun to wonder what all the fuss was about outside of work. Edward didn't see the need to take time off because it was a waste of time. He had procrastinated for years regarding any kind of self-nurturance, whether that meant taking time off for a one-hour massage, a game of tennis or a two-week vacation.*
>
> *However, once he began to explore the emotional deprivation of his childhood, he began to see that he literally did not know what he'd been missing.*

In many respects, Edward's case was similar to my own. As a child, I'd spent hours with what I now see was a reading addiction; it served as a perfect apprenticeship to my later problems with workaholism. In time I developed a "reader's block" for fiction. I could only read fiction if it was part of an academic assignment. Then I would read it with an analytic vengeance but I was too far removed from the world of real emotions to deal with the feelings the book was meant to arouse.

Then, as I began to succeed more and more in the academic realm, I took on the serious pace of a workaholic and proceeded to extend that pattern into the next decade of work positions as well.

It was only after I was able to release the shame involved in my childhood experiences that I finally started to see just what it was that I'd been missing for so many years by procrastinating in terms of human relationships, relaxation and good old-fashioned self-actualization. But now that I'm out of procrastination prison, I'm determined to stay out. The cost of recidivism is just too high. Reading books like Diane Fassel's *Working Ourselves to Death* or Bryan Robinson's *Overdoing It: How to Slow Down and Take Care of Yourself* may be helpful to you in overcoming this debilitating pattern as well.

* * * *

Exchanging Compulsion for Competence and Completion

Obviously, the antidote for compulsive behaviors is shame release. However, even though such techniques as those discussed in chapter 6 can be very helpful in terms of shame release, giving up compulsive and addictive behaviors is never an easy task. You can't just yank your inner child out of the protective layers involved in the process of procrastination, but instead must encourage him or her to come out to "play." Try not to order him or her to produce at your command—that sounds too much like those who shamed you in the past. Rather, it is essential that you are compassionate with that frightened inner self who's been hiding beneath all of your compulsive behaviors, and coax him or her out so that you'll no longer need to engage in compulsive-avoidant behaviors to mask your shame.

But this is easier said than done, because compulsive-addictive behaviors offer immediate gratification and relief. The long-term devastating side effects tend to get lost in one's perspective, to say the very least. Trying to release your shame is difficult if you are masking it with compulsive behaviors.

For many individuals, 12-Step organizations such as Workaholics Anonymous can be helpful in initiating and maintaining abstinence from compulsive behaviors as a prelude to shame release. For others, it is helpful to begin with a more physiological approach, such as acupuncture treatments, Ayurvedic medicine, antidepressants, herbal remedies, vitamin therapies, yoga, meditation or moderate exercise. It may also be important to seek out a competent psychotherapist so you can discover the source of the shame that triggered your use of compulsive-addictive behaviors as a form of procrastination.

Although it may seem impossible to think of your life without using compulsive behavior to cope, it is well worth the risk to find out how much better you can feel once your life is truly your own. Being in charge of your own life is the antidote to procrastination, and once you've had a drop or two of that magical elixir, you'll find it easier to let go of the compulsive behaviors that have continued to poison your life.

8

And If That Doesn't Stop You: The Role of Physiological Factors in Procrastination

*I know people who are
totally paralyzed—who have no
control over their bodies—people who are in
prison, and these people are joyful because they
are choosing to be.*

—Bernie Siegel

Physiological Factors That Create Spasms in Levels of Productivity

When a client first comes into my office seeking relief from procrastination, I am always aware that it's important to determine if any physiological problems are present that may be aggravating the problem and intensifying the urge for addictive behaviors, such as compulsive eating or substance abuse. The possibility of physiological factors that can intensify procrastination patterns is, of course, endless. Table 4 lists some of the more common problems I have seen that can cause SPASMS in productivity, creativity or effective decision-making. Although these factors are usually sporadic in nature, when they are added to a chronic pattern of procrastination, the results can be devastating. However, what is most crucial in treating these physiologically com-pounded cases of procrastination is not the physical problem per se, but rather the shame associated with the physical problem, or the pre-existing shame that has been displaced onto the physiological problem.

TABLE 4
Physiological Factors That Create
SPASMS in Levels of Productivity

S Serious Medical Problems

P Premenstrual Syndrome

A Attention-Deficit/Hyperactivity Disorder

S Seasonal Affective Disorder

M Menopause/Andropause

S Stress-Related Illness

In terms of our spiritual destinies, it's important to remember that the genetic blueprint for these problems, as well as the shame and procrastination that often accompany them, is present at birth, and thus part of our life lessons. Our bodies have fault lines, or potential fracture sites, where stress is most likely to cause an eruption. On the pages that follow, I will discuss a few of these possible fault lines and some remedies. The intent is to illustrate the fact that the problem of procrastination is multifaceted and that the entire human "organism" must be considered during diagnosis; otherwise, both client and counselor are likely to perceive "resistance" that may, in actuality, only be a bad case of premenstrual syndrome or perhaps attention-deficit/hyperactivity disorder.

Serious Medical Problems

Serious and even minor medical problems must be treated with top priority before we apply ourselves to other tasks. However, in the cases that I have seen, it is usually the issue of shame rather than the medical illness per se that seems to aggravate the problem of procrastination.

I once worked with a young man who had been born with facial deformities. After years of surgeries, even Todd agreed that his appearance was quite "normal." He had attained a certain level of self-confidence, despite years of ridicule by other grade-school children. However, for years Todd had procrastinated regarding his return to college, fearful of being "the new kid in the class" again.

Upon closer scrutiny, it became apparent that Todd had suffered from maternal neglect from early childhood until early adulthood. His shame at not being properly loved by his depressive, aloof mother had been masked by his shame over his physical appearance. Once Todd was able to access his feelings about his mother, he was well on the way to releasing the shame that had blocked him—and well on his way back to college as well.

* * *

A similar case occurred with a young photographer who had chronic fatigue syndrome. Although Janice was quite talented, she feared being successful. She even had difficulty collecting payment for the work she was producing. For years, she had delayed finding full-time employment because she had a son with severe health problems. In addition, Janice's battle with chronic fatigue often left her without energy. She had explored the use of hypnosis as part of her "mind-body" healing program but had been unable to benefit from it.

Once Janice began to explore her anxiety on a deeper level, she realized that she was terrified of going to work full-time. She feared the idea of not being a "good" parent to her son since she herself had been emotionally neglected as a child. It was her own sense of shame and inadequacy, generated by her sense of emotional deprivation as a child, that was leading Janice to conclude that she was not permitted to pursue her dream of working full-time. Instead, she felt that she must put herself in the full servitude of her son and continue to neglect herself—the way her parents had. Eventually, Janice chose to remain a part-time photographer, which was sensible, given her tendency toward physical fatigue. However, she did learn to stand up for herself and ask for payment upon completion of her photography assignments.

* * *

In another case involving serious medical problems, procrastination was also a central issue. Mitch denied the seriousness of his battle with heart disease and diabetes, to himself and others. He was a single man in his late 50s who was forced to change his lifestyle and admit that he could no longer hold down a full-time job as a high-pressured executive. Plagued by depression, Mitch had procrastinated for nearly a year regarding the necessary paperwork to make a claim on his disability insurance policy. Although he was entitled to receive the benefits, Mitch was terrified to admit that he was "disabled," since that meant he was no longer independent and in control of his life. He had always been financially responsible and did not want to be dependent on others for his survival.

Once he focused on these issues, Mitch was able to see that his fear of being dependent on others was clearly rooted in his relationship with his mother. Since the mother had been controlling, hypercritical and openly rejecting, Mitch had learned to take care of himself at an early age, ensuring that he would never be indebted to his mother. Thus, the shame of such maternal rejection had followed Mitch throughout his life; it had already cost him thousands of dollars in insurance benefits as a result of his late application. However, by finally filling out the paperwork, Mitch took the first step in adjusting to his new status in life. Even more amazing, he began to accept—and expect—help from friends and neighbors.

I have also worked with other clients whose genetic blueprints had set them up for breast tumors. The resulting complications of their removal have led to breast implants and eventual silicone poisoning with chronic fatigue syndrome, among other autoimmune problems, as a complication. In several of these cases, procrastination was a central issue. Some of these women were single, divorced or widowed; they had delayed dating again, since they felt like "damaged merchandise." Although the shame that these women felt appeared to be related primarily to their breast disfigurement, often this shame was related to childhood feelings of deprivation or loss. Once the earlier issues were addressed, these women were able to take a more realistic stance toward their medical problems and toward their personal appearance. They came to see that others wouldn't necessarily run away in horror upon seeing that they no longer had "perfect" breasts.

In other cases of silicone poisoning, procrastination was more directly linked to the medical condition—at least at first glance. Although the silicone implants in some of these women had ruptured, the clients had avoided seeking medical assistance for their resultant pain, chronic fatigue and depression. While they knew implant removal would help, they deprived themselves of potential relief. They reasoned that having the implants removed meant further disfigurement, since the cosmetic results with "uplifts" (rebuilding breast tissue from body material taken from the stomach or elsewhere) were never guaranteed.

In some of these cases, what came to light was the fact that pre-existing fears and a sense of shame about not being attractive enough were at the core of this procrastination regarding medical attention.

One case in particular illustrates just how this early emphasis on physical attractiveness can cause irrationality in later life, especially when one is facing surgery. During art therapy and a photohistory session, one woman who had suffered silicone poisoning from breast implants was startled to see that from infancy on, she and her twin sister had been dressed like little dolls and posed for the camera in every shot. She recalled how important it was for the children in her family to look attractive, no matter what the occasion.

Pam was doubly confused about her self-worth because her grandmother (who had raised Pam after the sudden death of her parents in a car accident) had been verbally critical of Pam as a child, constantly fussing over her appearance. The message was loud and clear: If you want my attention you must be physically appealing.

Thus Pam's fear of possible disfigurement was rooted in the shame she had felt as a child for not being loved. If she were to risk an operation, she'd also be risking reliving the pain of rejection. Once Pam faced these old dynamics and made the decision to have the implants removed, she began to feel a sense of hope that her life could improve and that she could feel good about herself.

In yet another case of medically aggravated procrastination, I worked with a young, HIV-positive male who had put off two of his major goals in life: achieving unconditional love and acceptance from his parents, and fulfilling the notion that he could have an intimate, loving relationship. Terry had kept both of these goals at bay because of a strong feeling that he didn't deserve love and attention. His story is a long and complicated tale of emotional, physical and sexual abuse—and yet what this young man knew that he wanted when all was said and done was simply love and the ability to forgive.

Though his parents had rejected him, Terry wanted to forgive his father for beating him and blaming him when, as a child, Terry had been led unwittingly into a sexually abusive encounter with an older man. Terry also wanted to forgive his mother for emotionally abusing him repeatedly as a child. And Terry wanted to experience genuine love, affection and intimacy in the context of a healthy relationship with a caring life partner.

After much soul-searching, making peace with his own son and forgiving his parents, Terry died as he had wished—in the loving arms of his parents who now knew and grieved deeply for what they had lost, and with the continuing love of a man who had stood by him to the end, a man he'd met by fulfilling his life's dream of going to Italy. And though he died before he was 25, Terry was finally able to conquer the shame-based procrastination that had kept his life unfulfilled—until the end, when he took all the love he needed with him.

* * * *

Premenstrual Syndrome

The problem of PMS (which can occur anywhere between days 14 to 28 of a woman's cycle, with day 1 being the first day of menstruation) has received a considerable amount of attention within the last few years. However, many women still don't know how to reduce the symptoms of this condition that affects anywhere from 30 to 90 percent of the female population, according to various experts such as Katharina Dalton.

Among the symptoms of PMS (some of which are listed in table 5 on the next page), the ability to concentrate is perhaps the most problematic in terms of procrastination. Many women will start a project, only to lose their momentum two weeks into it, right after ovulation triggers a plummeting level of endorphins and serotonin in their hormonal systems. They begin to crave foods that will replenish these mood-enhancing neurotransmitters—foods high in sugar, white flour and fat—and quickly become lethargic and unable to concentrate. Or they may crave salty foods, which increase irritability and weaken concentration due to water retention. To combat feelings of lethargy, many women will drink coffee or colas containing caffeine, which will in turn trigger a "stress response" in the body and eventually increase irritability and further reduce concentration. (Or they may have a few drinks to "relax" because they feel so tense, without realizing they'll have a much more intense "hangover" the next day during the PMS phase.) Additionally, the feelings of helplessness and worthlessness that accompany PMS not only feed into any pre-existing pool of shame a woman might have, but they also can lead the woman to question the worth of the procrastinated project at hand in the first place.

Table 5
Common Symptoms of PMS That
Trigger Procrastination

Food cravings:	Increased consumption of white flour products, sugar, fat: can lead to irritability, lethargy, apathy and subsequent overconsumption of caffeine (which in turn can heighten irritability)
Alcohol cravings:	Increase in desire for alcohol, decrease in ability to tolerate alcohol: can lead to quick intoxication and hypoglycemic symptoms of low frustration tolerance, tearfulness and poor concentration
Mood swings:	From angry to sad to apathetic: can interfere with clarity of thought
Energy level:	Edgy feelings or lethargy: can decrease motivation to complete tasks or make decisions
Concentration:	Easily irritated and distracted: can lead to task avoidance

One client, a very intelligent woman in her 30s, had a severe case of PMS that interfered with her ability to pass her medical school exams. Ruth would often procrastinate instead of studying. We quickly traced this avoidance of success to her history of childhood abuse. However, I began to notice a cyclical pattern in her behavior. At times Ruth seemed motivated to study, but at other times she was not. Once she was diagnosed with PMS, the problem was clarified. Every two weeks, Ruth would shift into a different frame of mind. Her mood would darken, she was prone to sudden outbursts of anger, and she could not concentrate on her reading.

Furthermore, like many women with PMS, Ruth compulsively overate the very foods that tend to aggravate PMS symptoms: white flour products, sugar, chocolate and salt. Like many women, her sex drive also increased during the few days just prior to menstruation, as did her cravings for caffeine and alcohol. What Ruth didn't know was that when she had PMS her tolerance for alcohol was lowered. She would become intoxicated on half the usual amount; feeling bloated and unattractive, she would fall into bed with the first man who paid attention to her. Aside from the heightened risk of HIV transmission, these physiological factors of PMS would of course aggravate Ruth's existing problems with procrastination. Intensely hung over, ashamed and exhausted, the last thing she felt like doing was memorizing the bones of the human body— she'd studied enough anatomy the night before, thank you.

Ruth was aware that her sexual abuse as a child was also a contributing factor to her sexual promiscuity. She was still trying to win the old battle for control, but she also began to see what a prominent role PMS was playing in her procrastination. She began to exercise moderately, eat a healthier diet, and take vitamins and various herbs such as evening primrose oil and ginger. She even sought out a competent acupuncture physician to reduce her PMS symptoms.

Table 6 offers a partial list of remedies for reducing or eliminating the symptoms of PMS. Further information can be found in Dr. Susan Lark's *Premenstrual Syndrome Self-Help Book,* which includes recipes, acupressure massage points, yoga exercises and nutritional recommendations for treating over 150 symptoms of PMS.

Table 6
Self-Help for PMS Symptoms

Medication	Natural progesterone, antidepressants
Nutrition	Avoid chocolate, caffeine, alcohol, sugar, excessive dairy products, white flour products, salt, food additives or chemicals ("processed foods"); eat plenty of fresh fruits/vegetables
Herbs, Vitamins, Minerals	Consult with your physician or herbalist to select appropriate herbal remedies, such as ginger, as well as a supplement that is high in B-complex vitamins and minerals, such as calcium and magnesium (see *Prescription for Nutritional Healing,* by James & Phyllis Balch)
Exercise	Moderate aerobic exercise (walking, jogging, swimming, bicycling), preferably every day for 20 to 45 minutes
Acupuncture, Acupressure Massage, Yoga, Meditation, Aromatherapy	See Lark's *Premenstrual Syndrome Self-Help Book*

* * * *

Attention-Deficit/Hyperactivity Disorder

In recent years, attention-deficit/hyperactivity disorder (ADHD) has received a good deal of attention. Teachers and parents are taking care to note the symptoms of ADHD (some of which are listed in table 7), rather than browbeating a child for not achieving or paying attention in school.

Many children carry the residual effects of ADHD into

adulthood; unfortunately, many ADHD sufferers don't even
know they have it. Since it tends to run in families, people
will often attribute outbursts of rage or poor impulse control
to the notion that "he's just like his father."

Table 7
Symptoms of ADHD in Adulthood

Underachievement

Undersocialized (inappropriate social responses)

Difficulty getting organized

Trouble starting projects

Trouble finishing projects

Poor impulse control

Easy distractibility

Difficulty with concentration

Easily bored

Mood swings

Sudden outbursts of anger

Restlessness

Impatience

Low self-esteem

Tendency to worry excessively

Tendency toward addictive behaviors

Tendency toward high intelligence

According to Dr. Edward Hallowell and Dr. John Ratey,
two psychiatrists with ADHD who have written a book
called *Driven to Distraction,* about 15 million Americans

suffer from ADHD; two-thirds of childhood ADHD sufferers do not outgrow it. Many of these adults were never diagnosed with ADHD as children, so they walk around tormenting themselves for being underachievers and procrastinators. People must realize that ADHD is thought to be caused by an imbalance in the body's neurotransmitters, specifically good old Aunt Serotonin, Uncle Dopamine and Cousin Norepinephrine—The Big Three when it comes to the physiological balance needed for clear thinking, motivation and the eradication of procrastination.

I worked with a woman whose ADHD was so severe that she had remained isolated, living at home with her parents into her mid-40s, with no job, no friends and no social life. Kristie was aware of her ADHD diagnosis, but her shame was so great that I had to attack that before I could treat her procrastination. During our first visit, this highly intelligent and creative woman constantly referred to herself as "lazy." Gently, I asked her to hand over that four-letter word, then I opened the window and "threw it" onto the street below. She understood immediately and seemed grateful not to be judged for her "problems."

It soon became apparent that the reason Kristie had procrastinated in getting a job or returning to college was because she was so ashamed of her past mistakes. During her childhood, she had failed repeatedly in her attempts to make friends, due to her demanding attitude and short temper. Furthermore, compulsive overeating, which had served as a stress release, was catching up with Kristie in terms of weight gain as well as increased levels of shame.

I felt it was essential to get Kristie on some form of medication. She had tried to use Ritalin, a stimulant used with ADHD sufferers, but the results had not been good. However, once I referred her to a psychiatrist who specialized in

ADHD, Kristie was put on a combination regimen of Ritalin and an antidepressant. The results were striking.

With the combined effects of our weekly therapy sessions and the psychiatrist's close monitoring, Kristie began to feel more confident, less depressed and more willing to make behavioral changes. She was able to concentrate and interact with others. She returned to college, picked up a part-time job and even began to experiment with social con-versation outside of therapy. By making lists, keeping to a schedule and mastering anger-management techniques (issues discussed in Driven to Distraction *as well as in Dr. Lynn Weiss's book,* Attention Deficit/Hyperactivity Disorder in Adults*), Kristie felt a stronger sense of control over her own life. She began to welcome the social and academic situations she had avoided as potential sources of shame.*

* * *

Another client with ADHD, a problem that most experts agree tends to strike males more than females, had turned to substance abuse in an attempt to self-medicate. Howard had procrastinated for two years regarding his career and wasn't quite sure why. An intelligent, highly resourceful 19-year-old man, Howard was unfocused and miserable. He had turned to cocaine and alcohol to cope with symp-toms that paralleled those of ADHD.

(According to Drs. Hallowell and Ratey, cocaine is very attractive to undiagnosed ADHD patients who may use it once on a lark, but quickly find that it helps them to focus rather than getting them "high," and they become chronic users. For them, cocaine is the closest thing to Ritalin, which they don't even know they might need.)

Howard had been sent into therapy by his parents as an ultimatum, but he really did seem to want out of the entrapment of his lifestyle. He was willing to quit abusing both alcohol and cocaine, but he also seemed to have a physiological need for these psychoactive substances. When I questioned Howard about his delay regarding a career change, he expressed a sense of futility that he would ever amount to anything. He admitted that he was filled with shame as a result of his underachievement and that his binges on alcohol and cocaine seemed to be his only relief.

Upon further exploration, it became clear that his verbally abusive boss, the top man in the company, was reminiscent of Howard's cruel older brother. Though I had some difficulty convincing Howard that his brother's severe physical abuse was still affecting him, Howard did begin to see the parallels in his current life in terms of his attempt to win the old battle for self-esteem and approval.

Once the connection to ADHD was made, Howard was able to release not only the shame attached to his childhood issues, but also the guilt of being an "underachiever." I can still see the pride in his face as he came back to report during his last session that he had found a new job with higher pay, more intellectual challenge, and respect— something that he finally had for himself now that he was no longer abusing alcohol or cocaine.

* * * *

Seasonal Affective Disorder

Seasonal affective disorder (SAD) also goes undiagnosed and untreated in many cases. Whenever I see a client whose procrastination or eating disorder tends to worsen during the autumn and/or winter months, I start looking at SAD as a possible culprit. In his recent book, *Winter Blues,* Dr. Norman Rosenthal discusses the fact that SAD tends to run in families and affects four times as many women as men. This seasonal pattern of depression occurs most often during the fall and winter months when there is less sunshine (although other seasonal patterns of this disorder can occur as well).

Without bright light, our bodies are unable to produce the correct amounts of melatonin and serotonin, substances that have both been implicated in the development of depression. Like other forms of depression, SAD results in decreased motivation, inability to concentrate and increased cravings for caffeine, alcohol and drugs—all of which can aggravate the problem of procrastination. In discussing treatments for SAD, Dr. Rosenthal, the director of light therapy studies at the National Institute of Mental Health, recommends not only "light therapy" but also changes in diet (eating carbohydrates can have the reverse effect of increasing rather than decreasing energy), more exercise, less sleep (melatonin is usually produced while one sleeps), psychotherapy and possibly antidepressant medication.

Once diagnosed, SAD sufferers who resist using such treatments are, in essence, saying they don't deserve to feel better. This, of course, indicates a pre-existing problem with shame that must be addressed in order to eradicate not only the symptoms of SAD, but also the problem of procrastination.

Because I currently practice in Florida, where only 1.4 percent of the population suffers from SAD (according to Dr. Rosenthal), my caseload is relatively free of individuals suffering from this malady. However, for me, living up north for some 30-odd years, I found myself more depressed during the fall and winter—as if my pre-existing level of depression wasn't enough! I was less productive during these two seasons as well.

However, once I began an exercise program, I noticed that the fall and winter months weren't nearly so bad for me, particularly since I had begun to jog outdoors, even in subfreezing weather, in the light of day. As I have stated earlier, I had other reasons for wanting to be outdoors in the light of day, away from the darkened households where I never felt safe, so it's difficult to say how much of my problem was SAD and how much was just plain "sad." If I ever move north again, you can bet I'll be on the lookout for my very own "standard 2500-lux light box"—which Dr. Rosenthal says could benefit 20 percent of the U.S. population—if I should ever hit the feeling of being sad in capital letters again!

* * * *

Menopause/Andropause

Menopause, the proverbial change of life, called by some experts "andropause" in men, is something we'll all have to face sooner or later, if we haven't already. This medical issue alone is often not enough to trigger a protracted case of procrastination. But when it's mixed with unresolved childhood issues, the effects of mid-life hormonal changes are compounded.

In several women I treated, it appeared on the surface that menopause was the primary factor in their procrastination. However, these women were taking normally effective dosages of antidepressants as well as hormone replacements, neither of which seemed to be helping. Upon closer scrutiny, it became clear that residual shame from childhood issues turned out to be a potent force in triggering problems with procrastination.

In one case, a menopausal client had been putting off a career as a sculptor. Although Betty had finally started to do a small amount of sculpting, she stated that she just felt "too close to tears from hormones all of the time," and therefore could not bring herself to enter any of her pieces into an art show for fear of public humiliation. Her reluctance was due not only to hormonally induced emotional distress, but to feelings of low self-worth stemming from her status as a child of an alcoholic. Gradually, she began to see that her fear of rejection was holding her back, not her hormones.

* * *

In another case, a woman with severe menopausal symptoms that were resistant to medical intervention came to see me for "depression." Jean had refused to "let go" of her deceased husband and get on with her life. Her inability to concentrate, her depressive episodes and extreme mood swings had made it virtually impossible for her to return to any type of work. When we delved more deeply into her past, it became clear that Jean's procrastination was a protective force to keep her from facing old issues.

Just as Jean's father had abandoned her family when she was five years old, leaving her feeling as if she "had done something wrong to make him leave," so had Jean's husband abandoned her suddenly. Without any warning signs of previous illness, he had died of a massive stroke. For Jean to return to work meant she would have to accept the loss of her husband and her previous way of life. She would have to face her feelings of abandonment. Although it appeared that Jean's menopausal symptoms were the primary factor involved with putting off her career, it was the age-old culprit of shame that was the real trigger when all was said and done.

* * * *

Stress-Related Illness

As mentioned earlier, physiological complications of procrastination can be seen in the genetic blueprint of an individual at birth—and stress-related disorders are no exception. From allergies to back problems, I could recite an entire litany of disorders that can interfere with one's concentration and motivation. I will focus on just a few examples in order to illustrate the fact that procrastination problems must be viewed with a wide-angle lens if we are to see the larger picture necessary for treatment. It is not just the physiological problem per se that triggers procrastination, but rather, the interactive effect of present shame and pre-existing shame that usually creates problems in motivation.

For example, allergies are much more prevalent than we think and are often triggered by stress, according to nutritionist Dr. Gary Null in his book entitled *No More Allergies*. Without a long digression on types of allergies and their symptoms, suffice it to say that I have worked with individuals who have had allergies of all kinds, and whose symptoms of lethargy, irritability and poor concentration had been able to wreak havoc with their level of productivity. However, it was usually earlier childhood events that had left these clients with the unconscious notion that they didn't deserve to feel better by seeing an allergist or by changing their living habits to accommodate their immune systems. Again, it's usually the interaction of shame and a physical problem that makes for a more protracted case of procrastination.

Similarly, I have worked with a number of clients whose stress triggered the re-enactment of old injuries, or at the very least prevented current injuries from healing, thereby interfering with motivation and productivity.

Richard is a highly intelligent young man whose physical limitations from a serious work-related accident had left him bereft of career choices (or so he thought). He worked part-time as a desk clerk in an executive office building, but was clearly dissatisfied. Richard came to me for treatment of procrastination, knowing that he was capable of accomplishing more. His constant physical pain usually left him feeling tired, and he spent a considerable amount of time going from one healer to another. The chiropractic and acupuncture work had abated some of Richard's physical pain, but now he wanted to work on his psychological pain, especially since stress increased his physical pain, which in turn limited him even further.

As we explored Richard's history, he started to see that he was ashamed whenever he was socializing (he feared telling others he wasn't gainfully employed), because he feared others would judge him as much as he judged himself. He was also afraid of being successful. Richard's parents had made it clear to him as a child that he was to meet their needs and that he was not to outshine them in any way. Unfortunately, the job-related accident had offered Richard a golden opportunity to fulfill his parents' unwritten rule. However, as he began to see that his physical pain was just a mask for his psychological shame, Richard was able to start making choices that could lead him out of procrastination prison and into a more meaningful and productive life.

Which is something we all deserve to have. Now.

9

Karma, Dharma and All That Jazz: How to Bargain in Good Faith with Destiny

He who perceives the Self everywhere never shrinks from anything . . .

—The Upanishads

A Final Report on Procrastination

Earlier in this book, I expounded on a plot line of a certain episode of *Star Trek* as an oracle for our times. Well, just yesterday, during the "reward" segment of my contingency management plan to finish this book, I was channel-surfing during a commercial in the middle of yet another *Star Trek* episode, and I happened upon an old film about Bernadette, the young French maiden who saw the famous visions of the Virgin Mary at Lourdes in 1858. She was telling a couple of other women that they must keep her secret.

"If Mama should hear of it, she might take a stick to me," she said.

Later on, the mother does find out the secret. She says, "Girls your age often see things that don't exist. You must put it out of your mind."

At first glance, this probably doesn't seem to have much to do with procrastination. But just as I said in chapter 1 that I wished I'd had this book as a clue to my inner self some 15 or 20 years ago, so, too, perhaps could we look to young Bernadette for a clue that could have helped us worldwide over 100 years ago. And with all due respect, I'm not talking about her vision of the Virgin Mary.

I'm talking about her automatic acceptance of "a stick" as a normal expression of parental displeasure, and her mother's automatic assumption that we must "put out of mind" anything that we can't see—as though that means it does not exist. In one brief flash, this scene encapsulates our tradition of childhood abuse as well as our denial of the things that really matter: self-esteem, tolerance for our children's individuality and openness to new ideas. Just as poor Bernadette faced the ridicule of the townspeople and the wrath of the religious authorities, so, too, do we challenge the notions of our ancestors, as well as our own integrity, when we search for the truth about the roots of our procrastination. When we give up the protection of procrastination to find the answers we need in order to heal, we have created a miraculous vision of a better future for humanity.

So what does this add up to when all is said and done? You can now see if nothing else that procrastination is not a simple matter. Whenever people ask me what causes procrastination, now I guess I'll have the luxury of handing them this book instead of saying, "Well, that's kind of a long story." When I first sought the answer for my problems with procrastination, I, too, thought I'd find one simple answer.

And although I could answer that question now with one word—shame—I'd still have to say that procrastination is a multifaceted issue when I look at the who, what, when, where, and why of it all.

Who

Who is likely to be prone to procrastination? Anyone currently living on Planet Earth.

I've stopped asking, "Why me?" when I look at my childhood experiences and the resulting years of shame and procrastination. I feel as if I have passed onto the third stage of recovery—from victim to survivor to thriver. What's important to me now is that I've learned some powerful lessons about compassion. And that's a gift I get to keep. I can think of easier ways to learn about compassion, mind you, but just because a gift isn't wrapped doesn't mean it's not a worthwhile gift.

You've probably never thought of procrastination as a gift. But it is. By protecting you from shame until you are ready to face it, and by being a prophet about your life lessons, procrastination can be seen as a gift in disguise.

Throughout this book, I have been asking you to discover the underlying dynamics of your problems and to work through the accompanying residual shame. If part of your inner pool of shame comes from intentional neglect or abuse, it's important—*after* you have worked through the pain—to forgive, but not to forget. If you forgive *before* you have worked through your pain, it's called good old-fashioned denial. If you forget what happened, you won't be able to protect the next generation from enduring similar forms of neglect or abuse. We're less likely to repeat mistakes once we realize that we were rejected as children simply because our caretakers were flawed, rather than because we were unlovable.

Once you have discovered the reasons underlying your problems with procrastination, and once you have done your fair share of weeping and wailing and gnashing of teeth, then it is time to forgive.

I didn't find it easy; I kept thinking that if I forgave my abusers, even if only in my heart rather than in person, then somehow I would be condoning what they did *to* me and what they didn't do *for* me. Gradually, I realized that was not true. As long as I held hatred in my heart for them, I was still allowing them to control me. *They were still in my heart.* It's like letting go of an ex-boyfriend or an ex-wife. As long as you still feel rage and hurt in your heart, then you're still attached to that person and cannot really move on. When you have moved from love to hate to indifference or even forgiveness, you are free. And once I realized that forgiving my abusers doesn't necessarily mean having relationships with them again—just because I changed doesn't mean they will—then I began to take those first few steps in letting go.

Some of my spiritual beliefs were of great assistance to me during this final step in moving from victim to survivor to thriver. You may find it helpful at this stage to consult a clergy person or to read some spiritually oriented books. For instance, I had just finished reading Joan Borysenko's book *Fire in the Soul,* regarding spiritual optimism—the idea that bad things really do happen for important reasons—and felt reassured once again that my beliefs were valid. After reading Borysenko's comments on Swami Paramananda's translation of the Hindu scriptures *The Upanishads,* I was reminded that, just like everyone and everything else, I was still a part of the One or God or Universe or whatever you want to call whoever is guiding this cosmos.

> *He who perceives the Self everywhere never shrinks from anything, because through his higher consciousness he feels united with all life. When a man sees God in all beings and all beings in God, and also God dwelling in his own Soul, how can he hate any living thing?*
>
> The Isa-Upanishad

I've tried to remember that my abusers were part of the One, too. After I had worked through my own pain, I tried to envision how they must have felt regarding their pain. From what I know about my abusers' childhood histories, their so-called "karma" wasn't much better than mine. I had never thought about applying such beliefs to my attempts at forgiveness. I started reading old texts on Eastern philosophies again, and began to realize that the way to forgiveness is through me—not through my abusers.

It goes like this: If we are all part of the One, when I hate my abusers (because of what they did to me out of ignorance and greed in an attempt to get their power back from *their* childhood abusers), I am hating myself. Until I forgive my abusers, I can't forgive myself. As long as I rail against them, I rail against myself. I had been essentially abusing myself—through procrastination and all of its accompanying symptoms and behaviors—for what they had done to me. I had simply picked up where they left off in terms of mistreating my "inner child."

Essentially, if we abuse ourselves, then we are abusing part of the Universe, the good and loving universe, and so abuse of the self in some ways is no better than abuse of the "other"—because both the self and the other person are part of the One.

If you have been able to avoid abusing others, then you have already stopped half the cycle. Yet it is up to self-abusers to forgive their perpetrators—not in order to condone the behaviors of their abusers, but in order to let go of the old conflict once and for all, so as stop abusing themselves, thereby completely stopping the cycle of abuse and neglect. In a world where "self" and "other" are both aspects of the same One, to stop self-abuse is equivalent to stopping the abuse of others. Keep in mind that if you are still being self-abusive or self-neglectful via procrastination and all of its accompanying symptoms, then you cannot possibly be fully present for your loved ones or for your children, who may then grow up feeling mildly neglected or confused—and the cycle, though in a diluted form, continues.

I learned a significant lesson along these lines, not from a neglected child, but from my faithful old dog. Through her I realized that although it isn't easy to forgive others for what they have done to me, it's even more difficult to forgive myself for what I did or didn't do. Unaware that my dog was near death, I had been promising her for weeks that we would go to the park, as soon as I finished my manuscript on my first book about the AIDS crisis. But on the day I mailed the text, she died. Although I was heartbroken that my friend of 16 years was suddenly gone, I have never forgotten the valuable lesson she taught me about the value of play and relationships versus work and accomplishments. I have asked her "spirit" to forgive me many times since that day, and I sense that she has. If she can forgive me for neglecting her in those last few days of her life, I guess I can forgive those who mistreated me as well. Granted, this lack of responsiveness to my dog is hardly comparable to childhood neglect or abuse, but regardless of the level of infraction, forgiving myself has been much harder for me than forgiving others.

Call me an eternal optimist (I frequently do), but I guess I think a lot like Anne Frank: I still believe, in spite of everything that's happened to me, that people are basically good at heart.

Some parents love and nurture their children and guide them so they can grow and learn. My parents and other misguided individuals abused and neglected me—but that doesn't mean I can't still grow and learn. Certainly, it seems to me that it's better to guide with love than with hatred. Regardless of what we're handed at birth in terms of environment or genetics, it's ours to do with what we will. We can choose to take it or leave it, but above all, we must learn from it.

What

Procrastination is a psychological as well as a potentially physiological problem, and thus treatment must be multi-faceted. We must address not just left-brain behavioral and cognitive solutions, but also the emotional components of procrastination, by using techniques that tap into the right side of the brain. We must also take note of the neurochem-ical aspects of depression, shame and such problems as ADHD, PMS or SAD because an appropriate balance of such neurotransmitters as serotonin, dopamine and norepineph-rine is essential to motivation, productivity and effective decision-making.

Accordingly, the use of antidepressant medication may be considered in order to intervene on a physiological level if the depression underlying procrastination has established a neurochemical imbalance, because regaining the feeling of wanting to be in a body again is often one of the first steps in overcoming shame-based procrastination.

When

The blueprint for the development of shame, which in turn triggers procrastination, is set at birth, in terms of what we are born with (genetics) and what we are born into (family and environment). In what now seems like the seed of my later problems with fully blossomed writer's block, I can remember purposely not studying for the grade school spelling bee when I was 12 years old, even though I was a sure winner if I had studied. Who knows how many times I may have procrastinated or held back in earlier years when it came to other activities, academic or otherwise? On some level, even at a very young age, I was trying to regain some semblance of control, although it may have meant short-circuiting my own development in the process. My clinical files abound with cases of clients who report similar lack of motivation during elementary school, in spite of teachers' statements that these young students held such "promise." Regardless of when you started to procrastinate, the time to learn how to stop is now.

Where

Where in our lives does procrastination create havoc? In our personal lives, we live in constant shame and stress, and cannot fully love. In our professional lives, we live in constant fear of being "found out," and cannot fully work. And in our spiritual lives, we live in a constant state of loss and confusion, and cannot fully embrace our spiritual destinies. It is up to each one of us to stop this pattern of loss and confusion, and to reach out for a better life for ourselves and for our loved ones. It is up to each one of us to take charge of our lives—now.

If your procrastination relates primarily to a creative endeavor such as writing, take heart in the words of death-and-dying expert Bernie Siegel, M.D., who said to me in a recent interview:

> *Everyone is mortal, so why not feel free? Go do something you love. . . . Just as there are doctors who say, "I hate being a doctor, I want to be a writer but my parents are worried I won't earn a living and they wouldn't be proud of me," you see, you have to wait until you're told you'll be dead in a year—then you'll keep a journal and write. No, you want to write, then write. Do what feels right and makes you happy.*

If your procrastination relates to the more mundane tasks of the day, take heart in the work of Mihaly Csikszentmihalyi, who says that by getting into the "flow" of your tasks in an almost meditative state, you can begin to see your chores as less aversive. Instead of thinking, "I have to do this task today," you can begin to think, "I choose to do this task today so that I can benefit from the consequence of completing it." No matter how you look at it, it *is* your life, to do what you will with it.

If you've always wanted to start your own business, don't let the idea of money stop you. Order up copies of books such as Laurie Blum's *Free Money from the Federal Government for Small Businesses and Entrepreneurs* or Stephen Harper's *The McGraw-Hill Guide to Starting Your Own Business.*

If you don't know exactly what you want to do with your life, try uncluttering your world by reading books such as Elaine St. James's *Simplify Your Life: 100 Ways to Slow Down and Enjoy the Things That Really Matter*—and see what happens to your ability to fulfill your dreams once the dust settles. And if you're just not sure where to begin, try Susan Kennedy's (a.k.a. "SARK") *Inspiration Sandwich,* just for the fun of it. The time to start living your life—and your dreams—is now!

Why

Why does procrastination plague us? As imperfect beings, we are prone to shame-based childrearing practices. And this development of shame triggers procrastination. Since I am not a spiritual advisor, I cannot say definitively why we must work our way out of these residual pools of shame. But no matter what your faith is, it all boils down to the same thing.

Many Western, Christian-based religions may say that we all have "a cross to bear," based on the residual effects of "original sin." Similarly, many Eastern religions say that we all have our own "karma" to work through. Both original sin and karma can be conceptualized as shame. Even if you are an agnostic, you could probably agree that working through shame is a mode of self-actualization that can lead to a more enlightened and enjoyable life. Regardless of your spiritual beliefs, letting go of shame means feeling the pain and learning to forgive—with emotional growth and spiritual evolution as a result.

While we must forgive to be free of shame, it is very important that we do not forget. If we forget, we will not be able to pass along our knowledge to future generations. Instead, we need to proceed with a combination of caution and compassion. In doing so, we are all contributing to the psychoevolutionary patterns of the human race. By being consciously aware that we are doing this, by releasing ourselves from such negative patterns that underlie perpetual problems such as procrastination, we not only shed shame, begin to savor success and embrace our essential destinies, but we also become part of the psychorevolutionary force that is now beginning to evolve all around us.

Think about it. Almost everywhere you look, whether it's on *Oprah* or in your neighborhood park, people are starting to question "the way we've always done things." No matter how you feel about blind faith, I think we can all agree that it's not a healthy pattern to accept blindly the "traditional" child-rearing practices developed by such imperfect beings as we are. To continue to do so would mean the destruction of the human race. Our flawed child-rearing practices have filled our streets and prisons with twisted souls whose only response to their own inner pain and shame are hatred and violence. We must all take a good look at ourselves and begin to lift the lid of denial regarding our imperfections, and finally, once and for all, exchange the protection offered by procrastination for the freedom of lifelong success and spiritual fulfillment.

And all we have to do, as Kurt Vonnegut says, is model ourselves after Stan Laurel and Oliver Hardy, two persevering men who, in the face of one calamity after another, "never failed to bargain in good faith with their destinies."

I will if you will.

References
for Further Reading

Procrastination and Time Management

Burka, J.B., and L.M. Yuen. *Procrastination.* Reading, Mass.: Addison-Wesley, 1983.

Culp, S. *How to Get Organized When You Don't Have the Time.* Cincinnati, Ohio: Writer's Digest Books, 1986.

_____. *Streamlining Your Life.* Cincinnati, Ohio: Writer's Digest Books, 1991.

Ellis, A., and W.J. Knaus. *Overcoming Procrastination.* New York: Signet/ Institute for Rational Living, 1977.

Fanning, T., and R. Fanning. *Get It All Done and Still Be Human.* Menlo Park, Calif.: Kali House, 1990.

Ferrari, J.R., J.L. Johnson, and W.G. McCown. *Procrastination and Task Avoidance.* New York: Plenum Press, 1995.

Roberts, M.S. *Living Without Procrastination.* Oakland, Calif.: New Harbinger, 1995.

Roesch, R. *The Working Woman's Guide to Managing Time.* Englewood Cliffs, N.J.: Prentice-Hall, 1996.

Schwarz, T. *Time Management for Writers.* Cincinnati, Ohio: Writer's Digest Books, 1988.

Creativity, Creative Blockage and Writer's Block

Bradbury, R. *Zen in the Art of Writing*. Santa Barbara, Calif.: Capra Press, 1990.

Cameron, J. *The Artist's Way*. New York: Jeremy P. Tarcher/Perigee Books, 1992.

Davis, G.B., and C.A. Parker. *Writing the Doctoral Dissertation: A Systematic Approach*. Woodbury, N.Y.: Barron's Educational Series, 1979.

Goldberg, N. *Writing Down the Bones*. Boston: Shambhala, 1986.

Hughes, E.F. *Writing from the Inner Self: Writing and Meditation Exercises That Free Your Creativity, Inspire Your Imagination, and Help You Overcome Writer's Block*. New York: HarperCollins, 1991.

Keyes, R. *The Courage to Write*. New York: Henry Holt & Co., 1995.

Klauser, H.A. *Writing on Both Sides of the Brain: Breakthrough Techniques for People Who Write*. New York: HarperCollins, 1987.

Lamott, A. *Bird by Bird: Some Instructions on Writing and Life*. New York: Pantheon Books, 1994.

Mack, K., and E. Skjei. *Overcoming Writing Blocks*. Los Angeles, Calif.: J.P. Tarcher, 1979.

May, R. *The Courage to Create*. New York: Bantam, 1975.

Nelson, V. *On Writer's Block*. Boston: Houghton Mifflin, 1993.

_____. *Writer's Block and How to Use It*. Cincinnati, Ohio: Writer's Digest Books, 1985.

Ray, R.J. *The Weekend Novelist*. New York: Dell, 1994.

Shekerjian, D. *Uncommon Genius*. New York: Penguin Books, 1990.

Storr, A. *The Dynamics of Creation*. New York: Ballantine, 1972.

_____. *Solitude: A Return to the Self*. New York: Free Press, 1988.

Wakefield, D. *Creating from the Spirit*. New York: Ballantine Books, 1996.

Psychology of Corporate Productivity

Bellman, G.M. *Getting Things Done When You Are Not in Charge.* San Francisco: Berrett-Koehler Publishers, 1992.

Bolles, R.N. *What Color Is Your Parachute? A Practical Manual for Job-hunters and Career-changers.* Berkeley, Calif.: Ten Speed Press, 1990.

Corbin, C. *Conquering Corporate Codependence.* Englewood Cliffs, N.J.: Prentice Hall, 1993.

Covey, S.R. *The Seven Habits of Highly Effective People.* New York: Simon & Schuster, 1989.

Lowman, R.L. *Counseling and Psychotherapy of Work Dysfunctions.* Washington, D.C.: American Psychological Association, 1993.

Stark, A. *Because I Said So: Recognize the Influence of Childhood Dynamics on Office Politics and Take Charge of Your Career.* New York: Pharos Books, 1992.

Right Brain/Left Brain

Edwards, B.E. *Drawing on the Right Side of the Brain,* rev. ed. Los Angeles: Jeremy P. Tarcher, 1989.

Joseph, R. *The Right Brain and the Unconscious.* New York: Plenum Press, 1992.

Klauser, H.A. *Writing on Both Sides of the Brain.* New York: HarperCollins, 1987.

Wonder, J., and P. Donovan. *Whole-brain Thinking.* New York: Quill/William Morrow, 1984.

Healthy Childhoods and Effective Parenting

Albrecht, D. *Raising a Child Who Has a Physical Disability.* New York: John Wiley & Sons, 1995.

Brazelton, T.B. *Touchpoints: Your Child's Emotional and Behavioral Development.* Reading, Mass.: Addison-Wesley, 1992.

Eisenberg, A., H.E. Murkoff, and S.E. Hathaway. *What to Expect: The Toddler Years.* New York: Workman Publishing, 1994.

_____. *What to Expect When You're Expecting.* New York: Workman Publishing, 1991.

Joslin, K.R. *Positive Parenting from A to Z.* New York: Ballantine, 1994.

Klaus, M.H., J.H. Kennell and P.H. Klaus. *Bonding.* Reading, Mass.: Addison-Wesley, 1995.

Leach, P. *Babyhood: Stage by Stage, From Birth to Age Two,* 2nd ed. New York: Alfred A. Knopf, 1994.

_____. *Your Baby and Child: From Birth to Age Five,* rev. ed. New York: Alfred A. Knopf, 1994.

Mrazek, D., W. Garrison, and L. Elliott, eds. *A to Z Guide to Your Child's Behavior.* New York: Perigee, 1993.

Seligman, M.E.P. *The Optimistic Child.* New York: Houghton Mifflin, 1995.

Tauscher, E.O. *The Child Care Sourcebook.* New York: Macmillan, 1995.

Weston, D.C., and M. Weston. *Playful Parenting.* New York: Putnam, 1993.

Creativity and Psychological Trauma

Duke, P., and G. Hochman. *A Brilliant Madness.* New York: Bantam, 1992.

Jamison, K.R. *Touched with Fire.* New York: Free Press, 1993.

Miller, A. *Banished Knowledge: Facing Childhood Injuries.* New York: Nan A. Talese/Doubleday, 1990.

_____. *Breaking Down the Wall of Silence.* New York: Dutton, 1991.

_____. *For Your Own Good: Hidden Cruelty in Child-rearing and the Roots of Violence.* New York: Noonday Press, 1990.

_____. *The Untouched Key: Tracing Childhood Trauma in Creativity and Destructiveness.* New York: Doubleday, 1990.

Rothenberg, A. *Creativity and Madness.* Baltimore, Md.: Johns Hopkins University Press, 1990.

Childhood
Abuse and Neglect

Bass, E., and L. Davis. *The Courage to Heal.* New York: Harper & Row, 1988.

Beattie, M. *Beyond Co-dependency.* New York: Harper & Row, 1989.

Blume, E. S. *Secret Survivors.* New York: Ballantine Books, 1990.

Bradshaw, J. *Healing the Shame That Binds You.* Deerfield Beach, Fla.: Health Communications, 1988.

_____. *Homecoming.* New York: Bantam, 1990.

Courtois, C. *Healing the Incest Wound.* New York: W.W. Norton, 1988.

Crowder, A. *Opening the Door.* New York: Breuner-Mazel, 1994.

Davis, L. *Allies in Healing.* New York: HarperPerennial, 1991.

_____. *The Courage to Heal Workbook: For Women and Men Survivors of Child Sexual Abuse.* New York: Harper & Row, 1990.

Evans, P. *The Verbally Abusive Relationship.* Holbrook, Mass.: Adams Media, 1992.

Gil, E. *Outgrowing the Pain: A Book For and About Adults Abused As Children.* New York: Dell, 1983.

_____. *Outgrowing the Pain Together.* New York: Bantam, 1992.

Hansen, P. *Survivors and Partners.* Longmont, Colo.: Heron Hill Publishing, 1992.

Lerner, R. *Daily Affirmations for the Inner Child.* Deerfield Beach, Fla.: Health Communications, 1990.

Lew, M. *Victims No Longer.* New York: Harper & Row, 1990.

Love, P., and J. Robinson. *The Emotional Incest Syndrome.* New York: Bantam, 1990.

McKay, M., and P. Fanning. *Self-Esteem,* 2nd ed. Oakland, Calif.: New Harbinger, 1992.

Whitfield, C.L. *Co-dependence.* Deerfield Beach, Fla: Health Communications, 1991.

_____. *Gift to Myself.* Deerfield Beach, Fla.: Health Communications, 1990.

_____. *Healing the Child Within.* Deerfield Beach, Fla.: Health Communications, 1987.

_____. *Memory and Abuse.* Deerfield Beach, Fla.: Health Communications, 1995.

Choosing Healthier Relationships

Beattie, M. *Co-dependent No More.* New York: Harper & Row, 1987.

Evans, P. *The Verbally Abusive Relationship.* Holbrook, Mass.: Adams Media, 1992.

Gray, J. *Mars and Venus in the Bedroom.* New York: HarperCollins, 1995.

_____. *Men Are From Mars, Women Are From Venus.* New York: HarperCollins, 1992.

Halpern, H. *How to Break Your Addiction to a Person.* New York: McGraw-Hill, 1982.

Hendrix, H. *Getting the Love You Want.* New York: Henry Holt, 1988.

Kreisman, J.J., and H. Straus. *I Hate You—Don't Leave Me.* New York: Avon Books, 1989.

Lerner, H. *The Dance of Intimacy.* New York: HarperPerennial, 1989.

Lerner, R. *Living in the Comfort Zone.* Deerfield Beach, Fla.: Health Communications, 1995.

Schaef, A. W. *Escape from Intimacy.* New York: Harper & Row, 1989.

Tannen, D. *Talking from 9 to 5.* New York: William Morrow & Co., 1994.

_____. *You Just Don't Understand.* New York: William Morrow & Co., 1990.

Whitfield, C. *Boundaries and Relationships.* Deerfield Beach, Fla.: Health Communications, 1993.

Woititz, J. G. *The Intimacy Struggle.* Deerfield Beach, Fla.: Health Communications, 1993.

Compulsive Behaviors

Abramson, E. *Emotional Eating.* New York: Lexington Books, 1993.

Adamse, M., and S. Motta. *Online Friendship, Chat-Room Romance and Cybersex.* Deerfield Beach, Fla.: Health Communications, 1996.

Carnes, P. *Don't Call It Love.* New York: Bantam, 1992.

_____. *Out of the Shadows.* Center City, Minn.: Hazelden, 1992.

Ellis, A., and E. Velten. *When AA Doesn't Work for You.* New York: Barricade Books, 1992.

Fassel, D. *Working Ourselves to Death.* New York: HarperCollins, 1990.

Fitzgerald, K.W. *Alcoholism: The Genetic Inheritance.* Lake Forest, Ill.: Whales Tale Press, 1995.

Goodwin, D.W. *Alcohol and the Writer.* New York: Penguin Books, 1988.

Hamilton B. [pseud.] *Getting Started in AA.* Center City, Minn.: Hazelden, 1995.

Huebner, H.F. *Endorphins, Eating Disorders, and Other Addictive Behaviors.* New York: W.W. Norton, 1993.

Kano, S. *Making Peace with Food,* rev. ed. New York: Harper & Row, 1989.

Katahn, M. *How to Quit Smoking Without Gaining Weight.* New York: W.W. Norton, 1994.

Klesges, R.C., and M. DeBon. *How Women Can Finally Stop Smoking.* Alameda, Calif.: Hunter House, 1994.

LeBlanc, D. *You Can't Quit Till You Know What's Eating You.* Deerfield Beach, Fla.: Health Communications, 1990.

Mellan, O., and S. Christie. *Overcoming Overspending.* New York: Walker, 1995.

Mundis, J. *How to Get Out of Debt, Stay Out of Debt, and Live Prosperously.* New York: Bantam, 1988.

Norden, M.J. *Beyond Prozac.* New York: Regan Books, 1995.

Robinson, B. *Overdoing It.* Deerfield Beach, Fla.: Health Communications, 1992.

Roth, G. *Feeding the Hungry Heart: The Experience of Compulsive Eating.* New York: Signet, 1982.

Trimpey, J. *The Small Book: A Revolutionary Alternative for Overcoming Alcohol and Drug Dependence.* New York: Doubleday, 1995.

Waterhouse, D. *Why Women Need Chocolate: How to Get the Body You Want by Eating the Foods You Crave.* New York: Hyperion, 1995.

Physiological Factors That Affect Productivity

Balch, J.F., and P.A. Balch. *Prescription for Nutritional Healing.* Garden City Park, N.Y.: Avery Publishing Group, 1990.

Bourne, E.J. *The Anxiety and Phobia Workbook,* 2nd ed. Oakland, Calif.: New Harbinger, 1995.

Burton-Goldberg Group. *Alternative Medicine.* Puyallup, Wash.: Future Medicine Publishing, 1994.

Chopra, D. *Perfect Health.* New York: Harmony Books, 1991.

_____. *Quantum Healing.* New York: Bantam, 1989.

Hallowell, E.M., and J.J. Ratey. *Driven to Distraction.* New York: Pantheon Books, 1994.

Jacobowitz, R.S. *150 Most-Asked Questions About Menopause: What Women Really Want to Know.* New York: Hearst Books, 1993.

Klein, D.F., and P.H. Wender. *Understanding Depression.* New York: Oxford University Press, 1993.

Lark, S.M. *Premenstrual Syndrome: Self-help Book.* Berkeley, Calif.: Celestial Arts, 1984.

Lehrer, P.M., and R.L. Woolfolk, eds. *Principles and Practice of Stress Management,* 2nd ed. New York: Guilford Press, 1993.

Null, G. *No More Allergies.* New York: Villard Books, 1992.

Rosenthal, N.E. *Winter Blues.* New York: Guilford Press, 1993.

Sheehy, G. *The Silent Passage: Menopause.* New York: Random House, 1991.

Utian, W.H., and R.S. Jacobowitz. *Managing Your Menopause.* New York: Prentice Hall Press, 1990.

Vasey, F.B., and J. Feldstein. *The Silicone Implant Controversy.* Freedom, Calif.: The Crossing Press, 1993.

Waterhouse, D. *Why Women Need Chocolate: How to Get the Body You Want by Eating the Foods You Crave.* New York: Hyperion, 1995.

Weiss, G., and L.T. Hechtman. *Hyperactive Children Grown Up: ADHD in Children, Adolescents, and Adults,* 2nd ed. New York: Guilford Press, 1993.

Weiss, L. *Attention Deficit Disorder in Adults: Practical Self-help for Sufferers and Their Spouses.* Dallas, Tex.: Taylor Publishing Co., 1992.

Winter, R. *A Consumer's Guide to Medicines in Food.* New York: Crown, 1995.

Young, J.E. *Total Well-being.* Miami, Fla.: Trihealth, Inc., 1994.

Anxiety and Stress Management

Beck, A.T., G. Emery, and R.L. Greenberg. *Anxiety Disorders and Phobias: A Cognitive Perspective.* New York: Basic Books, 1985.

Bilodeau, L. *The Anger Workbook.* Center City, Minn.: Hazelden, 1992.

Borysenko, J. *Minding the Body, Mending the Mind.* New York: Bantam, 1987.

Bourne, E.J. *The Anxiety and Phobia Workbook,* 2nd ed. Oakland, Calif.: New Harbinger, 1995.

Davis, M., E.R. Eshelman and M. McKay. *The Relaxation and Stress Reduction Workbook,* 4th ed. Oakland, Calif.: New Harbinger, 1995.

Dowling, C. *You Mean I Don't Have to Feel This Way?* New York: Bantam, 1991.

Fisher, S. *Discovering the Power of Self-hypnosis: A New Approach for Enabling Change and Promoting Healing.* New York: HarperCollins, 1991.

McKay, M., P. Rogers, and J. McKay. *When Anger Hurts.* Oakland, Calif.: New Harbinger, 1989.

Potter-Efron, R. *Angry All the Time.* Oakland, Calif.: New Harbinger, 1994.

Potter-Efron, R., and P. Potter-Efron. *Letting Go of Anger.* Oakland, Calif.: New Harbinger, 1995.

Stone, H., and S. Stone. *Embracing Your Inner Critic.* New York: HarperSanFrancisco, 1993.

Thayer, R.E. *Origin of Everyday Moods: Managing Energy, Tension & Stress.* New York: Oxford University Press, 1996.

Wells, V. *The Joy of Visualization: 75 Creative Ways to Improve Your Life.* San Francisco: Chronicle Books, 1990.

Psychotherapeutic Fiction

Allison, D. *Bastard Out of Carolina.* New York: Dutton, 1992.

Angelou, M. *I Know Why the Caged Bird Sings.* New York: Bantam, 1980.

Banks, R. *Success Stories.* New York: Ballantine Books, 1986.

Bloom, A. *Come to Me.* New York: HarperPerennial, 1993.

Fowler, C.M. *Before Women Had Wings.* New York: Putnam, 1996.

_____. *River of Hidden Dreams.* New York: Putnam, 1994.

_____. *Sugar Cage.* New York: Putnam, 1992.

Gibbons, K. *Ellen Foster.* New York: Vintage Books, 1987.

Jolley, E. *Cabin Fever.* New York: HarperPerennial, 1990.

McMillan, T. *Waiting to Exhale.* New York: Viking, 1992.

Morrison, T. *The Bluest Eye.* New York: Pocket Books, 1970.

Shea, L. *Hula.* New York: W.W. Norton, 1994.

Walker, A. *The Color Purple.* New York: Pocket Books, 1982.

Spirituality and Productivity

Borysenko, J. *Fire in the Soul.* New York: Warner Books, 1993.

_____. *Guilt Is the Teacher, Love Is the Lesson.* New York: Warner Books, 1990.

Canfield, J., and M.V. Hansen, eds. *Chicken Soup for the Soul.* Deerfield Beach, Fla.: Health Communications, 1993.

_____. *A 2nd Helping of Chicken Soup for the Soul.* Deerfield Beach, Fla.: Health Communications, 1995.

_____. *A 3rd Serving of Chicken Soup for the Soul.* Deerfield Beach, Fla.: Health Communications, 1996.

Chopra, D. *The Seven Spiritual Laws of Success.* San Rafael, Calif.: Amber-Allen Publishing/New World Library, 1994.

Csikszentmihalyi, M. *Flow: The Psychology of Optimal Experience.* New York: Harper & Row, 1990.

Epstein, M. *Thoughts Without a Thinker: Psychotherapy from a Buddhist Perspective.* New York: Basic Books, 1995.

Moore, T. *Care of the Soul.* New York: HarperCollins, 1992.

Peck, M.S. *Further Along the Road Less Traveled.* New York: Simon & Schuster, 1993.

Redfield, J. *The Celestine Prophecy.* New York: Warner Books, 1993.

SARK. *Inspiration Sandwich: Stories to Inspire Our Creative Freedom.* Berkeley, Calif.: Celestial Arts, 1992.

Siegel, B.S. *How to Live Between Office Visits.* New York: HarperCollins, 1994.

_____. *Love, Medicine and Miracles.* New York: HarperCollins, 1986.

_____. *Peace, Love, and Healing.* New York: HarperCollins, 1990.

Sinetar, M. *To Build the Life You Want, Create the Work You Love.* New York: St. Martin's Press, 1995.

St. James, E. *Simplify Your Life.* New York: Hyperion, 1994.

Weiss, B.L. *Through Time into Healing.* New York: Simon & Schuster, 1992.

Williamson, M. *Return to Love.* New York: HarperCollins, 1994.

Bibliography

Abramson, E. *Emotional Eating: A Practical Guide to Taking Control.* New York: Lexington Books, 1993.

Ainsworth, M. "Infant-Mother Attachment." *American Psychologist,* (34) 1979: 932-937.

Ainsworth, M.D.S. "Attachments and Other Affectional Bonds Across the Life Cycle." In *Attachment Across the Life Cycle.* Eds. C.M. Parkes, J. Stevenson-Hinde, and P. Marris. London: Tavistock/Routledge, 1991, pp. 33-51.

Ainsworth, M.D.S., and C. Eichberg. "Effects on Infant-Mother Attachment of Mother's Unresolved Loss of an Attachment Figure, or Other Traumatic Experience." In *Attachment Across the Life Cycle.* Eds. C.M. Parkes, J. Stevenson-Hinde, and P. Marris. London: Tavistock/Routledge, 1991, pp. 160-183.

Ainsworth, M.D.S., et al. *Patterns of Attachment: A Psychological Study of the Strange Situation.* Hillsdale, N.J.: Erlbaum, 1978.

Albrecht, D. *Raising a Child Who Has a Physical Disability.* New York: John Wiley & Sons, 1995.

Allan, J., and J. Bertoia. *Written Paths to Healing: Education and Jungian Child Counseling.* Dallas, Tex.: Spring Publications, 1992.

Allison, D. *Bastard Out of Carolina.* New York: Dutton, 1992.

Arieti, S. *Creativity: The Magic Synthesis.* New York: Basic Books, 1976.

Bailey, K. "Therapeutic Massage with Survivors of Abuse." *Massage Therapy Journal,* summer 1992.

Balch, J.F. and P.A. Balch. *Prescription for Nutritional Healing.* Garden City Park, N.Y.: Avery Publishing Group, 1990.

Banks, R. *Success Stories.* New York: Ballantine Books, 1986.

Basic Behavioral Science Task Force of the National Advisory Mental Health Council. "Basic Behavioral Science Research for Mental Health: Vulnerability and Resilience." *American Psychologist,* 51 (1) 1996: 22-28.

Bass, E., and L. Davis. *The Courage to Heal: A Guide for Women Survivors of Child Sexual Abuse.* New York: Harper & Row, 1988.

Beattie, M. *Beyond Co-dependency.* New York: Harper & Row, 1989.

_____. *Co-dependent No More.* New York: Harper & Row, 1987.

Beck, A.T., G. Emery, and R.L. Greenberg. *Anxiety Disorders and Phobias: A Cognitive Perspective.* New York: Basic Books, 1985.

Bennett, E.M., and K.J. Kemper. "Is Abuse During Childhood a Risk Factor for Developing Substance Abuse Problems as an Adult?" *Journal of Developmental and Behavioral Pediatrics,* 15 (6) 1994: 426-429.

Bennett, K., and S. C. Rhodes. "Writing Apprehension and Writing Intensity in Business and Industry." *Journal of Business Communication,* 25 (1) 1988: 25-39.

Bernard, A. *Rotten Rejections: A Literary Companion.* Wainscott, N.Y.: Pushcart Press, 1990.

Betensky, M. *What Do You See?: Phenomenology of Therapeutic Art Expression.* London: Jessica Kingsley Publishers/Bristol, Penn.: Taylor & Francis, 1995.

Bifulco, A., G.W. Brown, and T.O. Harris. "Childhood Experience of Care and Abuse (CECA): A Retrospective Interview Measure." *Journal of Child Psychology & Psychiatry & Allied Disciplines,* 35 (8) 1994: 1419-1435.

Bilodeau, L. *The Anger Workbook.* Center City, Minn.: Hazelden, 1992.

Blatt, S.J. "The Destructiveness of Perfectionism: Implications for the Treatment of Depression." *American Psychologist,* 50 (12) 1995: 1003-1020.

Bloom, A. *Come to Me.* New York: HarperPerennial, 1993.

Bloom, L., K. Coburn, and J. Pearlman. *The New Assertive Woman.* New York: Dell, 1975.

Bloomberg, M., ed. *Creativity: Theory and Research.* New Haven, Conn.: College & University Press, 1973.

Blum, L. *Free Money from the Federal Government for Small Businesses and Entrepreneurs.* New York: John Wiley & Sons, 1993.

Blume, E.S. *Secret Survivors: Uncovering Incest and its Aftereffects in Women.* New York: Ballantine Books, 1990.

Bohmer, C., and A. Parrot. *Sexual Assault on Campus: The Problem and the Solution.* New York: Lexington Books, 1993.

Boice, R. "Cognitive Components of Blocking." *Written Communication,* 2 (1) 1985: 91-104.

_____. "Contingency Management in Writing and the Appearance of Creative Ideas: Implications for the Treatment of Writing Blocks." *Behavior Research and Therapy,* 21, 1983: 537-543.

Bolton, F.G., L.A. Morris, and A.E. MacEachron. *Males at Risk: The Other Side of Child Sexual Abuse.* Newbury Park, Calif.: Sage Publications, 1989.

Borysenko, J. *Fire in the Soul: A New Psychology of Spiritual Optimism.* New York: Warner Books, 1993.

_____. *Guilt Is the Teacher, Love Is the Lesson.* New York: Warner Books, 1990.

_____. *Minding the Body, Mending the Mind.* New York: Bantam, 1987.

Bourne, E.J. *The Anxiety and Phobia Workbook,* 2nd ed. Oakland, Calif.: New Harbinger, 1995.

Bowlby, J. *Attachment and Loss, Vol. 1: Attachment.* New York: Basic Books, 1969.

_____. *Attachment and Loss, Vol. 2: Separation—Anxiety and Anger.* New York: Basic Books, 1973.

_____. *Attachment and Loss, Vol. 3: Loss—Sadness and Depression.* New York: Basic Books, 1980.

Bradbury, R. *Zen in the Art of Writing.* Santa Barbara, Calif.: Capra Press, 1990.

Bradshaw, J. *Bradshaw On: The Family—A New Way of Creating Solid Self-Esteem,* rev. ed. Deerfield Beach, Fla.: Health Communications, 1996.

_____. *Healing the Shame That Binds You.* Deerfield Beach, Fla.: Health Communications, 1988.

_____. *Homecoming: Reclaiming and Championing Your Inner Child.* New York: Bantam, 1990.

Brazelton, T.B. *Touchpoints: Your Child's Emotional and Behavioral Development.* Reading, Mass.: Addison-Wesley, 1992.

Bretherton, I. "The Roots and Growing Points of Attachment Theory." In *Attachment Across the Life Cycle.* Eds. C.M. Parkes, J. Stevenson-Hinde, and P. Marris. London: Tavistock/Routledge, 1991, pp. 9-32.

Brunning, N. *Breast Implants: Everything You Want to Know.* Alameda, Calif.: Hunter House, 1992.

Burack, S.K., ed. "Dick Francis: An Interview." *The Writer's Handbook.* Boston: The Writer, Inc., 1992, pp. 221-223.

Burka, J.B., and L.M. Yuen. *Procrastination: Why You Do It, What to Do About It.* Reading, Mass.: Addison-Wesley, 1983.

Burns, D.D. *Feeling Good: The New Mood Therapy.* New York: Signet, 1980.

Burton-Goldberg Group. *Alternative Medicine: The Definitive Guide.* Puyallup, Wash.: Future Medicine Publishing, 1994.

Cameron, J. *The Artist's Way: A Spiritual Path to Higher Creativity.* New York: Jeremy P. Tarcher/Perigee Books, 1992.

Carnes, P. *Contrary to Love.* Center City, Minn.: Hazelden, 1989.

_____. *Don't Call It Love.* New York: Bantam, 1992.

_____. *Out of the Shadows: Understanding Sexual Addiction.* Center City, Minn.: Hazelden, 1992.

"Child-Abuse Data Said to Argue for Funding." *National Association of Social Workers News,* May, 1996: 7.

Chira, S. "Study Says Babies in Child Care Keep Secure Bonds to Mothers." *The New York Times,* April 21, 1996: 1, 11.

Chopra, D. *Perfect Health: The Complete Mind/Body Guide.* New York: Harmony Books, 1991.

_____. *Quantum Healing: Exploring the Frontiers of Mind/Body Medicine.* New York: Bantam, 1989.

Cochran, S.D., and V.M. Mays. "Depressive Distress Among Homosexually Active African American Men and Women." *American Journal of Psychiatry,* 151 (4) 1994: 524-529.

Cole, D.A., and M. Milstead. "Behavioral Correlates of Depression: Antecedents or Consequences?" *Journal of Counseling Psychology,* 36 (4) 1989: 408-416.

Colgrove, M., H.H. Bloomfield, and P. McWilliams. *How to Survive the Loss of a Love.* Toronto: Bantam, 1976.

Consumer Reports. "Alternative Medicine: The Facts." January, 1994: 51-59.

_____. "Mental Health: Does Therapy Help?" November, 1995: 734-739.

Costanzo, G. "The Smallest Thing on Earth." In *In the Aviary.* Pittsburgh, Penna.: Coyne & Chenoweth, 1991.

Courtois, C. *Healing the Incest Wound: Adult Survivors in Therapy.* New York: W.W. Norton, 1988.

Croom, E.A. *Unpuzzling Your Past: A Basic Guide to Genealogy,* 3rd ed. Cincinnati, Ohio: Betterway Books, 1995.

Crowder, A. *Opening the Door: A Treatment Model for Therapy with Male Survivors of Sexual Abuse.* New York: Breuner-Mazel, 1994.

Csikszentmihalyi, M. *Flow: The Psychology of Optimal Experience.* New York: Harper & Row, 1990.

Dalton, K. *Once a Month: The Original Premenstrual Syndrome Handbook,* 4th ed. Claremont, Calif.: Hunter House, 1990.

Davis, G.B., and C.A. Parker. *Writing the Doctoral Dissertation: A Systematic Approach.* Woodbury, N.Y.: Barron's Educational Series, 1979.

Davis, L. *Allies in Healing: When the Person You Love Was Sexually Abused as a Child.* New York: HarperPerennial, 1991.

_____. *The Courage to Heal Workbook: For Women and Men Survivors of Child Sexual Abuse.* New York: Harper & Row, 1990.

Davis, M., E.R. Eshelman, and M. McKay. *The Relaxation and Stress Reduction Workbook,* 4th ed. Oakland, Calif.: New Harbinger, 1995.

DeAngelis, T. "New Threat Associated with Child Abuse." *APA Monitor,* April, 1995: 1, 38.

DeBono, E. *Serious Creativity: Using the Power of Lateral Thinking to Create New Ideas.* New York: HarperBusiness, 1992.

Deffenbacher, J.L., et al. "Social Skills and Cognitive-Relaxation Approaches to General Anger Reduction." *Journal of Counseling Psychology,* 41 (3) 1994: 386-396.

Dowling, C. *You Mean I Don't Have to Feel This Way? New Help for Depression, Anxiety, and Addiction.* New York: Bantam, 1991.

Dumas, J.E., and W.J. Serketich. "Maternal Depressive Symptomatology and Child Maladjustment: A Comparison of Three Process Models." *Behavior Therapy,* 25 (2) 1994: 161-181.

Eagle, R. "The Separation Experience of Children in Long-term Care: Theory, Research, and Implications for Practice." *American Journal of Orthopsychiatry,* 64 (3) 1994: 421-434.

Edwards, B.E. *Drawing on the Right Side of the Brain: A Course in Enhancing Creativity and Artistic Confidence,* rev. ed. Los Angeles, Calif.: Jeremy P. Tarcher, 1989.

Effert, B.R., and J.R. Ferrari. "Decisional Procrastination: Examining Personality Correlates." *Journal of Social Behavior and Personality,* 4 (1) 1989: 151-161.

Eisenberg, A., H.E. Murkoff, and S.E. Hathaway. *What to Expect: The Toddler Years.* New York: Workman Publishing, 1994.

_____. *What to Expect the First Year.* New York: Workman Publishing, 1989.

Eisenberg, D.M., et al. "Unconventional Medicine in the United States: Prevalence, Costs, and Patterns of Use." *New England Journal of Medicine,* 328, 1993: 246-252.

Elliott, D. M. "Impaired Object Relations in Professional Women Molested as Children." *Psychotherapy,* 31 (1) 1994: 79-86.

Ellis, A., and W.J. Knaus. *Overcoming Procrastination: Or, How to Think and Act Rationally in Spite of Life's Inevitable Hassles.* New York: Signet/Institute for Rational Living, 1977.

Ellis, A., and E. Velten. *When AA Doesn't Work for You.* New York: Barricade Books, 1992.

Erikson, E. *Childhood and Society,* 2nd ed. New York: W.W. Norton, 1963.

Evans, P. *The Verbally Abusive Relationship.* Holbrook, Mass.: Adams Media, 1992.

Fassel, D. *Working Ourselves to Death.* New York: HarperCollins, 1990.

Feldman-Summers, S., and K.S. Pope. "The Experience of 'Forgetting' Childhood Abuse: A National Survey of Psychologists." *Journal of Consulting and Clinical Psychology,* 62 (3) 1994: 636-639.

Ferrari, J.R., J.L. Johnson, and W.G. McCown. "An Overview of Procrastination." In *Procrastination and Task Avoidance: Theory, Research, and Treatment.* Eds. J.R. Ferrari, J.L. Johnson, and W. G. McCown. New York: Plenum, 1995, pp. 1-20.

_____, eds. *Procrastination and Task Avoidance: Theory, Research, and Treatment.* New York: Plenum, 1995.

_____. "Procrastination Research: A Synopsis of Existing Research Perspectives." In *Procrastination and Task Avoidance: Theory, Research, and Treatment.* Eds. J.R. Ferrari, J.L. Johnson, and W. G. McCown. New York: Plenum, 1995, pp. 21-46.

_____. "The Role of Personality Disorders and Characterological Tendencies in Procrastination." In *Procrastination and Task Avoidance: Theory, Research, and Treatment.* Eds. J.R. Ferrari, J.L. Johnson, and W. G. McCown. New York: Plenum, 1995, pp. 169-186.

Ferrari, J.R., and M.J. Olivette. "Parental Authority Influences on the Development of Female Dysfunctional Procrastination." *Journal of Research in Personality,* 28 (1) 1994: 87-100.

_____. "Perceptions of Parental Control and the Development of Indecision Among Late Adolescent Females." *Adolescence,* (28) 1993: 963-970.

Fichtner, M. "Russell Banks' Real World." *The Miami Herald,* March 7, 1995: E1-2.

Finkelhor, D., et al. "Sexual Abuse in the National Survey of Adult Men and Women: Prevalence, Characteristics, and Risk Factors." *Child Abuse and Neglect,* (14) 1990: 19-28.

Fisher, S. *Discovering the Power of Self-Hypnosis: A New Approach for Enabling Change and Promoting Healing.* New York: HarperCollins, 1991.

Fitzgerald, K.W. *Alcoholism: The Genetic Inheritance.* Lake Forest, Ill.: Whales Tale Press, 1995.

Flett, G.L., Blankstein, K.R., & Martin, T.R. "Procrastination, Negative Self-evaluation, and Stress in Depression and Anxiety: A Review and Preliminary Model." In *Procrastination and Task Avoidance: Theory, Research, and Treatment.* Eds. J.R. Ferrari, J.L. Johnson, and W. G. McCown. New York: Plenum, 1995, pp. 137-167.

Flett, G.L., Hewitt, P.L., & Martin, T.R. "Dimensions of Perfectionism and Procrastination." In *Procrastination and Task Avoidance: Theory, Research, and Treatment.* Eds. J.R. Ferrari, J.L. Johnson, and W. G. McCown. New York: Plenum, 1995, pp. 113-136.

Fossum, M.A., and M.J. Mason. *Facing Shame: Families in Recovery.* New York: W.W. Norton, 1986.

Fox, N.A. "If It's Not Left, It's Right: Electroencephalograph Asymmetry and the Development of Emotion." *American Psychologist,* 46 (8) 1991: 863-872.

Frank, B., D.N. Dixon and H.J. Grosz. "Conjoint Monitoring of Symptoms of Premenstrual Syndrome: Impact on Marital Satisfaction." *Journal of Counseling Psychology,* 40(1) 1993: 109-114.

Fredericks, C. *Psychonutrition.* New York: Berkley Books, 1976.

Freiberg, P. "Research Identifies Kids at Risk for Problem Gambling." *APA Monitor,* December, 1995: 36.

Friedlander, M.L., and S.M. Siegel. "Separation-Individuation Difficulties and Cognitive-Behavioral Indicators of Eating Disorders Among College Women." *Journal of Counseling Psychology,* 37 (1) 1990: 74-78.

Friedman, R.J., and M.M. Katz, eds. *The Psychology of Depression: Contemporary Theory and Research.* Washington, D.C.: Winston-Wiley, 1974.

Gardner, H., ed. "Bonds of Attachment." In *Developmental Psychology,* 2nd ed. Boston: Little, Brown, & Co., 1982, pp. 27-56.

Gardner, J. Foreword to *Becoming a Writer,* by D. Brande. Los Angeles: J.P. Tarcher, 1981.

Gawain, S. *Creative Visualization.* San Rafael, Calif.: New World Library, 1978.

Gerber, R. *Vibrational Medicine: New Choices for Healing Ourselves.* Santa Fe, N.M.: Bear & Co., 1988.

Gibbons, K. *Ellen Foster.* New York: Vintage Books, 1987.

Gil, E. *Outgrowing the Pain: A Book For and About Adults Abused as Children.* New York: Dell, 1983.

_____. *Outgrowing the Pain Together.* New York: Bantam, 1992.

Gold, M.S. *Drugs of Abuse: A Comprehensive Series for Clinicians, Vol. 1: Marijuana.* New York: Plenum, 1989.

_____. *Drugs of Abuse: A Comprehensive Series for Clinicians, Vol. 3: Cocaine.* New York: Plenum, 1993.

_____. *The Good News About Depression: Cures and Treatments in the New Age of Psychiatry.* New York: Villard Books, 1986.

Gold, M.S., and N.S. Miller. *Drugs of Abuse: A Comprehensive Series for Clinicians, Vol. 2: Alcohol.* New York: Plenum, 1991.

Goodman, L. A., et al. "Male Violence Against Women: Current Research and Future Directions." *American Psychologist,* 48 (10) 1993: 1054-1058.

Goodwin, D.W. *Alcohol and the Writer.* New York: Penguin Books, 1988.

Hallowell, E.M., and J.J. Ratey. *Driven to Distraction: Recognizing and Coping with Attention Deficit Disorder from Childhood Through Adulthood.* New York: Pantheon Books, 1994.

Hamilton B. [pseud.] *Getting Started in AA.* Center City, Minn.: Hazelden, 1995.

Hammond, D.C., et al. *Clinical Hypnosis and Memory: Guidelines for Clinicians and for Forensic Hypnosis.* Seattle, Wash.: American Society of Clinical Hypnosis Press, 1995.

Hansen, P. *Survivors and Partners: Healing the Relationships of Sexual Abuse Survivors.* Longmont, Colo.: Heron Hill Publishing, 1992.

Harlow, H. "The Nature of Love." *American Psychologist,* (13) 1958: 637-685.

Harper, S.C. *The McGraw-Hill Guide to Starting Your Own Business.* New York: McGraw-Hill, 1991.

Hay, W. "Budgies: Nature's Antidepressants." *Bird Talk Magazine,* January 1994: 66-69.

Hoblitzelle, W. "Differentiating and Measuring Shame and Guilt: The Relation Between Shame and Depression." In *The Role of Shame in Symptom Formation.* Ed. H.B. Lewis. Hillsdale, N.J.: Lawrence Erlbaum Associates, 1987, pp. 207-235.

Hopkins, J. "Failure of the Holding Relationship: Some Effects of Physical Rejection on the Child's Attachment and Inner Experience." In *Attachment Across the Life Cycle.* Eds. C.M. Parkes, J. Stevenson-Hinde, and P. Marris. London: Tavistock/Routledge, 1991, pp. 187-198.

Huebner, H.F. *Endorphins, Eating Disorders, and Other Addictive Behaviors.* New York: W.W. Norton, 1993.

Humphreys, C. *The Wisdom of Buddhism.* London: Curzon Press/Humanities Press International, 1987.

Ingrassia, M. "As American as Blaming Mother." *Newsweek,* November 28, 1994: 63.

Jacobowitz, R.S. *150 Most-Asked Questions About Menopause: What Women Really Want to Know.* New York: Hearst Books, 1993.

Jennings, S., and A. Minde. *Art Therapy and Dramatherapy: Masks of the Soul.* London: Jessica Kingsley Publishers/Bristol, Penna.: Taylor & Francis, 1994.

John-Roger and P. McWilliams. *DO IT! Let's Get Off Our Buts.* New York: Prelude, 1991.

Joseph, R. "The Four Ego Personalities and the Unconscious Child and Parent Within." In *The Right Brain and the Unconscious: Discovering the Stranger Within.* Ed. R. Joseph. New York: Plenum Press, 1992, pp. 165-183.

_____. "The Limbic System and the Most Primitive Regions of the Unconscious." In *The Right Brain and the Unconscious: Discovering the Stranger Within.* Ed. R. Joseph. New York: Plenum Press, 1992, pp. 107-137.

_____. "Repetition and Rejection: Dreaming, Self-Fulfilling Prophecies, and the Seeking of Failure." In *The Right Brain and the Unconscious: Discovering the Stranger Within.* Ed. R. Joseph. New York: Plenum Press, 1992, pp. 251-280.

_____. *The Right Brain and the Unconscious: Discovering the Stranger Within.* New York: Plenum Press, 1992.

_____. "Right Brain-Left Brain and the Conscious and Unconscious Mind." In *The Right Brain and the Unconscious: Discovering the Stranger Within.* Ed. R. Joseph. New York: Plenum Press, 1992, pp. 29-56.

_____. "Right-Brain Limbic Language and Long-Lost Childhood Memories." In *The Right Brain and the Unconscious: Discovering the Stranger Within.* Ed. R. Joseph. New York: Plenum Press, 1992, pp. 75-90.

Joslin, K.R. *Positive Parenting from A to Z.* New York: Ballantine, 1994.

Kagan, J., and N. Snidman. "Temperamental Factors in Human Development." *American Psychologist,* 46 (8) 1991: 856-862.

Kahle, A.L., and M.L. Kelley. "Children's Homework Problems: A Comparison of Goal Setting and Parent Training." *Behavior Therapy,* 25 (2) 1994: 275-290.

Kanner, E. "Connie May Fowler: Writing in Order to Reaffirm the Past." *Publisher's Weekly,* May 13, 1996: 50-51.

Kano, S. *Making Peace with Food: Freeing Yourself from the Diet-Weight Obsession,* rev. ed. New York: Harper & Row, 1989.

Katahn, M. *How to Quit Smoking Without Gaining Weight.* New York: W.W. Norton, 1994.

Kaufman, G. *The Psychology of Shame: Theory and Treatment of Shame-Based Syndromes.* New York: Springer Publishing Co., 1989.

Kelly, P., ed. *The Uses of Writing in Psychotherapy.* New York: Haworth Press, 1990.

Kelly, S.F., and R.J. Kelly. *Imagine Yourself Well: Better Health Through Self-Hypnosis.* New York: Insight Books, 1995.

Kenny, M.E., and K. Hart. "Relationship Between Parental Attachment and Eating Disorders in an Inpatient and a College Sample." *Journal of Counseling Psychology,* 39 (4) 1992: 521-526.

Klaus, M.H., J.H. Kennell, and P.H. Klaus. *Bonding: Building the Foundations of Secure Attachment and Independence.* Reading, Mass.: Addison-Wesley, 1995.

Klauser, H.A. *Writing on Both Sides of the Brain: Breakthrough Techniques for People Who Write.* New York: HarperCollins, 1987.

Klein, D.F., and P.H. Wender. *Understanding Depression: A Complete Guide to Its Diagnosis and Treatment.* New York: Oxford University Press, 1993.

Klesges, R.C., and M. DeBon. *How Women Can Finally Stop Smoking.* Alameda, Calif.: Hunter House, 1994.

Lam, R.W., et al. "A Controlled Study of Light Therapy for Bulimia Nervosa." *American Journal of Psychiatry,* 151 (5) 1994: 744-750.

Lamott, A. *Bird by Bird: Some Instructions on Writing and Life.* New York: Pantheon Books, 1994.

Lark, S.M. *Premenstrual Syndrome: Self-Help Book.* Berkeley, Calif.: Celestial Arts, 1984.

Lay, C.H. "Trait Procrastination, Agitation, Dejection, and Self-Discrepancy." In *Procrastination and Task Avoidance: Theory, Research, and Treatment.* Eds. J.R. Ferrari, J.L. Johnson, and W. G. McCown. New York: Plenum, 1995, pp. 97-112.

Le Blanc, D. *You Can't Quit Till You Know What's Eating You: Overcoming Compulsive Eating.* Deerfield Beach, Fla.: Health Communications, 1990.

Leach, P. *Your Baby and Child: From Birth to Age Five,* rev. ed. New York: Alfred A. Knopf, 1994.

Lee, R.G. and G. Wheeler, eds. *The Voice of Shame: Silence and Connection in Psychotherapy.* San Francisco, Calif.: Jossey-Bass Publishers, 1996.

Lehrer, P.M., and R.L. Woolfolk, eds. *Principles and Practice of Stress Management,* 2nd ed. New York: Guilford Press, 1993.

Lew, M. *Victims No Longer: Men Recovering from Incest and Other Sexual Child Abuse.* New York: Harper & Row, 1990.

Lewis, H.B. "The Role of Shame in Depression Over the Life Span." In *The Role of Shame in Symptom Formation.* Ed. H.B. Lewis. Hillsdale, N.J.: Lawrence Erlbaum Associates, 1987, pp. 29-50.

_____. *Shame and Guilt in Neurosis.* New York: International Universities Press, 1971.

Lewis, H.B., ed. *The Role of Shame in Symptom Formation.* Hillsdale, N.J.: Lawrence Erlbaum Associates, 1987.

Liebmann, M. *Art Therapy in Practice.* London: Jessica Kingsley Publishers/Bristol, Penna.: Taylor & Francis, 1990.

Lipsitz, J.D., et al. "Childhood Separation Anxiety Disorder in Patients with Adult Anxiety Disorders." *American Journal of Psychiatry,* 151 (6) 1994: 927-929.

Llera, C. "Emotions and Chiropractic." *Spotlight,* August, 1992: 29.

Love, P., and J. Robinson. *The Emotional Incest Syndrome: What to Do When a Parent's Love Rules Your Life.* New York: Bantam, 1990.

Lowman, R.L. *Counseling and Psychotherapy of Work Dysfunctions.* Washington, D.C.: American Psychological Association, 1993.

Luntz, B.K., and C.S. Widom. "Antisocial Personality Disorder in Abused and Neglected Children Grown Up." *American Journal of Psychiatry,* 151 (5) 1994: 670-674.

Mahalik, J.R., and D.M. Kivlighan. "Self-Help Treatment for Depression: Who Succeeds?" *Journal of Counseling Psychology,* 35 (3) 1988: 237-242.

Main, M. "Metacognitive Knowledge, Metacognitive Monitoring, and Singular (Coherent) vs. Multiple (Incoherent) Model of Attachment: Findings and Directions for Future Research." In *Attachment Across the*

Life Cycle. Eds. C.M. Parkes, J. Stevenson-Hinde, and P. Marris. London: Tavistock/Routledge, 1991, pp. 127-159.

Main, M., and E. Hesse. "Discovery of a Second-Generation Effect of Unresolved Trauma: Lapses in a Parent's Reasoning or Discourse in Discussing Traumatic Experiences Predict Disorganized Infant Strange-Situation Behavior." Unpublished monograph, submitted for publication, 1989.

_____. "Parents' Unresolved Traumatic Experiences Are Related to Infant Disorganized Attachment Status: Is Frightened and/or Frightening Parental Behavior the Linking Mechanism?" In *Attachment in the Preschool Years: Theory, Research, and Intervention.* Eds. M. T. Greenberg, D. Cicchetti, and E.M. Cummings. Chicago, Illinois: University of Chicago Press, 1990, pp. 161-182.

Main, M., and R. Goldwyn. "Adult Attachment Classification System," rev. Unpublished manual, Department of Psychology, Univ. of California, Berkeley, 1989.

_____. "Predicting Rejection of Her Infant from Mother's Representation of Her Own Experiences: Implications for the Abused-Abusing Intergenerational Cycle." *International Journal of Child Abuse & Neglect,* 8 (2) 1984: 203-217.

Mallinckrodt, B. "Childhood Emotional Bonds with Parents, Development of Adult Social Competencies, and Availability of Social Support." *Journal of Counseling Psychology,* 39 (4) 1992: 453-461.

Mallinckrodt, B., B.A. McCreary, and A.K. Roberston, "Co-occurrence of Eating Disorders and Incest: The Role of Attachment, Family Environment, and Social Competencies." *Journal of Counseling Psychology,* 42 (2) 1995: 178-186.

Mann, J.J., and S. Kapur. "A Dopaminergic Hypothesis of Major Depression." *Clinical Neuropharmacology,* 18 (Suppl. 1) 1995: S57-S65.

Mason, D., and D. Ingersoll. *Breastfeeding and the Working Mother.* New York: St. Martin's Press, 1986.

Matsakis, A. *Post-Traumatic Stress Disorder: A Complete Treatment Guide.* Oakland, Calif.: New Harbinger, 1994.

May, R. *The Courage to Create.* New York: Bantam, 1975.

McCown, W., D. Carise, and J. Johnson. "Trait Procrastination in Self-Described Adult Children of Excessive Drinkers: An Exploratory Study." *Journal of Social Behavior and Personality,* 6 (1) 1991: 147-151.

McKay, M., P. Rogers, and J. McKay. *When Anger Hurts.* Oakland, Calif.: New Harbinger, 1989.

McKean, K.J. "Using Multiple Risk Factors to Assess the Behavioral, Cognitive, and Affective Effects of Learned Helplessness." *Journal of Psychology,* 128 (2) 1994: 177-183.

McMillan, T. *Waiting to Exhale.* New York: Viking, 1992.

Mellan, O., and S. Christie. *Overcoming Overspending.* New York: Walker, 1995.

The Miami Herald. "Drug Against Alcoholism Approved by the FDA." January 17, 1995: 5-A.

Michaud, E., R. Wild, and eds. of *Prevention Magazine. Boost Your Brain Power: A Total Program to Strengthen and Expand Your Most Important Resource.* New York: MJF Books, 1991.

Miller, A. *Breaking Down the Wall of Silence: The Liberating Experience of Facing Painful Truth.* New York: Dutton, 1991.

_____. *The Drama of the Gifted Child.* New York: Basic Books, 1981.

_____. *Thou Shalt Not Be Aware: Society's Betrayal of the Child.* New York: Meridian, 1984.

Mintz, L.B., and N.E. Betz. "Prevalence and Correlates of Eating Disordered Behaviors Among Undergraduate Women." *Journal of Counseling Psychology,* 35 (4) 1988: 463-471.

Morris, J. *Creative Breakthroughs: Tap the Power of Your Unconscious Mind.* New York: Warner Books, 1992.

Morrison, N. "The Role of Shame in Schizophrenia." In *The Role of Shame in Symptom Formation.* Ed. H.B. Lewis. Hillsdale, N.J.: Lawrence Erlbaum Associates, 1987, pp. 51-87.

Morrow, S.L., and M.L. Smith. "Constructions of Survival and Coping by Women Who Have Survived Childhood Sexual Abuse." *Journal of Counseling Psychology,* 42 (1) 1995: 24-33.

Mrazek, D., W. Garrison, and L. Elliott, eds. *A to Z Guide to Your Child's Behavior.* New York: Perigee, 1993.

Mundis, J. *How to Get Out of Debt, Stay Out of Debt, and Live Prosperously.* New York: Bantam, 1988.

Mutter, C.B. "Ethics and Informed Consent, False Memory Issues — Guidelines." Paper presented at the meeting of the American Society of Clinical Hypnosis, Fort Lauderdale, Fla., December 1995.

Nathanson, D.L. *Shame and Pride: Affect, Sex, and the Birth of the Self.* New York: W.W. Norton, 1992.

Nelson-Zlupko, L., E. Kauffman, and M.M. Dore. "Gender Differences in Drug Addiction and Treatment: Implications for Social Work Intervention with Substance-Abusing Women." *Social Work,* 40 (19) 1995: 45-54.

Newcomb, M.D., et al. "Cognitive Motivations for Drug Use Among Adolescents: Longitudinal Tests of Gender Differences and Predictors of Change in Drug Use." *Journal of Counseling Psychology,* 35 (4) 1988: 426-438.

Newman, M., and B. Berkowitz. *How to Take Charge of Your Life.* New York: Bantam, 1977.

Norden, M.J. *Beyond Prozac: Brain-Toxic Lifestyles, Natural Antidotes, and New Generation Antidepressants.* New York: Regan Books, 1995.

Null, G. *No More Allergies: Identifying and Eliminating Allergies and Sensitivity Reactions to Everything in Your Environment.* New York: Villard Books, 1992.

Ogles, B.M., M.J. Lambert, and D.E. Craig. "Comparison of Self-help Books for Coping with Loss: Expectations and Attributions." *Journal of Counseling Psychology,* 38 (4) 1991: 387-393.

Orbach, S. *Fat is a Feminist Issue: A Self-help Guide for Compulsive Overeaters.* New York: Berkley Books, 1978.

Pandit, B. *The Hindu Mind: Fundamentals of Hindu Religion and Philosophy for All Ages,* 2nd ed. Glen Ellyn, Ill.: B & V Enterprises, 1993.

Paramananda, S., trans. *The Upanishads.* Cohasset, Mass.: Vedanta Centre Publishers, 1981.

Parkes, C.M. "Attachment, Bonding, and Psychiatric Problems After Bereavement in Adult Life." In *Attachment Across the Life Cycle.* Eds. C.M. Parkes, J. Stevenson-Hinde, and P. Marris. London: Tavistock/Routledge, 1991, pp. 268-292.

Parkes, C.M., J. Stevenson-Hinde, and P. Marris, eds. *Attachment Across the Life Cycle.* London: Tavistock/Routledge, 1991.

Pearson, D., and S. Shaw. *Life Extension: A Practical Scientific Approach.* New York: Warner Books, 1982.

Pennebaker, J.W. *Opening Up: The Healing Power of Confiding in Others.* New York: Avon Books, 1990.

People with AIDS Coalition. *Surviving and Thriving with AIDS: Hints for the Newly Diagnosed.* New York: PWA Coalition, 1987.

Peterson, C., S.F. Maier, and M.E.P. Seligman. *Learned Helplessness: A Theory for the Age of Personal Control.* New York: Oxford University Press, 1993.

Peterson, K.E. "Hidden Populations at High Risk for HIV Infection." In *AIDS Prevention and Treatment: Hope, Humor, and Healing.* Eds. M.R. Seligson and K.E. Peterson. New York: Hemisphere, 1992, pp. 153-172.

_____. "Kurt Vonnegut: Exorcism of an Autobiographical Gallows Humorist." Master's thesis, University of Akron, Akron, Ohio, 1982.

_____. "Relationships Among Measures of Writer's Block, Writing Anxiety, and Procrastination." Ph.D. diss., Ohio State Univ., Columbus, Ohio, 1987.

Phillips, C. "Holocaust's Effects Are Passed to the Children." *APA Monitor,* April, 1996: 40-41.

Piaget, J., and B. Inhelder. *The Psychology of the Child.* New York: Basic Books, 1968.

Pope, K.S., and B.G. Tabachnick. "Therapists as Patients: A National Survey of Psychologists' Experiences, Problems, and Beliefs." *Professional Psychology: Research and Practice,* 25 (3) 1994: 247-258.

Potter-Efron, R. *Angry All the Time.* Oakland, Calif.: New Harbinger, 1994.

Potter-Efron, R., and P. Potter-Efron. *Letting Go of Anger.* Oakland, Calif.: New Harbinger, 1995.

Poulton, R.G., and G. Andrews. "Appraisal of Danger and Proximity in Social Phobics." *Behaviour Research and Therapy,* 32 (6) 1994: 639-642.

Prevention Magazine. "The Best of Alternative Medicine." December, 1994: 65-96, 136-143.

Prochaska, J.O., C.C. DiClemente, and J.C. Norcross. "In Search of How People Change: Applications to Addictive Behaviors." *American Psychologist,* 47 (9) 1992: 1102-1114.

Progoff, I. *At a Journal Workshop.* New York: Dialogue House Library, 1975.

Radke-Yarrow, M. "Attachment Patterns in Children of Depressed Mothers." In *Attachment Across the Life Cycle.* Eds. C.M. Parkes, J. Stevenson-Hinde, and P. Marris. London: Tavistock/Routledge, 1991, pp. 115-126.

Redfield, J. *The Celestine Prophecy.* New York: Warner Books, 1993.

Retzinger, S. "Resentment and Laughter: Video Studies of the Shame-Rage Spiral." In *The Role of Shame in Symptom Formation*. Ed. H.B. Lewis. Hillsdale, N.J.: Lawrence Erlbaum Associates, 1987, pp. 151-181.

Rhodewalt, F. "Conceptions of Ability, Achievement, Goals and Individual Differences in Self-handicapping Behavior: On The Application of Implicit Theories." *Journal of Personality,* 62 (1) 1994: 67-85.

Rico, G.L. *Pain and Possibility: Writing Your Way Through Personal Crisis.* Los Angeles, Calif: Jeremy P. Tarcher, 1991.

Robinson, B. *Overdoing It: How to Slow Down and Take Care of Yourself.* Deerfield Beach, Fla.: Health Communications, 1992.

Rose, M. *Writer's Block: The Cognitive Dimension.* Carbondale, Ill.: Southern Illinois University Press, 1984.

Rosen, A., and R. Osmo. "Client Locus of Control, Problem Perception, and Interview Behavior." *Journal of Counseling Psychology,* 31 (3) 1984: 314-321.

Rosenthal, N.E. *Winter Blues: Seasonal Affective Disorder, What It Is and How to Overcome It.* New York: Guilford Press, 1993.

Rossi, E.L. *The Psychobiology of Mind-Body Healing: New Concepts of Therapeutic Hypnosis,* rev. ed. New York: W.W. Norton, 1993.

Roth, G. *Feeding the Hungry Heart: The Experience of Compulsive Eating.* New York: Signet, 1982.

Rothblum, E.D., L.J. Solomon, and J. Murakami. "Affective, Cognitive, and Behavioral Differences Between High and Low Procrastinators." *Journal of Counseling Psychology,* 33 (4) 1986: 387-394.

Russell, D.E.H. *The Secret Trauma: Incest in the Lives of Girls and Women.* New York: Basic Books, 1986.

Ryan, N.E., V.S. Solberg, and S.D. Brown. "Family Dysfunction, Parental Attachment, and Career Search Self-efficacy Among Community College Students." *Journal of Counseling Psychology,* 43 (1) 1996: 84-89.

Sanday, P.R. *Fraternity Gang Rape: Sex, Brotherhood, and Privilege on Campus.* New York: New York University Press, 1990.

Santrock, J.W., A.M. Minnett, and B.D. Campbell. *The Authoritative Guide to Self-help Books.* New York: Guilford Press, 1994.

SARK. *Inspiration Sandwich: Stories to Inspire Our Creative Freedom.* Berkeley, Calif.: Celestial Arts, 1992.

Scarf, M. *Intimate Worlds: Life Inside the Family.* New York: Random House, 1995.

Scheff, T.J. "The Shame-Rage Spiral: A Case Study of an Interminable Quarrel." In *The Role of Shame in Symptom Formation.* Ed. H.B. Lewis. Hillsdale, N.J.: Lawrence Erlbaum Associates, 1987, pp. 109-149.

Schouwenburg, H.C. "Academic Procrastination: Theoretical Notions, Measurement, and Research." In *Procrastination and Task Avoidance: Theory, Research, and Treatment.* Eds. J.R. Ferrari, J.L. Johnson, and W. G. McCown. New York: Plenum, 1995, pp. 71-96.

Seligman, M.E.P. "Depression and Learned Helplessness." In *The Psychology of Depression: Contemporary Theory and Research.* Eds. R.J. Friedman and M.M. Katz. Washington, D.C.: Winston-Wiley, 1974.

_____. "The Effectiveness of Psychotherapy: The *Consumer Reports* Study." *American Psychologist,* 50 (12) 1995: 965-974.

_____. *The Optimistic Child: A Revolutionary Program That Safeguards Children Against Depression & Builds Lifelong Resilience.* New York: Houghton Mifflin, 1995.

Seligson, M.R., and K. E. Peterson, eds. *AIDS Prevention and Treatment: Hope, Humor, and Healing.* New York: Hemisphere, 1992.

Serling, D.A., and N.E. Betz. "Development and Evaluation of a Measure of Fear of Commitment." *Journal of Counseling Psychology,* 37 (1) 1990: 91-97.

Shea, L. *Hula.* New York: W.W. Norton, 1994.

Sheehy, G. *The Silent Passage: Menopause.* New York: Random House, 1991.

Shekerjian, D. *Uncommon Genius: How Great Ideas Are Born.* New York: Penguin Books, 1990.

Sherwood, K. *Chakra Therapy: For Personal Growth and Healing.* St. Paul, Minn.: Llewellyn Publications, 1993.

Siegel, B.S. *How to Live Between Office Visits.* New York: HarperCollins, 1994.

_____. *Love, Medicine, and Miracles.* New York: Harper & Row, 1986.

_____. *Peace, Love, and Healing.* New York: Harper & Row, 1990.

Simonds, S.L. *Bridging the Silence: Nonverbal Modalities in the Treatment of Adult Survivors of Childhood Sexual Abuse.* New York: W.W. Norton, 1994.

Sinetar, M. *Do What You Love, the Money Will Follow.* New York: Dell, 1989.

_____. *Reel Power.* New York/Liguori, Miss.: Triumph Books/ Liguori, 1993.

_____. *To Build the Life You Want, Create the Work You Love.* New York: St. Martin's Press, 1995.

Solomon, L.J., and E.D. Rothblum. "Academic Procrastination: Frequency and Cognitive-behavioral Correlates." *Journal of Counseling Psychology,* 31 (4) 1984: 503-509.

St. James, E. *Simplify Your Life: 100 Ways to Slow Down and Enjoy the Things That Really Matter.* New York: Hyperion, 1994.

Steinem, G. *Revolution from Within: A Book of Self-Esteem.* Boston: Little, Brown & Co., 1992.

Sternberg, R.J., ed. *The Nature of Creativity: Contemporary Psychological Perspectives.* Cambridge: Cambridge University Press, 1988.

Stinson, M.H., and S.S. Hendrick. "Reported Childhood Sexual Abuse in University Counseling Center Clients." *Journal of Counseling Psychology,* 39 (3) 1992: 370-374.

Stipek, D. "The Development of Pride and Shame in Toddlers." In *Self-Conscious Emotions: The Psychology of Shame, Guilt, Embarrassment, and Pride.* Eds. J. P. Tangney and K. W. Fischer. New York: Guilford Press, 1995, pp. 237-252.

Stone, H., and S. Stone. *Embracing Your Inner Critic: Turning Self-criticism into a Creative Asset.* New York: HarperSanFrancisco, 1993.

Storr, A. *The Dynamics of Creation.* New York: Ballantine Books, 1972.

_____. *Solitude: A Return to the Self.* New York: Free Press, 1988.

Stott-Kendall, P. *Torn Illusions: One Woman's Tragic Experience with the Silicone Conspiracy.* Far Hills, N.J.: New Horizon Press, 1994.

Tangney, J.P., and K.W. Fischer, eds. *Self-Conscious Emotions: The Psychology of Shame, Guilt, Embarrassment, and Pride.* New York: Guilford Press, 1995.

Tangney, J.P., S.A. Burggraf, and P.E. Wagner. "Shame-Proneness, Guilt-Proneness, and Psychological Symptoms." In *Self-Conscious Emotions: The Psychology of Shame, Guilt, Embarrassment, and Pride.* Eds. J. P. Tangney and K. W. Fischer. New York: Guilford Press, 1995, pp. 343-367.

Taylor, C.L. *The Inner Child Workbook: What to Do With Your Past When It Just Won't Go Away.* New York: Jeremy P. Tarcher/Putnam Books, 1991.

Temoshok, L., and H. Dreher. *The Type C Connection: The Behavioral Links to Cancer and Your Health.* New York: Random House, 1992.

Thelan, M.H., et al. "Bulimia and Interpersonal Relationships: A Longitudinal Study." *Journal of Counseling Psychology,* 37 (1) 1990: 85-90.

Thombs, D.L., K.H. Beck, and C.A. Mahoney. "Effects of Social Context and Gender on Drinking Patterns of Young Adults." *Journal of Counseling Psychology,* 40 (1) 1993: 115-119.

Trimpey, J. *The Small Book: A Revolutionary Alternative for Overcoming Alcohol and Drug Dependence.* New York: Doubleday, 1995.

Ullman, A.D., and A. Orenstein. "Why Some Children of Alcoholics Become Alcoholics: Emulations of the Drinker." *Adolescence,* 29 (113) 1994: 1-11.

Utian, W.H., and R.S. Jacobowitz. *Managing Your Menopause.* New York: Prentice Hall Press, 1990.

Valkenburg, P., and T.H.A. Van der Voort. "Influence of TV on Daydreaming and Creative Imagination: A Review of Research." *Psychological Bulletin,* 116 (2) 1994: 316-339.

Vasey, F.B., and J. Feldstein. *The Silicone Implant Controversy.* Freedom, Calif.: The Crossing Press, 1993.

Vonnegut, K. "In The Capital of the World." In *Palm Sunday.* New York: Delacorte Press, 1981.

_____. *"Playboy* Interview." In *Wampeters, Foma, and Granfalloons.* New York: Dell, 1974.

_____. *Slapstick.* New York: Delacorte Press/Seymour Lawrence, 1976.

Wallis, C. "Why New Age Medicine is Catching On." *Time,* November 4, 1991:. 68-76.

Waterhouse, D. *Why Women Need Chocolate: How to Get the Body You Want by Eating the Foods You Crave.* New York: Hyperion, 1995.

Weiser, J. *PhotoTherapy Techniques: Exploring the Secrets of Personal Snapshots and Family Albums.* San Francisco: Josey-Bass, 1993.

Weiss, G. and L.T. Hechtman. *Hyperactive Children Grown Up: ADHD in Children, Adolescents, and Adults,* 2nd ed. New York: Guilford Press, 1993.

Weiss, L. *Attention Deficit Disorder in Adults: Practical Self-Help for Sufferers and Their Spouses.* Dallas, Tex.: Taylor Publishing Co., 1992.

Wells, V. *The Joy of Visualization: 75 Creative Ways to Improve Your Life.* San Francisco: Chronicle Books, 1990.

Wenar, C., ed. "Normal Development." In *Psychopathology from Infancy Through Adolescence: A Developmental Approach.* New York: Random House, 1982, pp. 37-71.

Weston, D.C., and M. Weston. *Playful Parenting.* New York: Putnam, 1993.

Whitfield, C.L. *Co-dependence: Healing the Human Condition.* Deerfield Beach, Fla.: Health Communications, 1991.

Winter, R. *A Consumer's Guide to Medicines in Food: Nutraceuticals That Help Prevent and Treat Physical and Emotional Illnesses.* New York: Crown, 1995.

Wise, S.R., and R.T. Elmore. "Integration of Hypnosis and Eye Movement Desensitization and Reprocessing (EMDR) in the Treatment of Traumatic Memories." Paper presented at the meeting of the American Society of Clinical Hypnosis, Fort Lauderdale, Fla., December 1995.

Wisner, K.L., and S.B. Wheeler. "Prevention of Recurrent Postpartum Major Depression." *Hospital and Community Psychiatry,* (45) 1994: 1191-1196.

Wonder, J., and P. Donovan. *Whole-brain Thinking: Working from Both Sides of the Brain to Achieve Peak Job Performance.* New York: Quill/William Morrow, 1984.

Wydra, N. "Is Your Bedroom Making You Ill? Create Healthy Interiors the Chinese Way." *Natural Health,* July/August, 1992: 50-53.

Young, J.E. *Total Well-Being: Integrated Balance of Body, Mind, and Spirit.* Miami, Fla.: Trihealth, Inc., 1994.

Zamostny, K. P., S.L. Slyter, and P. Rios. "Narcissistic Injury and Its Relationship to Early Trauma, Early Resources, and Adjustment to College." *Journal of Counseling Psychology,* 40 (4) 1993: 501-510.

Zilbergeld, B., M.G. Edelstein, and D.L. Araoz, eds. *Hypnosis: Questions & Answers.* New York: W.W. Norton, 1986.

Zimbardo, P. *Shyness.* Reading, Mass.: Addison-Wesley, 1987.

Zuckerman, A. *Writing the Blockbuster Novel.* Cincinnati, Ohio: Writer's Digest Books, 1993.

Zuroff, D.C., R. Koestner, and T.A. Powers. "Self-Criticism at Age 12: A Longitudinal Study of Adjustment." *Cognitive Therapy & Research,* 18 (4) 1994: 367-385.